Make It BIG!

Make It BIG!

49 Secrets for Building a
Life of Extreme Success

Frank McKinney

with

Victoria St. George

JOHN WILEY & SONS, INC.

Published by John Wiley & Sons, Inc., New York.
Published simultaneously in Canada.

Library of Congress Cataloging-in-Publication Data:

McKinney, Frank E., 1963–
    Make it big! : 49 secrets for building a life of extreme success / Frank E. McKinney with Victoria St. George.
        p. cm.
    Includes index.
    ISBN 0-471-44399-9 (alk. paper)
    I. Success—Psychological aspects.   I. Title.

BF637.S8 M3642   2002
158—dc21   2002026434

Printed in the United States of America.

10   9   8   7   6   5   4   3   2   1

To—

my mom, Katie McKinney, who has shown me the compassionate side of life;

my late father, Frank McKinney, who I believe would be very proud of this book;

my lovely wife, Nilsa, for all her patience and support;

and God, for blessing me with the privilege of sharing this book with you

Contents

Acknowledgments

A book isn't just made of words. Like life, it's composed with the support, help, and guidance of the people we encounter along the way. My life has been blessed with many such great and positive influences, without whom I would never be able to write a word about extreme success.

My beautiful wife, Nilsa, has been with me practically from the first real estate deal. Not many women would be willing to live in an efficiency apartment or servants' quarters for four years while their husbands put every single dime into making it big, but Nilsa is special in so many ways, not to mention being a real trouper. She has always been a driving part of the artistic vision of the estates I create. I rely on her impeccable taste, her ability to help me complete projects at lightning speed, as well as her willingness to support her husband's trendsetting ideas. She is so good that every time I go out of town she seems to be able to accomplish more than if I were around!

My daughter, Laura Katherine, brings joy to my life every day and reminds me to stay connected to that little boy inside my own heart. She makes my very existence complete. I hope that one day she reads this book and is touched in the same way she touches me.

My mother, Katie McKinney, has a raft of gray hairs due to my wild teenage years, but to me she has always epitomized the ideal combination of "tough" and unconditional love every mom should offer her kids. Mom taught me more about compassion, understanding, and persistence than any other human being. I'm just glad I'm finally able to give her something to brag about. My four sisters, Martie, Marlen, Madeleine, and Heather, have each been an inspiration to me in different ways. They have contributed to my success, and while we may not always get along, I will never forget what they did to help me succeed. Now that we're all grown up, I hope I can be a great "big brother" to them.

Even though my brother, Bob, is 10 years younger than me, I consider him a sounding board, a confidant, and my absolute best friend in this world. He is in the same line of work and also produces the finest homes in the Midwest. I speak to him every day for guidance and laughs. I know someday he will eclipse my successes (unless I can ever convince him to come to Florida and work with me). Another Bob, Bob Berry, is my uncle, and it's a privilege to have him as my president of construction. I look forward to collaborating with him for many years to come.

Through the years, many individuals have inspired me and kept me on the right track, even when I was doing my darnedest to take the low road. Brother David Downey, the Benedictine monk who was the prefect at the Abbey School in Cañon City, Colorado, threw me out after less than a year but stayed in touch with me constantly, telling me I'd be all right. I appreciated the combination of discipline, firmness, and encouragement he offered to someone others saw as a "throwaway" kid. I value the friendship we developed and maintain to this day. Charlie Harrell was president of Indiana University when I squeaked out of high school with my 1.8 grade point average. He let me spend a summer at IU to see if I wanted to go there, and continued to send me inspirational notes for many years after I moved to Florida. For someone of his caliber to believe in me meant a lot in those early days, and I thank him for his faith in me. Many other souls have helped me along the way to living these Philosophies, so I'd like to thank Eddie Madden, my Grandmama, Harry Bindner, Walter Ogilvie, Joe Barnette, Martha (Bindley) Moore, Cam and Jim Clark, Linda Paul, Jim Browning, Uncle Gil Berry, Father Larry Kanyike, Virginia Sparing, John Young, Mike Moore, Al Smith, Bob Hunt, Clark French, the Linder family, Tom Lynch, and Barbara Wynne.

Through my business I have met many people I admire, but two men in particular have made a big difference in my life. After I sold one of our estates to George Valassis, he became almost a surrogate father to me. I feel I can confide in him and seek direction from someone who has achieved enormous success. George has been generous with his time and support of my endeavors. He's gone to the mat for me several times with banks and other clients, and I appreciate his candor and his willingness to mentor me.

I am extremely proud that Rich De Vos agreed to write the Foreword for this book. He's who I'd like to be at age 70 or so: successful, fulfilled, spiritual, balanced, well-respected, generous with his time, willing to give others a helping hand as they climb the ladder of success. Rich De Vos is a living hero of mine, and someone I feel privileged to know.

When I started building in the exclusive oceanfront town of Manalapan, Florida, many old-time residents didn't want Frank McKinney coming into their town and changing things. But from the beginning, there were two men who realized my true intention and welcomed me with open minds. I thank Peter Blum and Tony Mauro for their support and confidence.

I would never be able to make it big without the professional support of all the guys and gals who have worked with me in my business. I can't drive a nail straight, so I have enormous admiration for all the skilled craftspeople who have renovated and built such magnificent mansions for me. Without their talents and their willingness to get in there every day and get the job done, all my success would be nothing but a lot of pipe dreams. The same goes for the people closest to me on my staff: Bob Berry, Ray Ferrera, Cathy Jorgens, Diane Berry, Shane George, Chris Cavalier, Paul Paulson, and Peggy Licata. I may make a fetish of being organized and getting things done, but they're the ones who provide the hands to do it. Special thanks go to Phyllis Bederka—den mother, surrogate mom when my mom's not around, my right-hand man even though she's a woman. No one could take better care of a boss.

In my line of work, a good banker is like the foundation of a house: When you have a solid one, you can build as high as you want. Joe Silk is my banker at Bank of America, and he has given my business the kind of solid foundation I needed to make it big. Joe has consistently worked "outside the box" and put together financing for projects that seemed impossible. Dick Ristine at Bank One also has demonstrated enormous flexibility and patience when it came to some of the loans I've asked him to approve!

Jeff Perlman has been a supporter of my efforts almost since I moved to Delray Beach. As a reporter, then editor, of a local newspaper, he helped me get my name established in oceanfront real estate. More important, he encouraged me to write a book about my Philosophies, and did many of the interviews that supplied stories you'll find in these pages. I rely on Jeff for friendship and advice. Jeff wants me eventually to open the "McKinney Institute for Spiritual Entrepreneurship," or MISE—who knows?

Because a large part of my life is giving back, I must mention some of my cohorts in contribution here in South Florida. Lula Butler and I founded the Greater Delray Beach Youth Council almost eight years ago. I've known Lula for 10 years, and nobody can figure out why we get along so well, including us! But I think it's because we respect and admire each other's dedication, attitude toward kids, and contribution. The same goes for Father Skehan, the pastor at St. Vincent's Catholic Church. We've worked together on fund-raising and other church activities, and somehow he's managed to put up with my unconventional approach. I'd like to acknowledge all the people I met through the Caring Kitchen organization, as well as those who have helped support my Caring House projects. Helping the homeless is never a glamorous endeavor, and I admire anyone who makes the time to make a difference.

If you've never tried to get a book published, you have no idea of what a perilous journey it can be from idea to hardcover. I want to thank all the agents and publishers who rejected this book in its first incarnation, because they just made me more determined to see this in print. An even bigger thank-you goes to Mike Hamilton of John Wiley & Sons. Mike read an article on me in *USA Today* in which I mentioned that I was writing this book. Based on that, he contacted me and became my publisher and editor. He has been instrumental in the direction the final, publishable version has taken. I regard Mike with the same appreciation I gave to the banker who gave me my very first loan, because I recognize the courage it takes to gamble on an unknown commodity. Mike has shown enormous enthusiasm for this first-time writer, and I trust he will be pleased with the results of his faith in me.

I also want to thank my agent, Carol Roth, who is a real class act. Carol kept in touch with me for over a year, checking in to see how things were going when the proposal was with another agent. She was even willing to take me on after I'd gotten 15 rejection letters from publishers! A very large thank-you goes to Paola Rana-Fernandez, my wonderful publicist. After 15 years of marketing my own properties I know a lot about PR, but Paola has guided me through the unfamiliar maze of publicizing a book. She's been an invaluable addition to my team, and if *Make It BIG!* is a success, to a large degree it will be due to her expertise. And special thanks go to my ghostwriter, Victoria St.

George, whom I believe is simply the best. Vicki has a talent for capturing what I want to say and expressing it with eloquence, while still making it sound like Frank McKinney. I appreciate her enthusiasm, her intelligence, and her stamina (considering how quickly John Wiley & Sons wanted us to complete the manuscript). Vicki and I also share a slightly warped sense of humor, so working with her has been a pleasure.

Finally and most important, I thank God—not just for the inspiration to write this, but also because I never would have survived my teenage years without some kind of divine protection and intervention. I am always grateful for the blessings He has sent my way, and I pray I may continue to try to live up to the vision of the man God wants me to be.

Foreword

A few years ago I attended the dedication of a new YMCA here in South Florida, and a young man came up to me and introduced himself as Frank McKinney. I had been hearing good things about this young developer of high-end oceanfront real estate—that he was an honest businessman committed to helping the homeless and youth in our community, a dedicated family man, and a faithful member of his church. However, it was a little hard to mesh what I had heard about Frank with the person standing in front of me, with his shoulder-length blond hair and a bright yellow sports jacket (which he told me I could borrow anytime). He looked like a cross between a rock star and a surfer who had somehow acquired a great, if unconventional, tailor. But when we talked a little, I discovered the reports I had heard of Frank's character were far more representative of who he was than his hair and attire indicated.

Since then I have gotten to know and appreciate Frank McKinney, not only for his business success and altruism but also for his commitment to live a life built upon solid, lasting, faith-based principles. His own rags to riches story is less Horatio Alger and more "Peck's Bad Boy makes good," but it is a testimonial to the power of persistence, courage, fairness, optimism, and the willingness to put in the time and effort required to build any successful business. More important, from a very early age Frank was sharing his success with others in a very hands-on way, fulfilling the command of Jesus that we feed the hungry, help the homeless, and uplift those who are down-trodden by circumstance. Frank believes, as do I, that those of us who enjoy a high or comfortable standard of living must thank God for what we have, and vow daily to be responsible, generous stewards of what we have been given.

Frank and I share another trait: the desire to share with others what we have learned from our experiences. In 2000 I wrote a book, *Hope from My Heart*, in which I pinpointed the "practical wisdom" I have gathered through the years, 10 lessons that I believe are the foundation of a successful life. I focused on hope, persistence, confidence, optimism, respect, accountability, family, freedom, faith, and grace, and how these lessons have illuminated my 70-plus years on this earth. When I look at Frank's 49 Philosophies, I see many of the same lessons in action—stated a little more outrageously, perhaps, but then that is Frank's style. Regardless, I believe that my lessons and Frank's Philosophies arise from the same desire: to live the life God wishes for us by using our talents to the best of our abilities, making a difference for others through our examples and our actions, loving our families, and helping the less fortunate.

There are never any shortcuts to success, but it is possible to follow the paths of those who have blazed a trail in their own fields of endeavor. Frank has created great success in the area of high-end real estate development. His oceanfront homes are some of the most magnificent in the world, and if you wish to enter the real estate profession, you will find much in these pages to help you. However, anyone can benefit from these 49 Philosophies and learn from the examples Frank describes. I believe the stories of succeeding against enormous odds, sacrificing personal comfort to put everything into your business, living according to your vision, putting in a full day's work day in and day out, contributing to others, and enjoying your life every moment can provide great inspiration no matter what your stage or status in life.

One of the most powerful forces in the world is the will of men and women who believe in themselves, who dare to hope and aim high, who go confidently after the things they want from life. Frank occasionally has been bad-mouthed by people who see his confidence, his success, his larger-than-life style, and equate it with arrogance. But what I see in Frank is not arrogance, but the confidence of a man who knows what he wants, who's willing to take the risks necessary to make his dreams come true, and who knows where to offer the credit for all his accomplishments. Frank says the Philosophies in this book have helped him create a life of what he calls "extreme success," encompassing business, family, community, faith, and fun. I believe they have given him the solid foundation of timeless, strong principles that must underpin any lasting success. I hope these Philosophies will do the same for you, so that you may achieve the success of your dreams. And, like Frank, I hope your success will blaze a trail for others who seek to learn how to make it big in every area of life.

RICH DE VOS
Cofounder, Amway

Make It BIG!

Introduction

Let me tell you, January's one helluva cold month in Indianapolis, Indiana. It's gray, dreary, and a good time to get out of town—which is exactly what I was doing. Permanently. At the tender age of 18, I put everything I owned into a duffel bag and headed to Indianapolis International Airport. I was following what I thought of even then as my "highest calling." Did I know what it was? Of course not! But I sure knew what I didn't want to be—a banker like my father—and where I didn't want to be—Indiana. I'm not dumping on Indiana; it's a fine place. But with my history there as a rebellious, out-of-control teenager, it wasn't a place that I thought offered much opportunity for me.

I also knew my destiny wouldn't include any more formal education. The summer before, I had graduated from high school by the skin of my teeth. Even with a grade point average of 1.8 and a track record of getting kicked out of several schools, I probably could have weaseled my way into some community college—but I was too much of a rebel. Besides, I wanted to be out on my own. I already had the itch, that little voice inside that was telling me, "Go for it—create something all your own. Even if you don't know what it is, the only way you'll find out is to risk everything" (which I'll admit at the time wasn't much).

So I used my savings to buy a one-way plane ticket to Palm Beach, Florida. I think my parents were sad to see me go, but they agreed it would probably be for the best. (I think they were relieved to have me out of their hair for a few months, which is all the time they thought I'd be gone. Boy, were they wrong!) I had vacationed in South Florida a few times with my family when I was 16 and 17. During our last visit I had basically told my folks, "I'm going to run away for a while," and went off on my own for a week. I liked Florida. I thought it

1

held a lot of opportunities—and I thought I'd fit in better there than I ever would in Indiana.

So on that January 11, 1982, I was standing in line at the Indianapolis Airport with a terrible hangover, waiting to check in for the flight to Palm Beach. As I pushed my duffel bag along with my feet, I took out my wallet and counted my cash. One bill, a $50—all the money I had in the world. Was I worried? I was 18, healthy, good-looking in a heavy metal kind of way, and, like most kids, I felt unstoppable. What do you think?

When I got to the counter, I dumped my duffel bag on the baggage scale, gave the woman at the counter my ticket, flashed my most charming smile, and said, "Any chance of an upgrade to first class?" She looked at me severely for a moment, and I thought, *Jeez, I didn't ask for your first-born child, lady—all I want is a bigger seat and a glass of wine on the flight!* She punched a few buttons on her keyboard, pulled a section out of my ticket, stamped it, stapled it to a boarding pass, and then handed the whole thing back to me.

"There you are, Mr. McKinney," she said, never cracking a smile. "Seat 1A—first class. Have a nice flight."

I almost jumped over the counter and kissed her, but I was afraid she'd have me arrested. I practically danced and skipped my way to the gate, waved good-bye to my parents, and got on the plane. I was risking everything in a way I had never done before, and it made me feel alive. I also felt as if I were indeed on the right track, following my highest calling. Whatever destiny awaited me in Florida, at least I would arrive there in style!

The flight seemed much shorter than I thought it would, probably because I was enjoying that first-class service. It seemed only a few minutes before the door of the plane opened and I walked down the stairs leading to the tarmac. I inhaled the balmy, humid breezes and soft fragrance of the Gulf Stream coast (combined with the heavy, oily smell of jet fuel) and shrugged off my coat in the 80-plus-degree heat. I must be a warm-climate person, because that scent and that temperature immediately energized and excited me.

I went down to baggage claim, got my duffel bag, and hopped into a taxi. "Take me to the nearest liquor store!" I told the driver grandly, as I settled back. He drove me to a place called Big Daddy's Liquor, where I bought a six-pack of Stroh's beer. (I was 18 and had only $50—that was my idea of a celebration.) Then I got back in the taxi and had the guy drive me to the Deerfield Beach pier.

I paid the driver, got out, and walked to the end of the pier, which stretches way out into the Atlantic Ocean. It was getting close to sunset. The fishermen were starting to bring up their lines, and the water was turning shades of pink and purple, picking up reflections from the sun. I sat right on the end of the pier and drank three beers as I watched the seagulls, the fishermen, and the water. I don't think I'd ever been happier in my life.

As the sky started getting really dark, I got up and walked back to the land. I didn't have enough money left from my original $50 to catch another cab, so using those plastic loops that hold a six-pack together, I attached the remaining three beers to my belt. Then I picked up my duffel bag and started walking toward the Deerfield Beach apartment I had arranged to share with some friends. It was a two-mile walk, but what did I care? I was 18, in Florida, following my highest calling; I had three beers inside me and three more for later; the night was warm, clear, and scented with tropical flowers. There were beautiful girls in bikinis riding their bikes home from the beach. This was as close to paradise as I had ever come.

In 1998, I found myself at the same airport in Palm Beach, but this time I was waiting to welcome two producers from Oprah Winfrey's television show. Oprah was putting together a program on successful young entrepreneurs, and she wanted to feature my latest creation: a $12 million mansion overlooking the Atlantic Ocean. In the 16 years since I arrived in Florida, I had gone from digging sand traps by hand at a local country club to getting the club manager to pay for my tennis instructor certification. I had parlayed that instructor certificate into my very first business—the Professional Tennis Service, which taught tennis at several clubs and condominium complexes in South Florida. I gave lessons 8 to 12 hours a day, and employed other tennis instructors as well. Within three years of my arrival in Florida my business was grossing over $100,000 a year, and I was driving a Ferrari and living in my own oceanfront condominium. But a little voice was still whispering that I hadn't yet found the fullest manifestation of my highest calling.

Several different people (including a couple of girlfriends) kept talking about real estate as a great business opportunity. One gentleman I respected greatly had done very well in a thing called "distressed real estate": buying and selling extremely low-end properties at foreclosure and tax sales. I decided to try it. After researching the field for six months, I made my first purchase: a Department of Housing and Urban Development (HUD) foreclosure that was falling down, graffiti-covered, and in a pretty poor neighborhood. I renovated the house and sold it at a profit, then did the same with two more, then two more. Over the course of five years I became an expert in finding low-end properties at the right price, fixing them up so they'd be the nicest homes in the neighborhood, and then selling them, mostly to first-time buyers, for profits of 100 percent or more.

But my success in distressed real estate wasn't why Oprah's producers were arriving on the plane that day. In 1991 I had made a sweeping move, from buying and selling foreclosures in marginal neighborhoods to doing the same thing with ultra-high-end homes on some of the most expensive real estate in the world: oceanfront property in Palm Beach County, Florida. Once I bought a property, I usually designed and built a new mansion on speculation ("on spec"), meaning I put up all the money and took all the risk. We're not talking little million-dollar homes, either: The custom-designed, custom-built mansions I create start at around $9 million and go up from there. I average about $100 million worth of property on my books at any given time. My paydays come once every year or two, when I sell one of my mansions. I've been called "the daredevil developer," "the undisputed king of the ultra-high-end speculative real estate market," and "the real estate rock czar"; they say I'm the best in the world at what I do.

But when I met the two *Oprah* producers at the airport, I could tell they were a little taken aback—they weren't expecting a guy with shoulder-length blond hair, a Versace vest, and motorcycle boots. I'm used to this kind of reaction; truthfully, I like keeping people off guard. I led the producers to my bright red Hummer, and took them on a quick tour of what's called Florida's "Gold Coast"—Palm Beach, Manalapan, Gulf Stream, Delray Beach. We drove past estates that were built in the 1920s for families with names like Biltmore, Vanderbilt, Post. I pointed out mansions occupied by those with newer money: Don King's beachfront house; the estate of Rich De Vos, cofounder of Amway; a palatial home I myself built and then sold to the chairman of a company that makes some of the finest china and crystal in the world.

Then we turned into the driveway of my latest masterpiece, La Marceaux. Television producers are supposed to be cool, but these two looked around with eyes wide and mouths agape. I designed and built La

Marceaux with inspiration drawn from the great French châteaus of the Loire Valley, combined with the open-air feel and luxurious style that are the hallmarks of Florida's Gold Coast. I pride myself on the fact that my estates are unique, with every detail crafted to make the most discriminating billionaire feel at home.

We drove through rows of Italian cypresses and date palms to the entry gate and checked in with the guard. (Security is a big issue for the ultrarich.) Then I pulled up to the mansion's front door, which was opened by my site foreman.

"Hey, Bob—how's it going?" I asked him.

"Great, Frank," he said. "You're set up for lunch upstairs on the sundeck."

Bob held the door for us, and the producers and I went inside. The first thing they saw was a two-story-high living room, with 30-foot-tall windows stretching from floor to ceiling, framing magnificent views of the Atlantic Ocean and the estate's private beach a few feet away. The decorating (done by my wife Nilsa's design firm) was impeccable—beautiful wood, sumptuously upholstered chairs, a grand piano, and a trompe l'oeil ceiling painting of a scene taken from the Ritz Hotel in Paris. Overlooking the living room were three galleries filled with art, mirrors, and more antiques. Fresh flowers were everywhere. Next to one of the many seating areas in the living room, a tray held the finest brandies and cigars, ready for a confidential after-dinner conversation.

"Wow!" one of the producers said. I smiled, because that's exactly the effect I want my creations to have. I believe that to attract the kind of clients I want, you must use the best of everything and take care of even the smallest detail in the most luxurious way possible.

"Let's take the tour," I told them, and we headed down a long gallery to the 3,000-square-foot master suite. Here, too, we were surrounded by a seductive combination of luxury and good taste. A rosewood fireplace graced one wall of the bedroom, and glass double doors opened onto a spacious walk and more views of the Atlantic. I showed the producers the suite's "his and hers" dressing rooms, the shower, steam room, sauna, and raised Jacuzzi (also with an ocean view).

From there we visited the dining room (where the table was set for a formal dinner for 14), the combination wine cellar/bar/tasting room (2,000 bottles of the world's finest wine at hand), the game room (where you can play darts, billiards, blackjack, or my personal favorite, pinball), the movie theatre (with THX surround sound), and the office (a replica of the White House Oval Office). After sauntering through the other bedroom suites upstairs, we took the glass elevator up to the third level and stepped out onto the sundeck, 60 feet above ocean level. Our lunch was set up right next to another Jacuzzi, which overlooked an expanse of white sand beach and incredibly blue water. The wind was blowing gently from the sea, carrying that indefinable, intoxicating scent of the Gulf Stream. I waved the producers to their seats. "Iced tea or champagne?" I offered with a smile.

Over lunch, they started interviewing me. "How old are you, Frank?"

"Thirty-three."

"How long have you been doing this?"

"Well, I bought my first piece of Florida real estate in 1986." (I didn't tell them it was a roach-infested teardown in the wrong part of town.) "However, my first million-dollar sale was Driftwood Dunes in 1992. Since then I've designed and built five houses with prices ranging from $2.2 million to $12 million. And my next project is a $30 million, 30,000-square-foot mansion."

The producers looked at each other; one of them whistled. "That's a lot of house, Frank. Where do *you* live? Have you built one of these for yourself?"

At that point I had to laugh out loud. "Sorry, folks," I said, wiping my eyes. "But I just moved into a nice three-bedroom house from a zero-bedroom efficiency apartment. It's the first time in six years my wife and I have lived in anything bigger than a thousand square feet."

Now they were *really* confused! I took pity on them and explained, "When I bought Driftwood Dunes, my first oceanfront property, I put everything into it. To raise the down payment, I sold the house that Nilsa and I were living in, and we moved into an efficiency apartment. We lived like that until Driftwood Dunes sold. Since then, we've been looking for a house that would suit our needs, and we just moved into a 1930s home in Delray Beach. It's comfortable, the kind of place you'd like to raise a family. My wife's pregnant, you know; she's due in a couple of months."

"Let me get this straight, Frank," the woman producer said. "You build some of the most opulent, luxurious mansions in the world, and yet up until recently you lived in a one-room apartment. Since you renovated your very first million-dollar house, you've spent money hand over fist to make sure everything was the absolute best, yet you had to sell everything, including your own home, to make that happen. Now you've got this amazing estate on the market," and she waved her hand to indicate where we were, "And I'm sure you've got a lot of money tied up in it. This place may sell tomorrow, and it may never sell at all. That's got to be an extreme amount of financial stress—yet you seem completely calm, collected, and content. How the heck do you do it? How do you sleep at night and keep that full head of hair?"

I smiled and shrugged. "Simple. Philosophy #25: 'Gently yet often exercise your risk threshold like a muscle. Eventually it will become stronger and able to withstand greater pressure.' I've been exercising my risk threshold for years so it will hold up under almost any kind of financial stress."

The other producer, a man, was intrigued. "What do you mean, 'Philosophy #25'?"

"Over the years I've come up with a list of 49 guiding Philosophies that have helped me to be successful," I answered. "I'll show them to you later, if you like. But before I do, there's another property I'd like you to see."

Just a few miles away from the oceanfront estates of Palm Beach, Manalapan, Gulf Stream, and Delray is a very different world: the section of Palm Beach County where I bought my first piece of property in 1986. It's the part of town where, as a volunteer for Caring Kitchen, every Monday night for four years I took a van out into the alleyways of crack neighborhoods and fed hot meals to the homeless. We drove through the "other" Palm Beach to a small house in a decent neighborhood.

Someone had obviously done a lot of work on the house; its paint and fixtures looked brand-new and well cared for. I pulled up in front and parked. "This is one of the projects I'm most proud of," I told the producers. "An 80-year-old man named Buster Rollins lives here. Buster was living in a one-bedroom rattrap of an apartment and paying more than half his Social Security check in rent. Then Buster's landlord decided to expand his funeral parlor business, and he took over the apartment. Buster had no place to live; he was going to be out on the street.

"As a volunteer for the Caring Kitchen, I used to serve meals out of the back of a van in some of the worst neighborhoods in Palm Beach County. Buster was one of the men we fed. When I heard he was being evicted, I knew I had to do something. So I bought this house, fixed it up, furnished it, and moved Buster in. Because I believe people feel more self-respect when they contribute instead of getting something for nothing, Buster pays me rent—$1 a month. Buster makes his money collecting aluminum cans, so considering how much work he has to do for that dollar, I feel it's a fair trade."

"Do you still keep in touch with Buster?" the woman producer asked.

"I come over here each month and collect the rent personally," I told her. "I really enjoy talking to Buster. I admire his determination, his willingness to work, his commitment to taking care of himself. He reminds me of lessons I apply every day in my life and my business."

"Like what?" the other producer asked as we got back in the Hummer and drove back to La Marceaux.

"Things like 'Proactively and creatively persist, day in and day out' and 'Take the "lunch pail" approach,' " I answered. "And 'Celebrate each humble victory as a triumphant achievement.' And my personal favorite, 'Many of us are fortunate to be blessed with the ability to succeed—not for our sole benefit, but so we may apply the result of our success to assist others.' "

"More of those Philosophies you talked about, Frank?" the guy asked.

"Yep," I said. "They cover every aspect of life. They're the reason I've been blessed with success. And they're the reason my life rocks!"

At that point I turned on the CD player, and my favorite rock music, Van Halen, started blasting. "Before we go back to the house, how about a ride on my bike?" I asked. "It's a Kawasaki ZX-12R, the world's fastest production motorcycle. I know a couple of places where we can take it out and really rip!"

———

How the heck did I do it? How did I go from being 18 and broke to providing homes to billionaires? How did I arrive in Florida a lousy student, a kid in trouble with the law, the black sheep of a well-respected family, and become a millionaire by my late twenties, building some of the most expensive mansions in the world, hobnobbing with people like Don King, Dave Thomas, Oprah Winfrey, Bruce Willis, Demi Moore, Richard De Vos, Jeff Gordon—all the while keeping my long hair, my motorcycles, and my unconventional attitude? At a relatively young age, how did I *dare* create a life most people would kill for? And why do I think I'm qualified to tell you how to succeed?

I believe that, along with every other area in business and life, the rules for success are changing. Today's generation doesn't want yesterday's version of success. We want our success harder, faster, bigger than ever before. We're willing to push the envelope in terms of risk, as long as it leads to big rewards. We want what I call *extreme* success: success at higher levels than ever before, not just in business, but in every area of life. In other words, we want to *make it big!*

I've always liked the word *extreme*—extreme sports, extreme games, extreme wealth. To me, *extreme* means the ability to handle large amounts of risk: to be willing to ski or skate or jump or do moves that no sane person would attempt. Well, that's exactly what I do in business. I take huge financial risks that go against the conventional wisdom of the real estate community. But I believe extreme success includes a lot more than selling the world's most opulent mansion, or creating the next hot company, or issuing the largest initial public offering (IPO), or discovering technology that will revolutionize the world. Don't get me wrong: Wealth, your own successful company (or companies), and creating something new are all great things—but extreme success means a lot more. It means succeeding in *every* area of your life: You have a great home and family. You have friends who value you for yourself, not for what you can do for them. You "spread the wealth" by helping others, giving of your time as well as your substance. You're in great shape physically, mentally, emotionally, and especially spiritually. You have a blast every day when you get up. You create a legacy that will live on after you're gone. And like extreme sports, you're pushing the envelope every single day, going beyond what anyone expects you to do, doing things bigger, better, faster than everyone else. Extreme success combines enormous business and financial accomplishment with love, friends, family, contribution, and every other element that makes up a life that truly rocks.

I'm happy to say that's the kind of life I have right now. I'm married to a fantastic woman, and we have a young daughter. I devote 15 percent of my time every week to philanthropic and community causes, which include my church, young people (I'm the cofounder of the Delray Beach Youth Council, which was formed to give teenagers a greater say in local government), and building housing for the homeless. I can honestly say I go to bed most nights a very happy man; I've managed to create the money I want and have the family I want, in the community I want, doing exactly what I want to do in the style I want to do it.

I've also spent the past 15 years figuring out why what I was doing worked so well—and why my life was a lot more exciting and fulfilling than those of most of the other hotshots I met along the way. Unlike most people (who seem to let life happen to them and never try to figure it out until they're sitting in a rocking chair at age 80), I started the practice of introspection when I founded my first business at age 19. (Okay, maybe it was at age 22, when I established the Young Entrepreneurial Society of Palm Beach County; at any rate, it was several years before I made my first million.) I kept asking myself, "Okay, why is this working? Why can I make the deal when someone else didn't? Why is my life turning out so well? What's the secret of this particular success?"

I studied other successful people, and saw how even the most astounding levels of financial wealth didn't keep them from being miserable human beings. I also saw how some of my contemporaries had given up on success because they were afraid of what it might cost them. It seemed my generation was running into what I thought of as the "same old, same old" problems: either (1) we wanted success but had no clue how to create it or (2) even if we were successful in business, often we had no idea how to be successful in the rest of our lives at the same time.

As I succeeded—and watched my contemporaries either making it big or going down in flames—I distilled my observations into a series of simple Philosophies, concise statements of why I was able to outdo others my own age (and older). Year after year, I added to the list. Today I have 49 Philosophies I try to live by every single day. They're my checklist; I use them every Saturday when I reflect on my life and plan my week. I believe they're the reason I continue to experience an ongoing level of success and happiness, not just in business, but in every area of life. They're also a part of my own personal legacy, far more important to me than the mansions I've built or the money I've accumulated. I hope they're the kind of legacy that will help others to create their own extreme success.

Now, I haven't mastered any of these Philosophies by any stretch of the imagination! There have been times I've forgotten, or gotten a little too busy, or yielded to temptation, or had my life get out of balance. Much of my weekly introspection consists of examining just how many ways I have failed to embody these principles. But when I do come back to them, it's like coming home. And when I'm living by them consistently, I'm in the zone; I feel like I can walk on water. Then, of course, I realize it's water and fall through once more! But I always pick myself up and try to live by them again, because through the years I have applied each and every one of them in different circumstances and seen their power in action.

A few years ago I started sharing these Philosophies whenever I speak to young entrepreneurs and teenagers. (Somehow I still fit in better with them than I do with businesspeople my own age—must have something to do with Philosophy #43, "Resist the temptation to act like an adult." Either that, or the fact that I refuse to cut my hair.) I also use them when I meet with these kids one-on-one. They come to my office or a project site, or maybe we just go for a walk on the beach, and they ask me, "Why am I here? What am I supposed to do with my life?" And I tell them, "First of all, that's a question you're going to spend your whole life answering. But I'll bet you already have a sense of which direction you want to go. So go for it. Take a risk. Life's going to teach you lessons along the way, and you should look for them and learn from them. And don't ignore the basics of success—things like being disciplined, being organized, working hard, and being willing to risk everything if you believe in what you're doing. Those kinds of principles aren't old-fashioned; they're time-less—because they work."

And I believe they'll work for you, too.

I invite you to use this book as your guide to extreme success. In each chapter I've used the story of my own life to illustrate how these principles work, in the hope you can use my mistakes and successes as a guide to creating the life you've always wanted. At the end of each Philosophy you'll find some suggested actions, ideas of some ways you can implement this Philosophy in your life. You'll also see a section called "Deal Points." In real estate, deal points are the key elements of a negotiation. Here, I use the Deal Points section to provide examples of how to apply the Philosophy in the contexts of real estate and business.

This book, and these Philosophies, may not be anything new to you. They surely won't provide you with a business plan for the next new thing. But they *will* show you how to train yourself to take risks, develop phenomenal relationships with customers and coworkers, create a niche in whatever marketplace you want, and become the go-to guy or gal in your industry. More important, it will show you how to live a life full of excitement, passion, and deep feelings of happiness. That kind of life doesn't come from your first, or five hundredth, million—it comes from living, giving, contributing, building a legacy, and doing it on your own terms. You *don't* have to do it someone else's way; you can buck the system and create a whole new category of success for yourself. And you can have a blast while doing it!

I believe it's simple to make it big—after all, if a guy like me can go from digging sand traps by hand on a Palm Beach golf course to building multimillion-dollar mansions a few miles away, anyone can make their dreams come true. So I dare you to succeed. Like Philosophy #25 says, "Gently yet often exercise your risk threshold like a muscle. Eventually it will become stronger and able to withstand greater pressure." So get in the psychological "gym" and build your risk muscle by exercising it a little every day. That's the only way you'll truly make it big!

Part One

Have a Vision for Your Passion

In the mid-1950s, my grandfather was offered a chance to get in on a business deal by a man he met through his good friend Bing Crosby. The man and my grandfather took an airboat out into the middle of the Everglades, where the gentleman said, "I envision a huge castle here, amusement rides the likes of which no one has ever experienced, a cartoon mouse, and all these other characters. People from around the world will come here and visit the park I'm going to build. Would you like to be part of it?" My grandfather turned to him and said, "Are you crazy? A castle? In the middle of the Everglades? Orlando as a tourist destination? I don't think so!" And he turned Walt Disney down on his offer to invest in Disney World.

A few years later, when Disney World was getting ready to open, Walt unfortunately had passed away, but his brother, Roy Disney, was there. Supposedly a reporter asked Roy about the sad fact that his brother wasn't there to see what had been created in Disney World. "Oh, Walt saw it," Roy replied. "You're seeing it now because he saw it years ago."

To make it big, you have to know where you want to go and have endless passion for getting there. You not only have to be able to go into the Everglades and see a Magic Kingdom; you also have to be excited and passionate about making that dream a reality. Each project I undertake has a vision driving it. For me, the most exciting moment of a multimillion-dollar project isn't when I sell it; it's when I buy the property that will give me the opportunity to create it. Walking in the door

13

of a house I've just bought, or walking across the raw dirt of a plot of land, and seeing in my mind's eye what that land or property will be transformed into when I'm through—that is the true magic moment. I literally see myself a year or 18 months later handing the house keys to the new owner, with this magnificent estate in the background. But I also know I will need plenty of passion, drive, and hard work to take that vision out of my head and create it on that plot of land. If you have one without the other—vision without passion, or passion without vision—you'll never have extreme success.

What Walt Disney called vision others (like my grandfather, unfortunately) called dreams. To me, a dream is a great fantasy with no possibility of coming true. I can dream I'm the King of England, but unless there's been a vast genealogical mistake somewhere I'm unlikely to sit on the throne. But what I would consider vision and aspiration far too many people call dreams. And here's the problem: Most people put their dreams up on pedestals, out of reach, and consider them unattainable. "I'll never get a date with him," they think, or "I'll never make the football team." When they get older, it's "I'll never get that promotion" or "I can't start my own business," or "I'll never own my own home." (I made quite a bit of money showing people how to turn that last dream into reality. You'll learn more about that in Part Two.) But all of those dreams are eminently attainable, aren't they? The only two things holding most people back are fear and lack of passion. The difference between those who attain their dreams and those whose dreams remain either entertaining fantasies or factories of regret is simply *the vision to see a dream as something you can and will turn into reality.*

I have never considered anything I've ever aspired to as a dream, because I knew that with enough vision and passion I could make it happen. In 1991 I had been in the distressed real estate business for six years. I had bought foreclosed and tax-sale houses at auction, renovated them nicely, and then sold them to first-time home buyers at a profit. I was doing very well for myself, but my vision was much bigger than that. One day I was walking on the beach, looking at the gorgeous homes overlooking the water. Some of them were gorgeous, anyway; others looked a little weather-beaten. I thought, *I could do the same thing on the oceanfront: buy property at the right price, fix it up, and then sell it. I'll bet I can make more profit in one sale of oceanfront property than I can in 20 of the smaller deals I'm doing now!*

But there was just one catch: I discovered I'd need 20 times the capital to put into that one oceanfront project up front. So I sold my own house, maxed out my credit, and bought my first piece of ocean-front property for $775,000—a big jump from paying $30,000 for a foreclosure property at auction. And all the $775,000 bought me was a house everyone considered a teardown, even if it was right on the water! A lot of people thought I was crazy. But I had a vision of what I could do, and I had the passion to carry through with it. And that vision has gotten me where I am today.

I'm proud of the fact that people here in South Florida have called me a visionary, but everyone has the gift of vision. A visionary is just someone who makes a conscious effort to look to the end of the deal and see it succeeding in a manner consistent with his or her plan. In other words, a visionary thinks in terms of the big picture. We have "big picture" meetings at our company all the time, and I insist that everyone take part in creating the vision. "Don't sit back and let me give you the big picture," I'll say. "Where do *you* think we ought to go?" When people get used to thinking in a visionary way, looking past their own personal concerns and seeing how everyone can work together to create something great, not only their work but also their lives can be transformed.

The kind of vision I'm talking about isn't confined to your profession, however; it touches every aspect of your life. It revolves around something I call a *highest calling*: the purpose of your life, why you were born. When you have a vision for your life that includes family, work, spirituality, and civic and charitable contributions, it's easy to have a passion for who you are and what you do. You can be comfortable even with the riskiest decisions because you know why you're making them, and you're driven to do whatever it takes to turn your vision into reality. (Here's one of the greatest things about vision: When people tell you no, you only get stronger.) A clear vision of your highest calling enables you to live with integrity. I won't say decision making becomes easier, as some decisions are always going to be difficult to make. But the *right* decision becomes a whole lot clearer when you have a vision for your life.

In this section you'll learn how you can create a vision for your life that will keep you passionate enough to make it big. You'll discover how to find your highest calling, the ultimate vision for your life. You'll learn how to take that highest calling and turn it into a personal vision or mission statement that you can use to direct your focus and actions on a daily, weekly, and yearly basis. You'll understand the need for introspection, spending time with yourself to evaluate how you're living up to your vision and mission. You'll see how to make decisions and take actions that reinforce your integrity rather than tear it down. You'll learn how to seek out the lessons life is trying to teach you and master them as quickly and painlessly as possible. You'll see why you must never compromise your beliefs or person just to close a deal or get ahead or any of the other excuses other people make. And you'll learn the importance of balancing your professional talents with your spiritual ones, and how both can help you succeed.

Before I set foot on a tennis court to start my tennis business, before I opened a newspaper to look for my first foreclosure, before I sought out my first oceanfront property, I always had a strong, clear vision of what I wanted to create and the passion to make the vision real. In this section you're going to hear many examples drawn from my own career; you'll learn ideas that I hope you'll be able to apply should you be in (or seek to enter) the real estate profession. But vision is so much more than any one profession or project. When your vision encompasses your life as well as your work, then no matter what—the market falls apart, the hurricane hits, your properties take a while to sell—you will keep right on dreaming, creating, and passionately living a life that will make a difference. And like Walt Disney, you may create a Magic Kingdom where one never existed before.

1

Recognize Your Highest Calling As Early As Possible in Life

This philosophy is first on my list because this is where it all starts. Why were you born? What were you put on this earth to do? What kind of legacy were you meant to leave? A highest calling is beyond your personal vision or mission. It's your destiny. It takes into account all of your life; it is literally the reason you were born. Recognizing your highest calling as early as possible should be your first priority. There's nothing sadder than seeing people in their thirties or even forties wandering aimlessly, with no idea of why they were put on this earth.

There are five criteria you should bring to bear when figuring out your highest calling. First, it should involve your heart; it should be *something you will find emotionally fulfilling.* Second, your head needs to get involved as well; your highest calling should be *something you have potential for.* Are you going to be able to succeed in this calling? Are you suited for it physically (in some cases), emotionally, and intellectually? If you want to be an opera singer but you can't carry a tune, perhaps that's not your highest calling. Third, it needs to be *something you want to do for a long time.* While a highest calling may change over the years, for anything to be classified as a highest calling you must be willing to put in time (perhaps a lifetime) pursuing it. Fourth, it must be *something you feel will utilize all your God-given gifts and talents.* I don't believe we're given certain aptitudes for nothing; your talents may provide a good indication of where your highest calling lies. And fifth, it must be *something that will make a difference in your life and ideally the lives of others.* Your highest calling will be a significant part of your time here on earth; make sure it has significance for both you and others.

A few people know right away what their highest calling is: They were born to be a musician, or an athlete, or a mathematician, for example. I envy such people but think they're pretty rare, because for most of us figuring out our highest calling is a process, one that often starts by figuring out what we *don't* want. When I was a teenager, growing up with a father in banking, I knew pretty quickly that I wasn't in the least interested in following in his footsteps. I also knew that formal education wouldn't be a part of my highest calling.

The stuff that doesn't work for us is usually pretty obvious, but then we have to zoom in on where our strengths and our hearts lie. Your highest calling had better start with your heart or you'll never be satisfied. What do you like to do? What are you yearning for? If you don't take those feelings into account, you'll never be happy with whatever profession you choose, and your career probably won't represent your true highest calling. It's like people who really want to be performers—actors or musicians or dancers. If they don't recognize that desire, either by going for it and trying to be successful in those professions or by incorporating those feelings into their lives in some other way, their chances for happiness and satisfaction are a lot more limited.

Luckily, I knew what I liked. I liked being on my own (I found that out when I went to boarding school for a year); I liked being my own boss; it was also pretty clear I liked risk taking and living on the edge.

And I wanted to be the best at whatever I chose. So I thought, "I'll become a stunt man!" I did some research and found a place where I could take a (short) course in stunt work before moving to Hollywood. But I had to earn the money for the course first—and that's where my highest calling started to take a turn.

Sometimes the signs of your highest calling come in very strange ways. I came to Florida when I was 18 simply because I liked this part of the world; it seemed like a great place to live and work while I earned the money for stunt school. But once I got here, I didn't want to leave—I had a change of heart. I also had a sense I could do more with my life than just taking falls for other people. I flirted briefly with being an actor, taking classes, even going out to Los Angeles for a summer and landing a few pitiful parts. But again, my head and heart weren't satisfied. For me, acting failed the fourth criterion; it didn't utilize all the talents I felt I had. (Many of us go through a process of elimination when seeking our highest calling. It's like college kids choosing a major: They may try and reject several before settling on the one that suits them.)

Meanwhile, I was using my talent for tennis to make money: I had convinced the manager of the country club where I was digging sand traps to sponsor me for a course to get my certification as a tennis instructor. With this certification, I then went to the condominium complexes that are all over South Florida and gave lessons on their courts. It was out of those lessons that the direction for my highest calling—to be an entrepreneur—began to appear. I thought, *What if instead of just teaching one person in this complex, I create a program for the whole place?* I approached the manager and got his agreement to start a tennis program, and then did the same with three other condominium complexes. Pretty soon I was running a business that grossed over $100,000 a year—and I was all of 20 years old. (It's not enough to want something with your heart; your highest calling must be something you have the potential for as well.)

After about two years I realized there was a limit to how long I could take the hot sun and how much I could really do with the business. I felt there was something more. (That feeling is a key indicator that you may not have found your highest calling yet.) So in 1986 I turned my entrepreneurial focus to real estate; and from the very first 600-square-foot house I bought, I have never looked back. I pursued my highest calling immediately and with intense persistence. My career meets all five of the "highest calling" criteria. I love what I do; it is mentally, emotionally, and financially challenging and rewarding. I'm good at what I do, and my results show it. I've been in real estate for 15 years and yet I'm constantly learning more every day. I seem to be using all of the talents that God has given me, both as a person and as a professional. I am working for the betterment of my family and the community in which I live. There may be other criteria that you feel must be met to satisfy your highest calling, but the bottom line is that you must feel in your heart that you would thoroughly enjoy pursuing this direction. Oh yes—you should also have an overwhelming sense of urgency to get going!

Your highest calling may or may not be a profession per se. My mom's highest calling was exactly that: being a mother to her six children, a tireless volunteer at our local church, and a contributor to the community. Your highest calling may be your avocation instead of your vocation. That's fine. I believe your highest calling can be applied both personally and professionally; for example, I apply my entrepreneurial talents by teaching teenagers how to become entrepreneurs (and keep themselves out of trouble in the process). And I don't think your highest calling necessarily means you have to choose one profession and stay with it forever. There are career changes, midlife changes, retirement. My highest calling has taken at least two different forms—buying and selling distressed properties and creating ultra-high-end custom oceanfront estates. At 38, I've still got many years ahead of me to pursue my highest calling, and I'm sure it will take other forms before I'm done. But remember: Your highest calling will lead directly to the legacy you leave here on earth. Whatever you believe is your highest calling, it's important to believe in it, commit to it, and follow it to the best of your ability.

That brings me to the final point about your highest calling: It's not about making money, although you may do very well. It's not about being successful, although it's easier to be successful following a calling than just doing a job. It's not even about being happy, although if you are truly pursuing your highest calling, happiness usually follows. When you pursue your highest calling, you will find yourself making a difference. You can't help it. Out of my highest calling of being a real estate entrepreneur has come an enormous desire to use my talents to help others, through coaching teens, building houses for the homeless, and feeding the hungry. Writing this book is an outgrowth of my highest calling. When you're following your highest calling, you're following a path laid out for your lifetime here on earth. And hopefully you'll live a life like George Bernard Shaw described when he wrote: "This is the true joy of life, the being used for a purpose recognized by yourself as a mighty one."

Actions

1. You may have a very clear idea of your own highest calling. If so, great! You might want to check your choice against the five criteria to affirm your choice.
2. If you're not sure you're in the right profession, or you don't even know whether you have a highest calling, relax. Remember, "as early as possible" does not mean when you're a teenager. It is *never* too late to recognize and pursue your highest calling.
3. Discovering your highest calling may be a process. Early in your career or your life you will undoubtedly experiment with what you might want to do, the same way college students often change majors. Start with your heart, add a healthy dose of reality—is this something you can do well and you'll be happy doing for a long time?—and make sure it fulfills the talents God gave you, and you'll be on the right track in no time.

Deal Points

Can your profession be an outlet for your highest calling? You'd better believe it—in fact, I believe the only way to really make it big is when your highest calling and your profession are in complete alignment. For most of us, our profession takes up a great deal of our focus, time, energy, and so on. And the only way we can put our heads and hearts into our profession is if we truly want to. And that usually means some involvement of your highest calling.

Check your profession to see whether it fulfills the five criteria listed in this chapter. First, do you enjoy your work? Is it emotionally fulfilling? Do you feel good about yourself at the end of the day? Next, do you feel you're succeeding? Is your potential being satisfied in your particular field? If you're just getting started, there may be some aspects of your potential that aren't being fulfilled yet. If this is the case, ask yourself, "If I continue in this profession and make manager (or agent, or own X number of properties), will I be fulfilling my potential?"

Third, is this profession or field something you'll be happy working in for the next 10, 20, 30 years—not the same job, hopefully, but in the same profession? Fourth, are you utilizing all your talents and gifts? If you're just starting out, you may have some talents that aren't being called upon; but could they be called upon if you continue to grow in this field? Finally, are you making a difference in your life and the lives of others? Doing a good job in your profession will almost automatically ensure that you are making some kind of contribution to life. If your profession or field meets all these criteria, then you're in the groove— you're able to mesh your highest calling with your profession in a truly fruitful partnership.

If your profession didn't score 100 percent on the highest calling test, examine the areas where it did and didn't match. Are there other areas of this profession that might be more suitable? Are there avocations you could pursue that would give you the satisfaction you can't get in this particular field? Remember, pursuing your highest calling is a matter for your whole life, not just your profession. If you can't make as big a contribution to others through your job, maybe you can spend time volunteering. If you have the itch to act or sing or dance and you're an accountant, are there other outlets where you could satisfy that need?

To really make it big and be happy while doing it, you need to find a profession that is part of your highest calling. Get clear about what your calling is, and then follow it. Even if you're at the end of your career, it's not too late; perhaps your highest calling will reach its greatest expression in retirement. But whenever, wherever, and however you do so, find your highest calling and follow it. It's the only way I know to truly make it big.

Know Where You're Going:
Create a Personal Vision or Mission Statement

Your highest calling can give you a sense of what your purpose in life will be. But how will you put that highest calling to work today, this week, this year, over the next five years? And how do you integrate your highest calling into the different parts of your life—personal and professional, family and friends, civic responsibilities and recreation? That's where a personal vision and/or mission statement comes in very handy. Have you ever asked AAA to plan a road trip for you? They'll give you what's called a "TripTik," a map of the suggested route for your entire trip, broken into one small segment per page, with your route marked in red. If you use the map and follow the route, you'll reach your destination safely and efficiently. Well, if your highest calling is the road of your life, your vision and mission statement is the "TripTik" of the next section.

There are plenty of people who dream about what they would do if they were rich. They fantasize about sports cars, beautiful homes, and trips to exotic, faraway places. But most people never spend the time coming up with a plan for how they might achieve their vision of success. Without a plan, success won't happen by chance unless you win the lottery. Your vision and mission statement is the blueprint for your success. It shows you how to get from point A, where you are now, to point B, where you want to go. It's not a list of goals; it goes deeper than that. This is a vision statement for your life. Just like our country has the Constitution of the United States of America, you could call this your personal constitution.

I started creating mission and vision statements when I was in my early twenties. I didn't call them that; they were just scribblings about where I saw myself in 10 years. But as soon as I committed my thoughts to paper, they seemed a lot more real. I believe the key to vision and mission statements is to *write them down*. The difference between a written mission statement and one that's in your head is the same as a written business plan and one that's still being formulated. As soon as you write something down, it ceases to be a pipe dream and becomes something you might eventually achieve. I go on a personal retreat each year, and use that time to create a personal vision and mission statement for the next 12 months. That statement (which is usually no more than a page) forms the basis of my efforts in every single area of my life. I refer to it weekly; I check my progress against it. It is a combination of my personal road map and my constitution—the rules and guidelines by which I live.

Stephen Covey's work helped make vision and mission statements popular. He is the master. You can use Covey's format to create your own vision and mission statement. In my planning process, I use some of Covey's questions and techniques, but ultimately I base my vision and mission statement on these three questions:

1. **What's my highest calling?** I always remember my highest calling when I'm creating my yearly vision and mission statement.
2. **What areas of my life am I focusing on at this time of my life?** Covey calls these your "roles," but to me they're just the different parts of my life that need attention.
3. **What is my vision for how I want to be in these areas?** Note that I'm not talking about what I want to accomplish. A vision statement is bigger than goals or accomplishments; it takes into account who you want to become rather than what you want to do. If I focus on becoming the person I envision, then I will take the actions necessary to create that person. If I try to take the actions first without that vision of who I want to become, that's a lot harder and means a longer road to success.

Once I have answered those three questions and written the answers down, I add one final question: **Is this vision something I can work on and create within the time frame I have set?** (In most cases the time frame would be a year.) If the answer is yes, then the list becomes my personal vision and mission statement for the year. On the page following is what I'm working on for 2002.

Notice a couple of things. First, the work from which I receive the most compensation and recognition is item number four—last on the list. That's a deliberate choice. In past years, I have focused too much on my work, and even though I have reaped great benefits from it, I know I

Personal Vision Statement
of Frank McKinney

In the areas of:

1. Family/Personal Growth Interests.
2. Philanthropy/Youth/Civic Involvements.
3. Building Relationships and Custom Projects.
4. Creating a Marketplace and the Success of My Personal Projects.

- Apply my God-given talents and awareness to procure for me and my family the security and peace necessary to allow me to assist those who can benefit from my blessings.
- Trust in and surrender all to God and His plan for me, for He shall bless me with success not for the sole benefit of myself but for those I shall assist.
- Learn to realize that time spent away from work will not leave me at a disadvantage. I will return sharper and refreshed. Recognize the need to address the truly important aspects of life first and worry not over my status in the marketplace.
- Give more than I receive—love and care for those less fortunate by providing compassion and expertise in order to ease the daily calvaries that life presents.
- Live by strong and correct principles. With consistent and diligent learning of life's lessons, review my principles on a regular basis.
- Understand that the space in time between stimulus and response is where integrity is built. Display patience and calm temperament in situations that appear to challenge my higher calling.
- Listen and understand prior to seeking to be understood.
- Keep in perspective what role I wish money to play in my life. Apply its powers and privileges in a responsible way.
- Work on fulfilling my marriage and needs of my family to the best of my ever-changing and improving ability.
- Recognize leadership qualities in others and encourage them to enhance God's gifts.
- Remember that by acting on any beneficial thoughts and compassionate feelings, a difference will be made in the lives of others as well as my own.

need more balance. I also know that it's easy for me to get most of my satisfaction from my work, so it will always be a temptation to focus there when I should be spending time elsewhere. Therefore, my family and my philanthropic interests are higher priorities for me at this time. That doesn't mean I won't focus on work—that's a given. But I want to keep my work in perspective.

Second, you may be thinking, "There's not a lot about success on this list!" You're right. Remember, this vision and mission statement is the latest in a series of more than 10 years of doing them. When I first began, there was a great deal more about creating a name for myself, succeeding at a higher level, and making money rather than determining its proper role in my life. But remember also, your vision and mission statement is supposed to be a representation of how you want to pursue your highest calling. And your highest calling always has to do with your purpose in life and how it can make a difference for yourself and others. Even when I was far more focused on increasing my success, I still put emphasis on philanthropic and civic involvements, on my relationships, and on my own personal growth. If your vision for your life is focused only on succeeding in business, you'll never really make it because you'll be leaving a large part of yourself behind.

(You also may notice that several of the Philosophies in this book are represented in my vision and mission statement. Many of these Philosophies were born out of my vision and mission statements through the years, and they are attributes and qualities I strive to embody on a daily basis.)

Once you've created your personal vision and mission statement, then you need a means to implement it. That's when I pull out my weekly organizational chart. Using this tool and my personal vision statement, I can plan the goals I need to accomplish in order to fulfill my vision and mission. I can organize my week around what's important rather than urgent (to use a Coveyism).

Turn the page for a sample chart.

You can see I took the four areas of focus from my personal vision statement and wrote them across the top of the page. Underneath each area, I list my goals for the week in order of importance (#1 for most important, #2 for next most important, and so on). When I'm finished, I have up to 20 goals, which I then transfer to my weekly calendar.

Now, that might be too much to get accomplished in one week. So which goals do you think I focus on? The first goal in each area. If I accomplish all my #1 goals, I will have made significant progress on my

Personal and Professional
Weekly Organizational Chart and Goals Agenda

Week beginning Monday, _____ ending Sunday, _____.

Important initiatives I wish to fulfill:

	#1 Family/ Personal Growth Interests	#2 Philanthropy/ Youth/ Civic Involvements	#3 Relationships/ Custom Projects	#4 Creating a Marketplace/ Personal Projects
#1				
#2				
#3				
#4				
#5				

❏ Nilsa   Other priorities to consider:
❏ Cathy
❏ Bob
❏ Peggy
❏ Crystal

Remember: Connect to Vision Statement and Transfer Goals to Weekly Calendar personal vision. Anything that I don't manage to accomplish I can move to the following week. Sure, I jump around. Monday morning at eight o'clock you'll probably find me focusing on my #1 goal in the area of Creating a Marketplace (which is my #4 priority). But by the end of the week, I'm pretty darn certain to have made progress on my #1 goals in each area.

I can also leverage these goals or get help on them from the people listed at the bottom of the page. These are major players in my life—my wife Nilsa (who's also the interior designer on my projects); my administrative assistant; my president of construction; the company bookkeeper/office manager; and so on. Calling upon their help in accomplishing the major goals of my life is just plain smart, to my way of thinking.

At the bottom of the chart you'll notice a line saying, "Other priorities to consider." This is where I list projects and items that aren't as time-sensitive or pressing as my goals for the week, but they're things that will become pressing if I put them off for too long. For example, I do quarterly performance reviews for my office and administrative staff, and I like to prepare for those reviews a month in advance. Three weeks before the review date, I might put "Prepare for performance reviews" in the section marked "Other priorities to consider." If during the week I complete all the goals I have listed in the "Important initiatives" area, then I can glance at my chart, see what other priorities I should handle, and start work on those reviews. If my week is busy and I don't get to my other priorities, I'll simply move the reviews into one of the goal boxes as needed.

This simple planning process—setting aside one weekend a year to create a new personal vision statement, and then taking a couple of hours each Saturday to establish the goals that will help me turn that vision into reality—has been the bedrock underlying my success for the past 10 years. Once I started doing this, I found a marked change in my life and in my results. Sure, I was accomplishing more, since I was taking the time to plan my week. But more than that, I was linking my weekly goals to the vision of who I wanted to be.

A personal vision and mission statement is the agreement you make with yourself that this is who you want to be, how you want to act, what you will and won't do, and how you want to appear in the world. It's also a living, breathing document that will change over the years. I know there are some people who like to create 5- and 10-year plans for their lives, but I'm not one of them. Sure, I can have a sense of who I want to be 10 years from now, but I have found that redoing my vision every year keeps it fresh. It allows me to take into account the progress I have or haven't made and set my direction based on what I see as my next step. After all, I have the big picture of my highest calling—as we discussed in Philosophy #1—that pulls me toward my ultimate future much more strongly than a 5- or 10-year plan.

But creating your own vision begins by your committing to paper what it is you want, and who it is you want to be. The vision statement doesn't have to be long; perhaps it's just one sentence, or a few things you want to make your priority for the year. But write it down. After all, what kind of country would we be if the founding fathers hadn't created a vision statement for the United States of America called the Constitution?

Actions

1. Create your personal vision and mission statement using the guidelines I've suggested. Or if you have another system you like (Stephen Covey's, for example), use that. Just make sure your vision is something you can concentrate on for the entire year, and it is focused on who you want to be as well as what you want to accomplish.
2. Read your personal vision statement at least once a week, preferably when you plan your week. (You *do* plan your week, don't you? We'll discuss that in Philosophy #24, "Organization is the key to success.") Use your vision to guide the goals you set and the areas in which you focus.

Deal Points

Every successful business has a plan, a vision of how to achieve goals and assure the continued health and vitality of the enterprise. Your business should have a vision and mission statement similar to your personal one. What is your vision for your business? What is its mission? How do you want your business to be viewed within the community? How will you set yourself apart from the real estate business around the corner? Your business's vision and mission statement is one of your best opportunities to start creating its identity in the marketplace or brand, which I'll discuss in depth in Part Two.

I create a vision statement for each project I undertake. I want the properties I build or renovate to be the finest, most unusual, most deluxe estates in the world. Do you think they would turn out that way if I didn't have a vision of the finished product long before we put a spade in the ground or a hammer to a wall? Each project has a fully articulated vision, which I share with all the major players—architects, designers, subcontractors, and so on. Whenever we have meetings, the comment you'll hear from me the most is, "Where does this decision fit into the big picture on this project?"

Working from a vision instead of just a set of mindless specifications helps all of my people make quality decisions. For example, say we're putting in a kitchen and I want a particular kind of granite for the countertops. However, none of our suppliers can locate that type of granite for me right now—it's not going to be available for another month. What do we do? Bob, my president of construction, takes a look at the problem within the context of the big picture. Is this particular kind of granite going to be the most important thing in that kitchen, the unique style element that the rest of the kitchen is built around? Or is it just a type of granite that Frank saw once and thought would be cool? What's more important: the granite or staying on schedule? And is there something else available right now that will maintain our uniqueness and standard of quality? If Bob knows my vision for this house, he can answer most of those questions and bring me a couple of possible solutions. And since I know he knows the big picture, I can trust him to take all those things into account when we talk.

For entrepreneurs, the line between corporate and personal vision often gets blurry, as the entrepreneur sets and drives the vision for the company. (In some cases—as was true for me throughout most of my years in distressed real estate—you're a company of one, anyway.) So it's even more important that your vision is clearly set and clearly articulated. And eventually it needs to be participatory as well. The people in your company will probably follow your vision to a certain point, but after they've been with you for a while it will be to your benefit to include them in the creation of your vision and the setting of goals to accomplish it. I've found people to be more enthusiastic and willing to do their best when they've been part of the vision- and goal-setting process.

Having a mission or vision statement for your business is the first step. Tying it to your goals is the next. Do your quarterly or yearly goals have anything whatsoever to do with your mission? I see so many entrepreneurs, banks, and other organizations with grandiose mission statements saying "Customers are our first priority," yet their phone systems are a joke, their web sites are confusing and inaccessible, and their salespeople seem to be trained only in getting the sale instead of taking care of customers. When I see that, I know their mission statements are nothing more than pretty wall decorations instead of true visions of how these companies wish to be.

Conversely, when a company's goals are tied to the vision of its corporate identity, you can tell. Think about all those Disney theme parks. Does Disney have a clear vision of its corporate identity? Do you think it is also pretty clear on its vision for what it wants to do? And do you think, given what you see of Disney employees, Disney movies and television shows, and Disney theme parks, that its goals are in alignment with its vision?

The last step is to make sure your daily efforts represent the goals you've set and the vision you've created. When your business spends its days pursuing goals based on your corporate vision, your customers as well as the business community will see you as having integrity. And isn't that the kind of reputation you want?

Setting a vision for your business is one of the most important tools in your entrepreneurial toolbox. A vision is what sets entrepreneurs or intrapreneurs apart from workers who do their nine-to-five and go home. A vision makes work not just earning a paycheck but a means of creating something great. Take the time to create a vision for yourself and your business. You never know what magic you will bring about as a result.

Figure Yourself Out:
Spend Time in Introspection

Once you know your highest calling and have a vision or mission statement as a guide for your daily life, how do you know you're on track? You spend time in introspection. You regularly take a look at what your actions are producing, both good results and failures, and see what you can learn from them. Over two thousand years ago the great philosopher Sophocles said, "The unexamined life is not worth living." The ability to turn inside, examine yourself, and learn from your successes and mistakes is absolutely essential if you want to make it big.

Now, I'm an exceedingly busy, "take action" kind of guy, and most people are surprised to discover I'm introspective, too. I believe it's important to spend time thinking about where we are and where we want to be. For the past six years I've scheduled time every week for private introspection. I also take a personal retreat each year to see how I did as a whole over the previous 12 months. It's the best way I know to keep my vision and mission on track.

You learned in Philosophy #2 about using an organizational chart to implement your vision. That chart is also a key part of my weekly introspection. Every Saturday afternoon (and I think I've missed perhaps two Saturdays in six years), I sit down with the previous week's chart and a copy of my personal vision statement. I review my vision statement first, to remember the big picture of what I want my life to be about this year. Then I look at the previous week's accomplishments and what hasn't gotten done, and I ask, "How was this week? How did I approach things? What did I do well? What did I do wrong? Where did I fail, not only professionally but personally? Where did I not live up to my personal vision statement?" Then I ask the most important questions: "What can I learn from this? How can I be a better person next time?" I write the answers to all those questions on the back of the previous week's chart. Once I have done my introspection, then—and only then—am I ready to plan a new week. Weekly introspection gives me the ability to grasp everything that's going on around me and, for the most part, to feel in control of the direction of my life.

The benefits of introspection really show up when I go on my personal retreat each year. I go off completely by myself, usually to a spot where I can be surrounded by nature's beauty and majesty. I take all the year's weekly sheets with me and spend a day or more reviewing them. It's like looking inside my own soul for the past year. What were my anxieties, my fears, my worries? What were my victories, both personal and professional? Where were the ups and downs? Where can I improve my thought processes? Where do I need to focus more of my time and energy? What habits and emotional traits do I need to eliminate to become happier and more successful? And in the same way I do every week, I write down the results of my introspection about my progress for the year. I wouldn't say the process is relieving, but it sure is enlightening. It's very easy to see where my hot buttons are, where I've been playing to my strengths, and where I need to focus my energy for the next year.

Let me give you a sample of a recent yearly introspection:

> *Just like the majesty and permanence of the mountains I'm looking at, the mountain of life will never fully be conquered. It's the climb that counts, and what a year full of mountaintops reached. A quick reflection: sold four multimillion-dollar properties, bought three others, was chairman of the board of the Delray Beach chamber of commerce, raised $3 million for St. Vincent's. . . .*
>
> *How blessed I am to have such a wonderful daughter and a loving and beautiful wife. I want to make a conscious effort to live a more content life. I want to be the best father and husband possible. I want to work on balancing my life and emotions, to work hard on patience and temperament. I shall continue to listen to my conscience. I shall give of God's gifts. My mantra for the year: a content life of integrity.*
>
> *I'm sure I will remain ambitious and continue to hone my business skills but in a relaxed, balanced way. I won't go soft; I'll only find more strength to live a principle-centered life. My life's calling is to succeed publicly and financially so that I might be able to assist others. That assistance does not always come in financial terms—it includes getting my message across so others may benefit, helping kids in the Youth Council, helping the hungry or homeless with the Caring House II project. There are so many opportunities to be kind and compassionate; I will strive to recognize them.*

As I embark on a content life of integrity, I know there will always be stumbling blocks along the way. If I pray for strength and courage, I shall conquer all shortcomings. I leave by saying thank you to God for my life's many blessings.

The habit of introspection keeps me on track with my personal vision but it also helps me keep on track with the little things, too. Every "spike" in my life—meaning an event that's out of the norm—makes me sit back and say, "Okay, what's going on here? Why did this happen? And what do I need to change, augment, appreciate, or correct?" (Quite honestly, this kind of introspection began when I started to work on my temperament, which used to be quite volatile. It's still not great, but it's better because of my introspection.) Introspection makes me evaluate everything to see if it's progress or a setback. And especially with the setbacks, I examine them in detail to find out what I did wrong, and how I can correct myself in the future.

Here's one example. A couple of years ago I was scheduled to do a presentation to the press about a $60 million house we had planned to build on a large oceanfront lot in Manalapan. There was a huge model of the house, and on it was a plaque with the architect's name. Well, while we were moving the model to the Manalapan site the architect's plaque fell off. I noticed it was missing when we got to the site, but I was so focused on getting everything else ready for the presentation to the press I didn't ask anybody to find it and put it back on the model. After the showing, the architect wrote me a letter and said how disappointed he was not to have his work acknowledged. Now, that was a trivial, understandable oversight on my part, right? But not to him. And when I examined the incident, I saw the kind of effect that seemingly small detail could have on my relationship with him, and possibly on my reputation. In terms of the 49 Philosophies, I had violated the idea of being generous (wasn't there enough credit to go around?) and having integrity (it certainly wasn't living up to who I am). What could have been just a trivial "oh, well" kind of incident turned into a valuable lesson. Introspection is really a process of self-correction; it's somewhat painful at times, but always important if you want to keep moving ahead.

Philosophy #35 is "When your conscience speaks, you'd better listen." With introspection, instead of listening to your conscience you're talking to it, determining whether your direction and actions are in alignment with your vision. It's like checking a map when you're on a trip: The more frequently you determine your position and whether you're on the right road, the easier it is to get where you want to go. When you spend time examining your life, you stand a much better chance of fulfilling your vision.

Actions

1. Use your weekly planning time not only to create the plan for your new week, but to examine your previous week as well. Look over your goals and accomplishments and ask, "Where did I succeed, both personally and professionally? Where did I fail, both personally and professionally? What can I learn? How do I want to improve/change my efforts next week based on what I have learned?" Write down what your introspection teaches you, and use it in planning your next week.
2. I strongly recommend you take a personal retreat once a year to review your life and set a direction for the next 12 months. Get away from any distractions, including family and friends. If you keep weekly sheets, take them with you. Write a summary of your accomplishments and setbacks for the year, focusing less on the details and more on the lessons learned or not learned. Use your introspections to create/revise your vision and mission statement for the new year.

Deal Points

Introspection is a valuable tool in any business. If you don't evaluate the results of your efforts on a consistent basis, you will keep making the same mistakes over and over again. Introspection allows you to catch even the smallest glitches early and nip them in the bud; it also helps you notice what you're doing right and build on your successes. Every single deal or interaction with a client, subcontractor, vendor, associate, boss, or anyone else is an opportunity to learn something about yourself and how you can do a better job the next time. Try taking a few moments after such meetings to ask yourself questions like, "What did I do well? Where did I fail or not succeed as I would have liked? What personal traits assisted me or got in my way in this meeting? What can I learn from this?" You might want to keep a journal or notebook and jot down what you learn.

I also use introspection as an entryway into creativity. I am always looking at the marketing plans for our properties, for instance, and using the introspection questions to evaluate our success or failure. What in this plan is working for us? Where is it failing to attract and close the kind of buyer we want? What aren't we seeing that we need to see? What can I learn from the results of this plan to improve it, starting now? The answers to these questions help spark my creativity, and direct its focus into new and better ways to impact our marketplace.

Act with Integrity:
Live Up to Your Own Idea of Who You Are

Recently the multinational financial services company Citibank changed its advertising. The new ads show fathers playing with their kids while a voice-over says, "It's a balance sheet, folks, not a scorecard." That's a good description of what this Philosophy is about. The word *integrity* has to do with being whole, being all of a piece. It's about living a life that takes into account *all* of your life, all the areas you address in that personal vision or mission statement you created. It's about living up to the best of who you can be rather than settling for anything less.

Living up to your highest potential is never easy. I have to remind myself of this Philosophy over and over again, because it's soooooo easy to slip. When you're trying to become that go-to person or create that marketplace, there are many temptations and shortcuts that supposedly can get you there even faster. In my early days of renovating foreclosure properties, for example, quite honestly I was guilty of taking some of those shortcuts. I'd put a coat of paint over the existing trim on a house rather than scraping it and doing it right. I focused on making the properties as attractive as possible so I could turn them around quickly. Sure, they were safe, and they gave the buyers value for their money, but I took shortcuts that I regret—not because people were upset, but because the houses didn't represent what I wanted a "Frank McKinney" house to be.

And that's the first and foremost reason to act with integrity: your reputation. One of the things I was most grateful for when I moved to Florida was the ability to leave behind my reputation of being a trouble-making kid and start fresh. In business, reputation is your calling card; in *my* business, it's 90 percent of why buyers will look at a property. And living by your word is where reputation starts and ends. Reputation is built slowly and crumbles quickly. You build a reputation by living by your word consistently, day after day, week after week, in every area of your life. If you're known as an honest businessperson but people see you drink and cheat at golf, what effect is that going to have on your reputation? If you are known as a pillar of your church but you'll under-cut your own brother to get a contract, is that a reputation of integrity? But when your life is part of one cohesive whole, when your actions in business, your conduct at home, and your relationships with others demonstrate an upstanding person, you can acquire and hopefully keep a reputation of honor and integrity.

I learned my lessons on reputation and integrity early, and now I try to live my life consistently as the best person I can be. In work, I use the best craftspeople I can. I don't cut any corners. I try to produce the absolute best property and sell it with equal integrity. I believe you act with integrity anytime you use your best abilities to produce the finest product, home, term paper, casserole, and so on. Your most challenging taskmaster should be your own conscience, urging you to act like the best "you" possible.

Living with integrity doesn't mean you won't be tempted to do otherwise almost every day. In business, there's a fine line between aggressive selling and misrepresentation, between presenting your product in the best possible light and lying. (In your own life, have you ever lied on a resume, or told a date something other than the strict truth when it came to your accomplishments?) In negotiations with subcontractors and vendors, I can be tempted to close a deal that will be good for me but unfair for them. (This also violates Philosophy #21, "Think win-win, be fair, then close the deal.") It's a temptation to spend all my time on my business and neglect my family, friends, and charitable and civic responsibilities. Along with everyone else, I can be tempted both professionally and personally to cut corners, give in to vices (see Philosophy #22), or do or say things that may seem to get me what I want but in truth make me less of a person in the process.

The problem arises when all these little breaches in the wall of your integrity begin to weaken its very structure. It's like water that seeps unnoticed into a basement, or termites that get a foothold in your house. You may not immediately see the damage these lies, exaggerations, shortcuts, and vices do, but if you let them continue unchecked your integrity will crumble and you'll find that you're a different person—one you may not like very much at all. Think about that reality TV program, *Temptation Island*, where four couples were plopped onto an island resort with all these eligible single people, whose whole focus was to tempt the couples to cheat on their partners—a revolting concept. How do you think those partners who thought about cheating felt about themselves? If they gave in to temptation, sure, it probably would feel good in the moment, but how would it change their idea of who they were? They'd go from being in love and faithful to being doubting and faithless. That's the price of violating your integrity, and to my mind, it's much too high a price.

What keeps my integrity intact? It's living by these 49 Philosophies. They are my compass, my guide, my personal code of honor. They allow me to create my vision on a daily basis. If I do my best each day to live up to them, then I will have lived with integrity. Sure, I mess up, but with these Philosophies, I'm a lot less likely to do so—and I'm a lot less likely to let myself off the hook when I do. And when I can look at my wife and daughter at the end of a day, knowing I've been the best Frank McKinney I could be for myself and for them, I go to sleep a happy and fulfilled man.

Actions

1. Look at your personal vision or mission statement and ask yourself, "Who is this person? What kind of life would he or she live?"
2. What temptations have you given in to in the past? How will you avoid or handle those temptations in the future?

Deal Points

To live with integrity in my business, I use a principle I call the "Holy Trinity." In every project there are three elements that must be considered: (1) the time invested; (2) the quality that I will require in materials, workmanship, and so forth; and (3) the budget—how much money the time and quality will cost. When these three elements are kept in balance, it's easier for me to stay in integrity and live up to the reputation I have built over 10 years of creating ultra-high-end oceanfront estates.

However, there are endless temptations to focus on one element more than another, and that's when you can lose your integrity and get into trouble. In my foreclosure days, I concentrated almost totally on budget and time. I made my money by bringing a project in, on, or under budget, and turning it around as quickly as possible. Quality? Well, quality came in third place, and was always outvoted by time and budget considerations.

But I know now that all three must be balanced. I've known builders, especially in the world of ultra-high-end real estate, who focus strictly on quality. They use the best of everything just to be able to say that's what they did. But it takes them years and years to get their houses on the market, and when they finally do the profit margins are so low they don't come anywhere near to paying for their efforts. If I focus completely on quality, not only will my budget be shot, but I won't get the property on the market in a timely fashion. And since I own most of the properties I build or renovate and I'm carrying all the expenses from month to month until the property is sold, time is important. (Also, here in Palm Beach County there is a "season" that runs from November to May when the really wealthy people converge on Florida to take advantage of the weather. I need to have my properties on the market during the season, because that's when the likeliest clientele are going to be here.)

However, if I focus only on time (which I tend to do—I'd rather spend a little more if I can get a property on the market faster), I can end up reducing my profit margins because I'm paying so much in overtime and rush charges. My quality can go out the window, too, either because I can't get the materials I want or because I don't have the time to install the materials properly. And in my marketplace, shoddy goods will come back to bite you every time. I'll never forget a set of outdoor cabinets I had installed at one of our properties. I thought we had used marine-grade plywood so the cabinets would stand up to the sea spray and salty air of the Florida oceanfront. But after two and a half years, the buyer called me to complain. "Frank, my outside cabinets are rotting! What are you going to do about it?" Now, my warranty on the house was for a year, but I can't say, "I'm sorry, Mr. Buyer, but the warranty period on your multimillion-dollar investment is over." This man can sell a house for me just by picking up the phone and calling a few of his friends. What do you think I did? Yep—I replaced his cabinets. And now we make sure we use only marine-grade plywood or even composite material for the outside cabinets at our properties.

I work hard to instill in everyone who works for me the need to balance each element of the Holy Trinity: time, quality, and budget. And it's no different for your business. How much time are you spending with this client? What quality of service are you providing? Are you keeping track of budget considerations so you can make an adequate profit? Above all, are you doing business in such a way that your customers see you as someone with integrity, someone they want to do business with? Once you have that reputation for integrity, treasure it. It's probably the most important property you'll ever own.

Be Sensitive to Life's Lessons and Learn from Them

I was an extremely slow learner as a kid—not necessarily in school (although I was no shining star there) but in terms of life lessons, the things you need to learn in order to make it in this world. I was incarcerated repeatedly in the juvenile detention center and even thrown in jail a few times before I realized I had to straighten out. When I moved to Florida, it took a whole lot of speeding tickets and court appearances before I realized, "Driving way over the speed limit is stupid." It took a few too many times getting drunk or wasted to ask myself at last, "Why am I poisoning my body like this?" and to stop. I'm just lucky God has a big baseball bat when it comes to teaching lessons, because it took a lot of hits "upside the head" for me to learn what I needed to know.

Life's always presenting us with lessons. They come in many forms: experiences like getting arrested for speeding; showing your very first house as a real estate professional; dealing with the death of a parent (as I had to do in 1992 when my dad died in a plane crash); having a child and becoming a parent yourself. Some of the lessons are pleasant; many are not. But it's up to us to recognize those lessons when they come along and learn them as quickly and as well as possible.

Winston Churchill once said, "Personally, I'm always ready to learn, although I do not always like being taught." Often it's the painful, tough lessons we remember the best. One of the toughest lessons I had to learn was the need to conform. There's a pretty significant part of any successful entrepreneur that is a nonconformist; we want to do it our way. I still enjoy pushing the envelope and being out in front of the crowd. But there are certain rules of society that you have to abide by if you're going to succeed. Now that I've become sensitive to this lesson, however, I actually have a little more latitude, because I know which boundaries to stretch and which to leave alone. I can dress the way I want, build the finest ultra-high-end oceanfront properties in the world, and support homeless causes, just as long as I get my permits, develop my relationships with clients and the Palm Beach County community as a whole, and maintain my integrity as a man and entrepreneur.

I believe one of the ways we develop a sense of our highest calling and mission is by being sensitive to the lessons life is teaching us. You may think your calling is in one direction, like an acting career, but if you keep getting rejection after rejection after rejection, that may be a clue your path lies elsewhere. Conversely, you may get a signal out of nowhere, like I did, that shows you where your true path lies (see Philosophy #9). If you're not sensitive to life's lessons, you may end up wandering aimlessly for 10, 15, 20 years, never finding your true calling. You have to be open to learn what you're being taught, whether you like the lesson or not. And the quicker you learn it, the quicker you can get on with your life.

Many people turn to books to learn these kinds of lessons, but I honestly prefer to learn in other ways—from other people, for example. I'm an avid observer. I'm always looking around to see what I can learn from others. I'll watch a lady ahead of me in the drugstore checkout line and learn something from the way she relates to the cashier, for instance, or how she's handling her cranky five-year-old with humor instead of anger. I also love learning from people who have achieved some mark of success in their careers or lives. (You'll learn about this in Philosophy #13.)

But mostly, I love to learn by doing. That Nike slogan, "Just do it," was written for me. On the job, I'll implement something, then sit back and see how it works out. Since I'm creating my own marketplace (see Part Two), a lot of the stuff I do hasn't been seen or even tried before, but I'm going to try it anyway. Take the koi pond idea. In late 2001 we were nearing completion on a $15 million property, and in the living room there was a sunken area that was basically a waste of space. I don't know what it was for originally; maybe a piano, maybe a planter, maybe it was a mistake in design. But I thought, *What about a koi pond inside the house? I've never seen that before.* We spent a lot of money converting the sunken space into a pond complete with 13 imported Japanese koi at $500 per fish. I don't know whether buyers will love it or hate it, but I did it anyway, and I'll look forward to learning more about my buyers based on their responses.

I'm teaching my three-year-old daughter to learn by doing. She'll come to me and say, "Daddy, help me turn on the light," and I'll tell her, "Honey, you know how to do it. Get your stool and turn it on yourself." I'd rather she try and fall down than not learn that she's capable of doing it. I want her to be eager to try new things whether she's good at them or not. Face it—if we do only what we're already good at, we're never going to expand our abilities. We've got to be willing to try something and look like an idiot for a while until we learn what we need to know.

One of the best life lessons I have learned, however, is how to make some lessons easier. Just this year, I took up snowboarding. I'm a self-taught skier who hadn't skied in about six years, but after watching *The "X" Games* on ESPN I decided snowboarding would be fun. Now, I could have just gotten a board and learned by myself. Instead, I was humble and smart enough to take a lesson from a kid who's a great snowboarder. I was able to shorten my learning curve considerably, and had a lot more fun faster as a result.

In business I feel the same way. If there are ways I can shorten my learning curve, I'll do it. When I'm getting ready to take action, I'll prepare like mad. I'll do my homework, study my market, talk to other people. I'll anticipate the possible consequences of my actions, both positive and negative. But once I've done all that, I'll still get in there and just do it. I'll deal with the consequences and learn from whatever happens. I'm not sitting on the sidelines waiting for life to teach me; I'm seeking those lessons so I can continue to grow.

Once you're presented with life's lessons, your final step is what we talked about in Philosophy #3: introspection. Introspection is how you take the raw material of your life and draw lessons from it. These weekly reflections keep me aware that life is constantly presenting me with lessons. Whether I'm sensitive enough to learn them remains to be seen—but I'm sure a lot better than I was!

Learning lessons is a large part of the reason we're on this earth.

Easy or hard, pleasant or unpleasant, whether we like it or not, we've gotta learn 'em. But don't make God have to get out the baseball bat, like I did. Be sensitive to life's lessons; seek them out. Then learn them, benefit from them, and move on.

Actions

1. What lessons have you learned or not learned in your life? What have they given you? Have they been pleasant or painful? Which ones do you remember the most vividly?
2. What's something you're faced with right now—a new experience or direction, perhaps—that might provide a lesson? What's it going to take for you to get off your butt and just do it?
3. How can you shorten your learning curve? When faced with a potential lesson, what can you do to prepare?
4. How will you make sure you are learning the lessons life is giving you? In your introspection time, you might ask questions like, "What have I learned from this? What did I do well? Where did I not accomplish what I wanted, and why? How can I do this better the next time?"

Deal Points

I learn from every single real estate meeting, transaction, negotiation, and deal I do—and you should do the same. Even if you're buying and selling identical townhouses or condominiums, each client is going to be able to teach you something about your marketplace, about what it takes to close a deal, and so on. Especially when you're first getting started, it's imperative that you learn everything you can. Go to classes and seminars if they are helpful; but more than that, I suggest you learn (1) one-on-one from others, and (2) from just getting out there, trying things and seeing what happens.

When learning one-on-one, develop your observation skills. Notice what your coworker Sue does when she talks to a client on the phone. Observe how your boss negotiates with the bank. Check out your competitors—maybe you can get some great ideas from them. (Certainly, you want to avoid any mistakes they may be making!) You can also go to people you admire and ask them what they have learned through the years. (People love to share this kind of information—see

Philosophy #13.) You might want to set up a system for capturing what you learn, perhaps a place in your personal organizer where you put all your observations. Then at least once a week, take a look at your observations, summarize them, and try to come up with the lessons these observations are teaching you.

Remember, however, that the most meaningful lessons come from doing. Get out there and try things. Do something no one's ever done at a showing in your area. Go into a neighborhood others aren't willing to enter. (That's how I made my first profits in real estate—by buying properties in neighborhoods other investors wouldn't consider. But I knew there were people in those neighborhoods who could afford to buy instead of rent, and I believed they would be eager to put their money into a house that had been well renovated and was fairly priced.) Prepare, yes; make sure you can handle the consequences of your actions. But try things and learn the lessons they bring. Some of the lessons will be painful, certainly, but others will help you jump ahead of your competition.

After each new action, take the time to ask yourself, "What did I learn? What's the lesson here? And how can I apply this to the next deal, and the next, and the next?" Introspection on your lessons will help you shorten your learning curve, make the painful lessons more valuable, and give you greater pleasure in your successes. Enjoy your lessons— they're part of the reason you're alive.

Don't Compromise Your Beliefs or Person, Ever!

In 1984 when I turned 21, I had been teaching tennis for two years. My tennis business was doing well but I wanted more, so I had decided to pursue a career in real estate. To learn about the business, I took courses and passed my real estate exam. The next step, I thought, would be to work with a large real estate brokerage firm for a year or so. I could learn the business from seasoned professionals and then go out on my own. This was the path for my life, and I was very excited to be pursuing a new direction.

I set up an interview with the local office of a well-respected national real estate brokerage company. I went to Burdine's department store and bought myself a very conservative business suit, a pair of those really uncomfortable black shoes with the skinny laces, black socks, a white dress shirt, and a boring maroon tie. I was ready, but something was missing. *Maybe I should get a haircut*, I thought. It was a tough decision. I had had long hair all my life, but I thought it made me look more like a tennis pro than a real estate professional. So I went to Super Cuts and paid $8 to have my hair chopped off. I was now the complete "package."

The next day I walked into the real estate office, confident and ready. The office manager (who was wearing a suit just like mine) shook my hand, slapped me on the back, and said, "Hi, Chuck, great to see you!" (He acted like he'd known me all my life, even though he didn't get my name right.) We sat down and did the interview. At the end of it, he said, "Even though you're young and don't have a lot of experience, you seem to have all the characteristics of a good real estate salesperson. Your scores are good, you're licensed, it sounds like you have contacts in the communities where you're teaching tennis. You're hired. When can you start?"

Excited, I told him, "As soon as you need me!" He nodded. "Great—but I have to ask you to do me one favor. You need to get a haircut before you can work here."

Time seemed to stand still. There I was, in my tight shoes and stiff, hot suit, and it hit me like a ton of bricks: I was compromising who I was. The suit, the shorter hair, the boring tie that I hated weren't enough: I was going to have to go *further* just to fit in with people like the guy sitting across from me. I started to laugh.

"What's so funny?" the office manager asked.

I shook my head and stood up. "Thanks, but I don't think I'll be working here." I walked out the door, took off the tie, went to 7-Eleven, and got a large Slurpee. When I paid the clerk, I gave him my tie, too.

That's as close as I have ever come to working for somebody. But the lesson it taught me about the peril of compromising your beliefs or person will last a lifetime. Anytime I am put into a position where I am tempted to compromise myself, I remember that moment in the real estate office and tell myself, "It's not worth it." *Compromise* is a horrible word when it has to do with who we are or what we truly believe.

We're faced with the temptation to compromise ourselves throughout our lives. A kid has the chance to cheat on an algebra test. A young lady's boyfriend wants her to have sex with him and it goes against her values. A businessperson is offered a slightly shady deal. An executive is asked to concoct a business plan that causes harm to the environment. Far too often we go along with what we think or are told is what we should do, rather than standing by our deepest instinct about what is true for us.

When I talk to college kids in university business classes, this subject comes up a lot. "How can I be myself and work in a big company?" they ask. "If I work for a bank, I'm going to have to act a certain way, aren't I?"

"Sure," I tell them. "You may have to change small things. But if you find yourself compromising who you really are, deep down, for any job or relationship or cause, then you should get out immediately, because that job, relationship, or cause isn't for you. You should *never* have to compromise who you really are."

Nothing's worth lying about when it comes to who you are and what you believe. If you do lie, eventually you start lying to yourself, and then you become the lie—and that will eat you alive inside. It's far better to cut yourself loose from the situation and find something where you can be yourself. Yes, you have to put food on the table and provide security for your family, but if you stand up for your principles and beliefs, more often than not you're going to come out of it with your paycheck. And you're going to feel a heck of a lot better about yourself for not selling out.

A few years ago I was at a loan closing for a multimillion-dollar deal. I had been negotiating with the bank on this for 14 months. I had read through every loan document and made sure I understood everything. Anything I didn't understand I had asked my attorney to explain to me. I had asked for some changes to the terms of the loan that I considered reasonable—allowing Nilsa to take over the loan and the business in case of my death instead of automatically defaulting, for example; some insurance issues; and so on. But the bankers refused to change the terms of the loan, so I refused to sign. "Forget it," I told them. "I'll find another way to make this happen if I need to. But as it stands, I will not do this deal." I wasn't willing to put myself in what I believed was a subservient position to a bank just because I was asking for a loan. I left the room and walked toward the elevator. In just a few minutes, however, the bank's attorney came running after me and offered to iron out whatever issues I had. Eventually we got to the point where the loan was a win both for the bank and for me (see Philosophy #21), and we closed. But rather than compromising and signing, I was perfectly happy to go elsewhere. And you should be, too.

Now, I'm not talking about being stubborn and stupid. Sure, I wear suits when it's appropriate. (I wear suits in colors that make me stand out, but that's another story—see Philosophy #15.) And I dress as a general contractor when I need to. In business, you have to adapt to the needs of others and the needs of the situation (see Philosophy #20). I also hope my sense of who I am and what I believe keeps evolving as I continue to learn and grow (see Philosophy #19). Still, there are some things I will not change just to make others feel comfortable, or to make a deal that's to my advantage. I have found one of the easiest ways to deal with change and challenge is never to compromise who you are or what you believe in. When you're very clear on what's absolutely important to you—your core values, the essence of what you believe about yourself and the world—it's like standing on a rock while the eddies of change whirl around the base.

This kind of consistency is something that people actually come to admire. Look at some of our most successful and highly respected individuals of the last few years: Herb Kelleher, founder of Southwest Airlines. Rich De Vos, cofounder of Amway. Politicians like Senator John McCain. Even Mother Teresa—she faced down the entire church establishment to help dying people in cities all over the world. Many figures who have been called "eccentric" I believe just never followed the masses, and ended up carving a wider and deeper niche as a result.

In 2000 the movie *Gladiator* was a huge hit. Critics lauded it as a return to the Roman spectacle movies like *Ben-Hur* and *Spartacus*. But why do audiences love these movies? Because their heroes refused to compromise who they were. We get a thrill whenever we see someone like Maximus or Ben-Hur or Spartacus standing up to the might of the entire Roman Empire, saying, "This is who I am and you cannot break me!" We admire their principles, their bravery, and their conviction; but most of all, we know clearly who these men are, and what they believe—and that they will never, ever compromise either themselves or their beliefs.

You do not have to sell out for your career, for love, or for social acceptance. Your soul should never be compromised. You can maintain your integrity and uniqueness and still get what you want out of life. Certain behavior is required to be successful—discipline and organization, for example. But you do not have to become co-opted in order to succeed. It's not worth it. Believe me, you'll sleep a lot better when you hit the pillow each night knowing you've lived the day in alignment with who you truly are.

Actions

1. The personal vision or mission statement you created in Philosophy #2 should be the basis of your "line in the sand," the beliefs and attitudes you will not compromise. Review it, and perhaps post it in your home or office so you see it every day.
2. Have you ever been placed in a position where you were forced to compromise your beliefs or person? What were the results? How did you feel about having to make that choice? What do you need to do from now on to ensure you will stand by your beliefs, even in the tough times?
3. Are you currently in a business, profession, or relationship in which you feel your beliefs or person are compromised? How can you change your situation so you can live by your principles? If necessary, are you prepared to leave the situation rather than continuing to compromise who you are?

Deal Points

Sometimes it's tough in business to stand on your principles when a client is asking you to bend a little, or a deal is just out of reach and will be yours if only you do this or that ("this or that" being something you believe is unfair or dishonest). "It's standard business practice," you'll hear. "We always slip so-and-so a little extra," or "The banks always treat us this way," or "The client expects us to ignore such-and-such." You have to be willing to draw your own line in the sand when it comes to conducting your business.

I believe that most real estate clients would prefer to deal with someone whom they see as an up-front kind of person, rather than getting a better deal from someone they can't trust. We've already talked about the importance of your reputation; well, compromise is one of the fastest ways to damage it. Once you're known as someone who will cut corners or turn a blind eye to things that need attention, what kind of clients do you think you'll attract? If you want to spend your time doing shady business, fine—but the money and success you achieve in that way provide a very shaky foundation.

Conversely, what kind of client will you attract with a reputation of being honest, fair, conscientious, strong, and willing to stand by your principles? Isn't that the kind of person you'd like to have on your side when it comes to real estate—or any business?

Coming from this position of strength will also help you in your relationships with banks, vendors, subcontractors, and so on. The people I work with may not always like my positions, but at least they're clear about what I stand for, and what I will not allow. The kind of strength I'm talking about is not being a bully or imposing your will on others. It's simply saying, "This is who I am; you choose whether you wish to deal with me or not." And those who do choose me I feel I can work with honestly, fairly, clearly. I feel we will do the best job possible together, because we respect ourselves and each other. Those kinds of relationships will help you to make it big while staying true to yourself.

Each of Us Has Not Only a Professional Talent but a Spiritual One As Well. Find Yours and Apply It

When you create a vision for your life—that passionate vision that will drive you to fulfill your purpose here on earth—if you're like most of us you'll think in terms of a profession first. "What will I do?" and "What will I make of my life?" are the questions you're looking to answer. And as we talked about in Philosophies #1 and #2, wherever your talents lie, that's where your focus goes. Whether you're a great tennis player or businessperson or writer or parent or teacher, you have a drive to find and develop your professional talents to their fullest.

But I believe that we have not only a professional talent but a *spiritual* one as well. A spiritual talent is that feeling inside that nudges us to do something selfless for others, to contribute and give back in recognition of both the gifts we've received from God and our common humanity with others. Even for those who don't believe in God, I believe there's an instinctive need to contribute to something bigger than ourselves for something other than our own benefit.

However, the professional talent is the one most people focus on. They don't work on their spiritual talent, which is equally important when it comes to creating real success, the kind that permeates every part of your life. I think we have an obligation to explore and use to their fullest *all* the blessings and talents we've been given. And I've found it actually helps your professional talent blossom when you find and develop your spiritual talent, too.

It would be very easy for me to be an absolute workaholic like I was when I was younger. During my first few years in Florida, everything I did was either real estate focused or for pure relaxation. But from the time I was a kid, I also was aware of my spiritual side. I was an altar boy; I went to a boarding school run by Benedictine monks. I knew I had a spiritual talent; I just didn't quite know what it was. Once I found it—and for me it's twofold, helping young people and helping the homeless—my life took off in ways I never could have imagined. My spiritual talent brings me riches that my professional talents will never match. Developing both of them to their highest level has filled my life with blessings.

When you have a talent, it's like having a child: You have to take care of it, bring it up, make the most of it. Sure, everybody has talent at different levels, but in order to succeed we have to take those talents as far as we can. And that applies spiritually as well as professionally. It's funny—the people I see struggling the most with their lives, or maybe only stagnating, are the ones who aren't in touch with their spiritual side. Some may even be extremely successful in their professions, but they aren't very successful as people. Conversely, I know other men and women who perhaps haven't attained a lot in their careers, but they are very fulfilled because their spiritual talents are utilized to the utmost.

There are so many outlets for your spiritual talent; one of them is sure to fit. Maybe for you it's feeding the homeless, or building homes with Habitat for Humanity like former president Jimmy Carter, or joining the Peace Corps, or visiting elderly shut-ins, or mentoring a student, or becoming an officer for your church group. You can march for causes, counsel teenagers, lead a food drive in your town. Your spiritual talent doesn't necessarily have to benefit the world. Perhaps your spiritual talent is praying for others, like many monks and nuns do. Whatever it might be, even if that spiritual talent simply makes you a happier person, it's going to influence and possibly uplift the people you meet.

My spiritual talent pulls me to help the homeless. Starting in 1992, every Monday night for four years I went with a group called the Caring Kitchen and fed the homeless out of the back of a van. Then I decided I could help more by combining my professional and spiritual talents, so I created the Caring House project, where I renovate houses (and eventually apartments as well) and rent them to the homeless for $1 a month. I also work with young people through an organization called the Greater Delray Beach Youth Council. I want to help kids channel their energy into productive directions instead of drugs and alcohol, so we teach kids between the ages of 12 and 17 how to be entrepreneurs.

Many of us recognize that internal itch of a spiritual talent; we just don't scratch it very often. For instance, because people know of my interest in the homeless, I get a lot of calls in November and December: "Frank, do you know of a soup kitchen or shelter where my family and I can serve Thanksgiving or Christmas dinner to the homeless?" While I'm delighted these people are nurturing their spiritual talents by feeding the homeless during the holidays, that's just once or twice a year. What if you were to feed your talent once a month? Once a week? Do you think that talent would grow and increase, and maybe you'd grow, too, as a result? We spend so much time on our professional talents, often 40 or more hours a week. What if we were to devote just one hour a week to our spiritual talents?

If you have a talent, you should pursue it. When it comes to your professional talent, it's really your approach on a day-to-day level that makes you a professional. You can be a professional house builder or a professional at McDonald's. It doesn't matter: You take the talent you're given and make the most of it. But I believe you have an equal obligation to find and develop the spiritual talent you've been given, too. When you do that, it's like the parable from the Bible about sowing seed in a fertile field: Everything you plant will come back to you a thousandfold.

Actions

1. What's your professional talent? You may have several, but one probably stands out. What are you doing to develop that professional talent to its fullest? Remember, being a professional is

only partly about talent, and mostly about approach. Choose your profession well, and then express your talent within that profession to its fullest.

2. What's your spiritual talent? Where are you pulled to contribute, give back, make a difference? How have you developed that spiritual talent? How will you develop it consistently from now on?

3. How will you balance your professional and spiritual talents? How will you integrate them into your vision or mission statement for your life?

Deal Points

I believe within each profession there is room for a wide variety of talents; it's just a question of finding yours. Do you have a professional talent that suits you for real estate? If you have the professional talent to be an entrepreneur, you'll probably be happy working on your own, perhaps buying and selling properties, building commercial real estate or custom homes, and so on. If your professional talent lies more in selling, perhaps you'll be a great broker. You may be an amazing team builder or leader; you might do your best work as the office manager of a real estate office, training and supervising agents or brokers. Perhaps you love numbers and details; your perfect profession might be researching title deeds and foreclosures, or handling all the finances for a more entrepreneurial partner. Whatever your particular talent, keep working with it until you develop it to its fullest.

But remember your spiritual talent, too; it can absolutely have an impact on your professional career, especially if it leads you in unexpected directions. Say you're working in a real estate office as an agent. You're doing okay but not great at selling houses, and you keep plugging away, doing your best every day to develop your talents. At the same time, you're part of a church group that focuses on supporting missionaries all over the world. When the group's elections roll around, somehow you end up as vice president. Now you have to go to monthly meetings with the church board. People are asking you to speak up about different issues and concerns. You have to make reports and collaborate with the other officers. You've taken on a lot more responsibility, you're learning to speak in public, and you're seen as someone who has valuable ideas. Do you think that experience might have an impact on how you do your job at the real estate office? Is it possible that the way you relate to others when you're speaking with caring and compassion about missions and helping starving children might affect your ability to communicate in a caring way with clients?

We haven't been given talents for them to go to waste. And often the talents we develop in one area can be used in another. Take your professional talents and apply them to help others. Take your spiritual talents and use them to support your professional endeavors. And use all your talents to support the vision and mission you have created for your life.

Part Two

Stake Your Territory:
Create a Unique Brand for You and Your Life

As the careers of Walt Disney, Donald Trump, Michael Dell, and Mary Kay Ash demonstrate, a lot of success starts with branding. How are you going to become the go-to guy if your clients and customers don't know who you are? Especially in today's media-driven world—where business celebrities like Alan Greenspan, Warren Buffett, and Bill Gates can get more coverage on the evening news than the president of the United States—developing a unique brand for yourself and establishing that brand in the marketplace are not simply a by-product of success. Instead, they are essential steps in making it big.

No matter what I have done, from taking care of golf courses to building the most expensive and luxurious spec homes in the world, I have always created a name for myself—an outrageous one, but one backed with a successful track record. My goal has been to create a business (and even an entire marketplace) that will take advantage of an underexploited niche. Then I work hard to make that business more successful than any potential competitors. Along the way I have created new markets, broken price barriers, and in some cases changed the way the industry itself operates. I have done my best to stay away from the safe, "same old, same old" approach. I constantly run up against people who tell me, "Frank, you're crazy—there's no way that's going to work!" Then I take pride in proving them wrong.

My goal is simple: I want my name to mean something unique in the ultra-high-end real estate market. I'd love it if clients would fight to

53

tour a Frank McKinney property because they know they will be dazzled and delighted. At the same time, I also want that brand to mean something when it comes to making a difference in the world. I'm not like Andrew Carnegie or Bill Gates; I don't have the means (yet) or the desire to plaster my name on universities. But if Frank McKinney's name means something to the homeless here in South Florida because I've provided hundreds of them with essentials like food and shelter, then that's a pretty good "brand" in my book.

There are two aspects to the kind of branding I'm talking about. First is your personal brand, the one you create for yourself. You must decide who you are and how you want to think, work, and act in the world. I hope what you learned in Part One—about following your highest calling, creating a vision, and so on—will help you create a personal brand of strength, creativity, and integrity. The second brand, what I'll call the public brand, is about relationships and how others perceive you. The personal brand is inwardly focused, while the public brand outwardly focused; both are vital components of a life of extreme success.

This entire book is designed to help you develop the best personal and professional brands possible. If you follow the philosophies and precepts in its pages, I believe you will have a strong foundation for your personal brand. At the same time, I have included suggestions and ideas drawn from my own experiences in developing what I consider a strong public brand, one where you can be seen as an excellent businessperson, committed to building and maintaining customer relationships. In this section, we're going to explore how to select and develop a marketplace in which you can allow that public brand to take hold.

When you are first starting to establish a public brand, finding your market is critical. Where is the niche in which you can create a unique presence? You need to be very attuned to the needs and desires of your proposed marketplace. Any marketplace can change very quickly, and if you don't keep up with its changes, you'll lose ground to your competitors. You have to keep working at establishing your niche, knowing your market, discovering your customers' needs, and filling them at ever-increasing levels.

When you develop a public brand, I believe it's best to specialize. You want your efforts to be efficient, effective, and timely; you want to develop a reputation of being great at what you do rather than merely competent. So concentrate your efforts. It's like the difference between using a shotgun or a rifle to shoot at a target: The end result may be the same, but the rifle does the job a lot more efficiently with a lot less mess! In Part Four I'll talk about starting small and building your risk threshold gradually, and you should build your public brand in exactly the same way. Begin by finding one area you want to focus on, start small, and get really good at it before you choose to expand or move on.

Some people tap into the pulse of their marketplace very naturally; but I've always had to work hard to investigate my marketplace, to get to know my prospective customers, and to do the kind of job that would make my brand memorable. I've also worked hard to distinguish my product and brand from everything else out there. It's not only the personal image I cultivate, although being called the "rock 'n' roll developer" hasn't hurt my visibility here in South Florida. More than that, it's the way I have approached the creation of my product, and the marketing I have used. When I was renovating some of the worst houses in Palm Beach County, I made sure those properties stood out because they were better than anything around them. I upgraded houses, and the people who bought them helped to upgrade their neighborhoods in turn. I have continued to do the same on the oceanfront. Each and every property I have renovated or built from the ground up has been unique, pushing the envelope in terms of quality and price point. I have been extremely effective at establishing a public brand in the niche marketplace I have chosen. I can say with confidence that I have helped to shape the market for ultra-high-end oceanfront real estate here in South Florida, and values along the entire Palm Beach County coast and beyond have risen as a result.

How do you become the go-to guy or gal in your chosen marketplace? Well, you'll need a lot of different elements to go your way. You'll need discipline, because it'll take you a while to establish a reputation with enough customers. It'll also take a lot of research into your marketplace or an amazing instinct, or both, about what your customers want—not just today, but tomorrow. It'll take focusing on the big picture, knowing where you are going, not letting yourself get bogged down or distracted by either failures or successes. It'll take the "lunch pail" approach you'll learn about in Part Three and a willingness to take on ever-increasing amounts of risk, as you'll learn in Part Four. It'll take a personal brand that's memorable, being someone your customers will trust, and a willingness to toot your own horn and seek out publicity, both for yourself and for your products. You have to be willing to bring attention to yourself, knowing you do so in service to the brand, reputation, and identity you are striving to create. I also think it will take someone who enjoys what they do! When you can do all of that—and you back everything up with delivering the best products targeted to the right market—then you'll be surprised at how quickly you're the person everyone goes to in your particular field.

One of your biggest allies (or enemies) in the creation of your public brand will be the media. In establishing a brand, word of mouth is powerful, but there is nothing better than media coverage to spread your name beyond your customers to new potential clients. I discovered the power of media when I marketed my first oceanfront property. I had gotten coverage through the years because of the Young Entrepreneurial Society (which I founded at age 22), and on a few of the larger renovation projects I had done. But when I moved to the oceanfront, all of a sudden the stakes were a lot higher, and I needed to generate more interest for the property. So I went to work. I created a detailed marketing plan that included a grand opening, lots of well-timed media coverage, stories leaked to selected reporters on specific newspapers, and so on. I learned how to create an interest in what I was doing, and how to think like a reporter so I could offer them an appealing story. I've become an expert in getting the kind of coverage that will help sell my properties, timed in such a way that the pieces will have maximum impact (very essential in my business, where I receive my paycheck only when a property sells). To this day, many of my competitors do not believe that, except for a few months surrounding the unveiling of our $30 million spec home, I had never had a public relations (PR) firm during the entire time I've been in the oceanfront real estate market. But I know how to make my personal and professional brands attractive to the media, and I work hard to get the word out as widely and as positively as possible.

As I said at the very beginning of this part, we're living in an age that is dominated by the media. The media are constantly on the lookout for content to feed their endless pipelines. With good branding, a little work, and a willingness to create a personal brand that is out of the ordinary and perhaps a little outrageous, you can turn that need for content to your advantage. I'll talk more about media and how they can help you in Philosophy #14.

Remember, however, that your public brand seldom relies on your efforts alone. As soon as you employ anyone else, or as soon as you are part of a team, your brand will be established, helped, or hindered by their successes or failures. As leader of a team or head of your business, you must provide the kind of inspiration, direction, and empowerment that will make others want to protect and enhance your brand. One of the best (and most rewarding) ways to do so is to help them enhance their own personal and public brands in the process.

Creating a brand isn't always pleasant. A lot of people feel threatened by anyone who is different or happens to stand out from the crowd. I've been criticized for my taste, my looks, my dress, my hair, even my politics. Through it all, I've followed the guidelines of Broadway personality George M. Cohan, who said, "I don't care what you say about me, as long as you say *something* about me, and as long as you spell my name right." When you're committed to create a brand, you learn to be thick-skinned; you learn resolve; you learn the power of perseverance. You also learn the power of living by your principles. I believe that as long as I continue to live by the Philosophies in this book, my brand, and my life, will be a testament instead of a warning.

In this part you're going to learn several ways to help you establish a unique brand and create a marketplace for yourself and your business. You'll see why, if you want to live an extraordinary life, you must resist anything that smacks of an ordinary approach. You'll learn about finding and filling your niche, the area of the marketplace currently missing or underserved—the place where you will get the greatest results for your efforts. You'll discover how important it is to avoid being distracted from that niche until you are ready. You'll see if you have the passion and enthusiasm needed to be an exceptional entrepreneur, how to apply that passion both at work and at home, and how to keep the naysayers and pessimists from distracting you as you pursue success. One of the most vital shortcuts I know to making it big is to learn from highly respected, successful people, and you'll discover how to do so. Then in the last two chapters of this part we'll talk about two touchy yet important subjects: ego and self-esteem. To create a powerful brand, you need both—leavened with a little humility and a lot of humor, please!

One of the things I am proudest of is the statement I've heard again and again from people who have bought one of my properties, as well as those I have bought from. They say, "Frank, nobody does it the way you do. It's a privilege to do business with you." To me, that means all the years spent developing my brand have paid off, in a reputation of quality and a legacy of satisfied customers. And that's the kind of brand I want, both in my business and in my life.

To Live an Extraordinary Life You Must Resist an Ordinary Approach

I have always resisted an ordinary approach to life. When I was a rebellious teenager, this took the form of a lot of unproductive behavior that got me in trouble. But ever since I learned to turn my horror of the ordinary into a desire to be *extraordinary*, this drive has been a major force in my success.

What is ordinary? It's what most people settle for; and it's usually the lowest common denominator. It's a life lived without passion, without anything to distinguish it from the billions of other lives on this planet. It's ordinary not to be disciplined. It's ordinary to be a little lazy. It's ordinary to sit in a chair in a cubicle and hate your job. It's ordinary not to push yourself. It's ordinary not to take chances. It's all too ordinary to depart this world without leaving any mark upon it other than a tombstone.

No one wants to be known or remembered as plain, boring, without impact, or ordinary. Inside our own minds, we see ourselves as unique and special—and we are. The problem is, not enough of us share our uniqueness and specialness with the world. And we don't put in the work that's necessary to create an extraordinary life.

Extraordinary people break away from the ordinary and make sure their lives matter. To be extraordinary, you have to be willing to set yourself apart from your fellow men and women and do what they will not. You have to put in the work that will create extraordinary results in whatever field you choose. Living an extraordinary life has little to do with *what* you do; it is more a function of *how* you do it. You don't have to make millions, but you can make great homemade apple butter. You don't have to be CEO of a multinational company, but you can run a happy household. You don't have to be the all-star sports hero, but you can be the best coach a Little League baseball team ever had.

Since I did not have the benefit of much formal education, I started very early to observe how the people I admired lived their lives. I discov-

ered that most extraordinary people are often ⸂
do. They avoid vices: the common ones lik
gambling, and so on, but also the more ⸂
overeating, complacency, laziness, compla⸍
tus, succumbing to peer pressure, accepting u⸍
velop traits that set them apart from the crowd—th⸍
steadfastness in their beliefs, introspection, risk taking,
say yes, and working to make their dreams come true. (You n⸍
nize many of these traits in the Philosophies contained in this booк.⸍

I also studied what was considered ordinary and normal, and discovered that I was best at pursuing the opposite. (I'm sure you're very surprised by that.) It was ordinary to dress conservatively when you're in business—luckily, I was allergic to anything that caused me to appear conservative. It was ordinary to be a follower—I wasn't interested in following in someone else's footsteps, and I certainly didn't want to do what the next guy was doing; I wanted to improve on it. It was ordinary to lack discipline—I developed a strong work ethic and enormous discipline. Every single character trait and approach I saw in the average person would make me head in the opposite direction. If you call it a conscious effort to be something other than ordinary, you're right, because I had no interest in being ordinary in anything that I did.

When I entered the distressed real estate market, I applied many of the principles of extraordinary people to help me create success. I also looked to see what everyone else was doing and if I could change it/ improve upon it/do the opposite. It wasn't usual for a beginning real estate entrepreneur with big dreams to buy falling-down foreclosures in extremely rough neighborhoods? I was right there. I didn't care if the properties were covered with graffiti, smelling of urine, infested with cockroaches the size of your thumb crawling all over the floor and walls, littered with used condoms and discarded needles lying next to a torn mattress on the bedroom floor. I knew I could turn these houses around with a little extraordinary effort, so that's what I did. (And because of my doing so, the people who lived in the neighborhoods where I had my properties started to improve their own houses. One of the benefits of living an extraordinary life is that you inspire others to do the same.)

It wasn't ordinary for the guy who was buying and selling the properties to be as hands-on as I was in the building or renovation process. Yet every moment I wasn't out looking at properties or at an auction, you'd find me at one of the job sites, helping the subcontractors in any way I could to move things along. And the way I sold those properties

nly not ordinary. Yes, we had the usual open houses (although
pice those up as much as we could; see Philosophy #46), but I
d that to reach our primary marketplace—the first-time home
r—I needed an extraordinary approach.

In the mid-1980s there were people who were shelling out more in
nt each month for a small one-bedroom apartment than it would cost
them for a monthly mortgage payment on one of the two-bedroom,
two-bath houses I was renovating. But no one had ever educated them
on how to go from renting to buying. So I put together these little seminars on how to own your own home. I would make up a flyer, and a
buddy of mine and I would walk the neighborhoods where we thought
good prospects for the seminars would be living. I'd pretend I was just
some guy who'd been hired by a company for $4.50 an hour to hand out
these flyers. I'd wear jeans and sneakers, and carry a Walkman. I'd knock
on a door and say, "Hey, there's a seminar at the grade school around the
corner this coming Saturday about how to buy your first home. I've
been reading the flyer and it looks pretty cool—I think I'm going to go."

On Saturday 30 or so people would show up, and I'd have a little
pamphlet of instructions to hand out. Then I'd teach them the basics:
how to check your credit, how to save for a down payment, how to apply for a loan, which banks to go to, and so on. I'd show them how to
calculate their monthly mortgage payment on different loans at different interest rates, and the advantages of buying versus continuing to
rent. At the end of the presentation, I'd say, "And by the way, there are
some properties listed in the back of your pamphlet in case you're ready
to start house hunting." Of course, they were all properties I currently
had on the market.

An extraordinary approach? At the time, absolutely—nobody was
teaching renters how to buy their first houses. Sure, it was more work
for me, but the ensuing benefits were enormous. I learned so much
about my marketplace, putting myself in the other guys' shoes and figuring out what they would need to buy my product. I was also able to
help a lot of people take that step up to home ownership while increasing my own list of potential buyers.

To this day, I continue to do my best to apply an extraordinary approach. The way I choose to build, renovate, and market my properties
is unique and far above the usual standards, even in the business of ultra-
high-end real estate. I try to create extraordinary relationships at home,
at work, with our buyers and sellers. I continue to observe both extraordinary and ordinary people in all walks of life, from the homeless to bil-

lionaires. I do my best to emulate their extraordinary qualities, and run as fast as I can from anything ordinary.

The Philosophies in this book constantly remind me to turn from the ordinary and choose another path, and I hope they help you do the same. For example, it's not ordinary to take the results of your success and make a conscious effort to go out and help people, but is there a place you can share your abundance with others? It's not ordinary to have a vision and discover your highest calling, but what quality of life ensues when you have that kind of clear direction? It's not ordinary to condition yourself to take risks, but how fast can you grow when you do so? It's not ordinary to live each day as if you were on the concert stage of life, but how much more fun will you have if you do so, no matter what your occupation or condition?

To live an extraordinary life you will have to sacrifice an ordinary approach, but with that sacrifice will come the rewards of a fuller, happier life. Look around you and study what ordinary people are doing (you'll have plenty of subjects), and make a commitment to do the opposite. Then seek out the people who are making a difference in any arena. You will observe they take a proactive approach to life rather than a reactive one. You'll find them stepping outside of their comfort zone and taking calculated chances, celebrating the pursuit of individuality while remaining accountable for their actions.

The great inventor Thomas Edison once said, "If we did all the things we are capable of doing, we would literally astound ourselves." Extraordinary rewards are the result of an extraordinary approach. It is your choice: to be ordinary or to step into the power you already possess inside. Choose to astound yourself and the world.

Actions

1. Whom do you admire? What extraordinary people would you like to model yourself upon? You don't have to become exactly like them; you can choose to emulate only the traits you feel have allowed them to be extraordinary. How will you put those traits into practice in your own life?
2. What do you consider ordinary? Make a list of the traits that in the past have kept you from taking an extraordinary approach, and commit to do the opposite. If you have been lazy, vow to be disciplined. If you've been fearful, apply your courage and

take a risk. If you've been selfish, help others. Focus on one trait a month, and make it a project to eliminate this destructive influence of the ordinary from your life forever.

Deal Points

One of the ways I take an extraordinary approach in business is in fostering relationships long after the sale is made. Like many builders, I will offer a year's warranty on any work I've done on a house, but I don't hold myself or the client to the terms of the warranty: I *exceed* the warranty every step of the way. I've learned to set aside a certain amount of the profits from a sale and earmark it for "relationship building." Any problem—and I mean *any* problem—a client brings me with one of our houses I will most likely fix and not charge for the repair. Does it affect my bottom line? Some. And I confess, being as bottom-line conscious as I am, it can irritate me if the requests go way past the warranty or end up costing me a lot. But I believe I have created an extraordinary property, using the finest materials available, and my follow-up needs to be of equal quality.

Now, sometimes there are clients who will take advantage of you if they think you're a pushover, and I do know when to stand firm with such people. But overall, I try to exceed customer expectations beyond anything even the ultrawealthy might expect. That small investment of time and money can make an enormous difference when it comes to establishing the kind of brand that will distinguish you from your competition.

An extraordinary approach doesn't have to be the opposite of what everyone else is doing; instead, try doing an extraordinary job when others are just getting along. Look for places where you can do things in a new, unique, more productive way. If your competitors are spending all day Saturday taking clients through house after house, can you have the clients come to your office instead and, using a high-quality, large-screen monitor, take them on virtual tours of four properties in an hour so they can narrow down the number of houses they wish to visit? Can you give buyers new to your area lists of local information, like the closest grocery store, a good dry cleaner, a beauty salon, or a great day-care center for their kids? (For my ultra-high-end buyers, I might help them hire staff for the house, set up hard to get tee times at a prestigious golf course, or arrange for them to meet people who can help them become members at one of the exclusive country clubs in the area.) Can you provide after-sale amenities that other realtors never consider? For example, in addition to the usual flower arrangement or candy, take a high-quality photo of the outside of their house (which you probably have already from your marketing materials), have it enlarged and framed, and then present it to them when they move in. The after-sale attention you give your clients will make all the difference in the number of referrals you'll receive.

Whatever your business, you can find hundreds of extraordinary approaches that will set you above the ordinary and apart from your competition. And I think you'll like the extraordinary rewards that will come your way as a result.

Find and Fill a Niche—an Area That You Believe Is Missing in the Marketplace

If you think of yourself and your life—and in particular your working life—as a brand, the best product placement is to be first in your category. That's the equivalent of a display at the end of a grocery store aisle, or your web site being the top listing on all the major search engines for the Internet. You're all alone out there where everyone will see you, and any competition is playing catch-up. If you're the first and the best, your brand can end up as a one-word description of an entire product or service category, like Kleenex for facial tissue, Xerox for copiers, and FedEx for overnight delivery. But how do you find a category to be first in? In a world crammed with products and services (and people pitching them), how can you identify that little piece of the American dream in which you can make it big?

The secret is to find what I call a *niche*—an area in the marketplace that is right for your product or service. I believe the best niches are found in areas (1) that are missing altogether, (2) that are underserved, (3) that are ripe for innovation and/or improvement, or (4) where demand far exceeds supply. FedEx made its mark by basically inventing overnight delivery service, an area of the market that had been missing altogether. Charles Schwab took advantage of a growing interest in stock investment by an underserved segment of middle-income Americans who didn't feel comfortable with big, snooty brokerages but were delighted to accept less broker contact in exchange for lower commissions. Wireless phone companies have capitalized on an endless stream of innovation and improvement to develop a growing niche in the telecommunications field. And in many communities—from San Francisco to Los Angeles in California, to the South of France and the Italian Riviera, certain parts of Hawaii, and, of course, Palm Beach County, Florida—the limited supply of prime real estate continues to affect real estate prices even in a volatile economy.

I had known from a very early age that I wanted to go into business. I liked the idea of creating something that other people would pay for, and I believed I'd have a knack for it. When I felt I was ready to start my first business (about six months after I moved to Florida in 1982), I knew how to do three things: (1) how to get into trouble, (2) how to dig sand traps, and (3) how to teach tennis. The decision on which one to go with for a business was pretty obvious. Unfortunately, the country club where I'd been maintaining courts said they couldn't hire me as a tennis instructor, so I started looking elsewhere. Within a few days I noticed something: There were a lot of single-family residential and condominium complexes springing up in South Florida in the early 1980s. Many of them had beautiful tennis courts but no tennis programs. Voilà! A niche. I went to several of the more affluent clubs and complexes and offered to create tennis programs for them. "You don't have to do anything other than let me have the court time," I said. "I'll get paid from the lessons I'll give, and you can tell your prospective condo buyers that you provide expanded leisure-time activities, including a first-class tennis program."

I had found a niche in an area of the marketplace that was missing altogether. It was a perfect fit: These clubs and complexes didn't have the money to hire tennis pros full time, so I provided a missing service to their customers. I called my business the Professional Tennis Service, or PTS. With a lot of legwork and hustle on my part (coupled with an ability to sell myself to both students and managers), my business was grossing $100,000 annually by the time I was 21.

After about two years, however, I started thinking. By that point I had enough business that I was hiring other tennis instructors to work for me, and PTS had expanded to serve five communities. But I knew I couldn't teach tennis forever. My body and my skin couldn't take year after year in the hot sun, and there was definitely a ceiling on how much I (or my business) could net. Besides, a couple of girl-friends (and their mothers) told me in no uncertain terms that being a tennis bum all my life wasn't a proper career. So I started looking around for a new niche. As you'll hear in later chapters, I learned from several places (including many of my affluent clients) that real estate was a great field to make your fortune in. My dad (the banker) had also spoken with admiration about real estate being a great investment. But what part of real estate should I pursue? Commercial? Building? Realtor? Condos? Rentals?

I believe it was a little luck, a little fate, and a little divine intervention that whispered the words "distressed real estate" into my ear. (Okay, it was an older gentleman you'll hear more about in Philosophy #13.) I did some investigating, and it seemed to me there was an excellent opportunity to create a niche for myself in the distressed real estate market. What was missing in the marketplace in South Florida? There were tons of midpriced condos and houses available for people who were trading up, but almost no well-built, well-restored houses within the price range of the first-time home buyer. *This market is seriously underserved*, I said to myself. *All I need to do is find inexpensive properties, fix them up so they're livable and even nice, then show renters how they can afford to move up to home ownership.* (This may not sound remarkable today with all the Fannie Mae advertising on television and the whole "no money down" thing, but remember, this was 20 years ago. I was the only one in South Florida who was targeting this particular segment of the market.)

So, where would I find these inexpensive properties? In distressed real estate: homes that had been either foreclosed, seized for nonpayment of county taxes or income taxes, or taken in drug raids. Every week there were at least 40 distressed properties on the auction block in Palm Beach County. Most of these houses were falling apart, in crack neighborhoods, infested with bugs—all of which kept buyers away. Except me: I saw potential for turnaround and profit in every graffiti-covered inch. For six months I studied the homes, the sales, the competition, everything I could learn about the industry. Then I took $30,000 I had saved from my tennis business, borrowed $70,000 from friends and some of my affluent tennis students, and bought my first property.

I figured I would do the renovations as quickly as possible, make the house as nice as I could within my budget, put the property on the market, sell it fast, and do it all over again. It took me four months from the time I bought my first property until the day it sold, and I cleared a whole $7,000. But it was the most significant money I ever earned, because it proved to me my concept worked! I could find property at the right price point; I could renovate it quickly yet well; I could market it in such a way that first-time buyers would be attracted; and I could make a good and (equally important) predictable profit in fairly short order.

In this case, I created a niche in a marketplace that was severely underserved. I was not only developing houses but also developing buyers through a series of seminars I taught on how to buy your first home (see Philosophy #8). By the time I moved from the distressed real estate market to the oceanfront market six years later, I was renovating around 16 to 20 houses a year and selling them for $100,000 each on average. In addition, my business wasn't just improving houses, it was upgrading whole neighborhoods. People who lived nearby would see how we'd turn a graffiti-covered, broken-down monstrosity of a property into a clean, neat, well-built house with a green lawn and white picket fence, and all of a sudden they'd get active. They'd start cleaning up their own homes and chasing the crack heads, drug dealers, prostitutes, and pimps off their streets. Parts of Palm Beach County I used to be afraid to ride through were becoming nice neighborhoods again—and I felt great that my business was helping in that process.

While I was buying and selling these houses, I was also running the Young Entrepreneurial Society (YES). At a meeting someone asked me, "Where do you want to go from here? How much longer do you see yourself doing these smaller projects? Where do you want to apply your talents next?" (That was one of the reasons I loved YES: People would ask you questions like that all the time. We were always looking to expand our horizons and raise the stakes.) Without much thought, I answered, "I'd like to do what I'm doing now, working with real estate, but I'd like to do it on the oceanfront where the stakes are higher." That offhand answer was both a harbinger of things to come and a reflection of my developing (and at that point, subliminal) sense of the marketplace.

Remember what I said earlier about there being a lot of housing choices for the midrange buyer who was trading up? I looked at that midrange market and saw it didn't meet a single one of my criteria for developing a niche. It was saturated instead of missing; it was over-served, both in terms of available properties and people who were building and selling them; the opportunities for innovation and/or improvement were limited because there was only so much money a midrange buyer could spend; and there was plenty of supply. So I followed up on my offhand remark at the YES meeting and started researching properties on the ocean.

At that time oceanfront real estate was selling for anywhere from $200,000 for a condo to $2 million for a house—a real jump in investment level for me from the $20,000 to $70,000 I had been paying in the distressed market. But the key for this niche was *supply and demand*. In the early 1990s, no one was really capitalizing on the limited supply of oceanfront real estate. It didn't take a rocket scientist to understand that Palm Beach was an extremely desirable location: an internationally recognized address with great weather, some of the most beautiful beaches in the world, direct ocean views and access, and a proven and internationally known home for the well-to-do. The buyers for properties in Palm Beach were some of the wealthiest people in the world, as had been true since the 1920s when the Vanderbilts, Biltmores, and Posts had built palatial winter homes here. But no one had looked to build those kinds of high-end, ultra-high-quality homes in places other than Palm Beach proper. I saw an opportunity to create a whole new niche in a marketplace that seemed to be continually capable of attracting new buyers for a limited supply of products.

I also believed I could take some of the principles I had applied with such great success in the distressed real estate market and do the same thing on the oceanfront. Do my research? I researched and looked at properties for almost a year before I found my first one. Distressed property? Nilsa and I found that first property, Driftwood Dunes, while we were driving to church one Sunday. It was on the oceanfront in Delray Beach, the Palm Beach County town where we resided, which is about 20 minutes south of the city of Palm Beach. The property showed all the telltale signs of being distressed: high grass, overgrown trees, weeds, a month's worth of unclaimed newspapers scattered around. The house was falling apart, boarded up, with peeling paint. On the plus side, however, it had nice beachfront, and I knew I could get it on the market quickly by adding onto the house and renovating instead of tearing it down and building new. The house also had character and charm—it had been owned by a shipping captain who ran cargo from Florida to the Bahamas, and was constructed to look like a boat with its prow pointing out to sea. Best of all, there was a for sale sign in the lot. I thought, *This is it!*

I'm a firm believer in being at the bottom or the top end of any market, but nowhere in between. Don't waste your time in the middle: It will put food on your table, but it's not going to yield the big prizes you'll find at either end. The oceanfront property I chose represented the most inexpensive of the high-end market. We paid $775,000 for the house and grounds. From researching comparable property in the area, I knew I could ask at least $2 million for it when I was done with the renovations, which I estimated at around $300,000. And it worked—I sold Driftwood Dunes for $1.9 million in 1992.

Since then I have continued to innovate and improve as I carved out my niche in ultra-high-end oceanfront property. I will confess I benefited greatly from timing, as I bought my first oceanfront house in 1991, right when the U.S. economy started its ten-year-plus up-swing. But one advantage of niches at either the high or low end of your market: They tend to be relatively recession-proof. On the low end of real estate, there will always be a need for affordable houses for first-time buyers, and as long as you do your acquiring at the right price, the profits will be there. On the high end—well, at certain levels of net worth even the most dire of recessions won't cause too much of a dent. And as I said, the market for this kind of property is international. When I sold that first estate in 1992, the typical buyer for ultra-high-end oceanfront real estate in South Florida (properties worth $3 million and up) was around 65 years old. Of 10 qualified buyers, 6 would be from another country (England, Switzer-land, Germany, Finland), and 4 from the United States. Today, the average age of a qualified buyer has dropped from 65 to 50, meaning we have as many 45-year-olds as 60-year-olds looking at our proper-ties. Even more staggering, the number of American buyers has in-creased; 8 of 10 are from the United States. (Which brings up another point about your niche: You must know it backward and forward, and track the changes in it so you can keep up and, hopefully, keep ahead of trends.)

I believe I have been successful in the niches I chose because each of them suited my particular talents and abilities. I am very good at putting deals together, ferreting out opportunities, and negotiating to get the best price point and terms that will work for both buyer and seller. I'm not intimidated by the number of zeros on a purchase price (very helpful when I moved to the oceanfront). I seem to have an instinct for what the higher-end buyer wants; and it's an instinct I feed every chance I get by learning as much as I can from affluent, successful people (see Philosophy #13). I'm not afraid to take risks and put everything on the line, to try something I believe will lead the market rather than follow it, yet I'll always precede those choices with thorough research. I have taken my niche in a new direction for the past nine years, setting new standards in quality and price for the oceanfront market. I have begun to establish the Frank McKinney brand in my part of the world. What's more, I believe you can use similar techniques and strategies in creating a niche in whatever market or industry you choose.

To find your niche in the marketplace, you must start by knowing yourself. Get a sense of where your strengths lie and what your interests are, and based on that sense, choose a marketplace. The marketplace itself doesn't really matter—it should simply be something that will keep you interested and passionate (see Philosophy #11) for a good long period of time. Once you've selected a marketplace, look for areas where you believe there is room for development. You're most likely to find your niche in an area (1) that is missing altogether, (2) that is underserved, (3) that is ripe for innovation and/or improvement, or (4) where demand far exceeds supply. Once you've found something, get to work. Do your research first; see what's out there, and figure out how what you have to offer will either augment the current market or break new ground. Then knuckle down and start working. At each step of the way, keep learning about the psychology of your customers. Listen to them. What do they want? What are they missing? How can you serve them better? How can you make your product or service stand out? Remember, the psychology of the marketplace will constantly evolve, and you must keep abreast of the changes. And once you've been in your niche for awhile, you may be able to start leading your customers instead of just filling their needs.

Once you have maxed out one niche, as I did with tennis, investigate another. Use what you learned in your first niche to build your brand even more efficiently and effectively the next time. Or expand your niche to include greater opportunities, as I did when I moved from distressed properties to oceanfront real estate. Above all, don't be afraid to take the risks necessary to give yourself a shot at extreme success. I guarantee that once you've found and built one niche, you can apply what you have learned to take any business to the highest levels of success. And if you do it right, you'll find you've not just built a business, but you also have created a whole new area of the marketplace that has your name on it. You will have become the go-to guy or girl in your particular field because you've carved a niche that's wider and deeper than those of your competitors.

Actions

1. Start by surveying yourself. What are your interests? What are your strengths? What kinds of endeavors attract you? Based on that, in what marketplaces do you think you might enjoy developing a niche? Don't confine yourself to the obvious, as, "I love music so I'm going to be a musician." Often you may find your niche by applying the whole range of your talents in a different part of the market. If you love music and also have a head for business, you could become a manager or an agent, or a concert promoter. You could establish a travel agency that caters to the needs of musicians. There are a million different niches out there that will accommodate your unique talents, abilities, and interests.

2. Once you've assessed yourself and your abilities and investigated marketplaces you might be interested in, look for niches (1) that are missing, (2) that are underserved, (3) that are ripe for innovation and improvement, or (4) have limited supply and lots of demand. How can you create a business that takes advantage of any of those conditions? Then start to work. Do your research, be willing to apply a lunch-pail approach, continually assess your customer's psychology, take risks, and enjoy the ride. If you keep at it, you stand a great chance of making it big in the niche you have chosen or, better yet, created.

Deal Points

If you're interested in real estate as a potential marketplace for your business, there are two keys I want to cover here. First is the importance of research and where you make your money. For most people just starting out, real estate is an expensive proposition. You can buy stock in a company for $5 a share and up, but even the smallest piece of raw land is going to set you back hundreds, thousands, or tens of thousands of dollars. It's in your best interest to do your research to determine what your profit potential will be from this particular piece of property. I spent six months learning the distressed real estate market before I put even one dollar into it. (And I paid too much for the first house I bought, and it cut into my profits significantly.) Even when I was buying and selling 16 to 20 properties a year, there were many opportunities I would walk away from because the profit potential wasn't great enough. In real estate, your profit is always made the day you *buy* your property, not when you sell it. The price you pay to acquire the property will determine your profit potential. If you're in a hot market, you can afford to pay a little more; but I prefer to acquire property for less money, invest some time and further capital to improve the underlying land or the structure itself, then sell at a greater profit margin.

Even though I've been in oceanfront property for ten years, I still consider myself in the distressed real estate market in a way, because I'm applying exactly the same principles as I did when I bought homes for $20,000, fixed them up, and sold them for $60,000. I look to acquire property that I believe is undervalued or will be so in the next year to 18 months. (Even in the current volatile economy, oceanfront land values in Palm Beach County are appreciating between 2 and 3.5 percent a month. That means I can buy a piece of oceanfront land for $10 million today and even if I do nothing to it, it will probably be worth between $12 and $14.2 million next year.) Then I increase the value of the property, either by constructing a beautiful new house on it with the best of everything or by completely renovating a relatively new house, upgrading nearly all major systems, replacing "nice" materials with the best the world has to offer, and furnishing the house down to the gold-plated toothbrush in the bathroom. Finally, I put the estate on the market at a price point that is almost always above that of the surrounding properties, but which I believe is justified by the increase in land values and the improvements I have made.

The key is still the price point at which I acquire the property. I'm looking for a minimum profit potential of 30 to 50 percent based on the acquisition price, the cost of renovations, and the selling price I believe I can get. If a deal doesn't meet my numbers, I walk away from it. I've had properties I've been salivating over but wouldn't buy them for the price that was being asked. When it comes to cash, I've always been a businessman and then a visionary.

The second key for developing a profitable niche in real estate is the psychology of the deal, the buying and selling. I'll talk a lot in Part Three about putting yourself in the other guy's shoes, thinking win-win, being fair, and closing the deal. But you have to know your own psychology as well as that of your buyers and sellers. Let's start on the buy side, where you're looking to acquire a certain piece of property. In a seller's market (which describes oceanfront real estate in South Florida) demand exceeds supply. To me, that means every property I buy represents almost a guaranteed opportunity, if I buy it at the right price. I take a look a year or so down the road and figure out what this property will be worth in that time (remembering those rising real estate values of about 24 to 36 percent a year). I look at the potential upside for any number of scenarios: selling the property as land only, selling the land and house as is, renovating and selling, or razing the house and building something new. I figure in all the variables like carrying costs, renovations, promotions, and so on. Then I look at possible downsides: natural disasters (hurricanes), delays, market downturns, overcommitment of assets, and possible lost opportunities. (I can maintain upwards of $100 million in inventory at any given time, but I have to consider whether this particular deal is the best use of my funds.)

Only after I have considered all of that do I start negotiating the price at which I will buy the property. Knowing my profit potential gives me great flexibility. Even though I think and act like every nickel of a deal is the most important nickel of my life, I know that based on the increases in this particular marketplace, if I overpay for the property by $50,000 or even $100,000 it's okay. I suggest that you, too, don't lose a good opportunity over the false pride represented by refusing to pay a few more dollars. I always weigh the purchase price against the opportunity to use this property to create a new price level, perhaps a whole new marketplace. Then I calculate my risk (see Philosophy #26) and I make my decision.

When it comes to selling the property to someone else, a whole new dynamic ensues. First, you have to be able to read your buyers to make sure they're qualified in the first place. In the ultra-high-end marketplace, there are a lot of (excuse me) flakes who represent themselves as being able to afford something that's actually way out of their league. On the other hand, at this level there's a lot more latitude on price than you'd expect. I tell brokers, "If you have clients who say their uppermost price point is $10 million, it's not. Show them the right $15 million house and they'll go for it." At the $2 million or $3 million or even $5 million level, your clients may be telling the truth when they say that's all they can afford. But once you move past that point, it gets a lot more flexible. I've had clients who came to look at one of our $5 million properties who eventually were considering ones in the $15 million range. Often brokers will ask me, "Is your price firm, Frank?" I respond, "It's real estate—what do you think?"

In negotiations on the sell side, I'm not calculating based on the amount I paid for the property plus improvement costs; I am looking for straight profit. How much am I going to make on this deal in real dollars? I have to take into account brokers' fees, carrying costs, selling versus keeping it on the market, and so on. Is it better for me to take a little less and put my profits into another opportunity? Or should I hold out for more profit and be willing to carry the property a little longer? And (something very important to me in creating a brand) if I sell at a lower price, what will that do to the prices I'm trying to establish in this marketplace? Every property sets a standard for its neighborhood and for the Frank McKinney brand, and I'm committed to making sure that brand represents enormous quality and increasing value. But remember, when I set my selling price at the outset, I'm usually priced above current levels anyway, and that gives me more wiggle room while maintaining my profit potential. I can set those kinds of prices because (1) it's a seller's market, with demand outstripping supply; and (2) I provide the kind of quality that buyers see as justifying the higher prices. In your particular market or niche, you may not have the same flexibility in setting price. That's why the buy side of the deal is always where you really make your money.

In the Deal Points in the next chapter I'll talk about the most important things you can know about the psychology of the marketplace itself—not just the psychology of your buyer or seller, but the psychology of each segment of the market (low end, middle range, and high end). I believe this information will help you make it big if you select a niche in residential real estate.

10

Apply True Focus to What You Do Best. Until You Are Ready, Do Not Be Distracted Outside Your Niche

Concentration and focus are powerful forces in building success. When you're learning to be a great tennis player, for example, you spend hours working on one element of your game at a time. You concentrate your efforts in that one area so you can master it. I think of my dad a lot when it comes to concentration and focus. He was a great swimmer, great enough to win gold, silver, and bronze medals in the 1956 and 1960 Olympics. He focused on the backstroke. Day after day, hour after hour, he'd swim up and down the pool, doing the backstroke, working on his technique (he invented the "bent arm" style all backstrokers use today), his breathing—whatever would make him better at that one thing. He didn't swim in freestyle races or breaststroke, and in relays of course he swam the backstroke leg. His niche, if you will, was the backstroke, and for quite some time he was the best there was, as evidenced by his world records.

You need to apply a similar level of concentration and focus within your own niche. Overnight success is a fairy tale; it usually takes time to achieve anything worth much. Above all, success takes focus and concentrated effort. Ask any successful entrepreneur how he or she made it; I'll just bet the individual had a level of focus that bordered on obsession. That may be a failing in terms of a personal life, but it's a valuable trait when it comes to filling a niche.

Unfortunately, it's very easy to get distracted. All kinds of things will pull your focus away. When you're first starting out, you may be indecisive: "Is this the right niche? Should I be trying something else? How long before I know whether I'll succeed at this or not?" It's like trying to choose just one ice cream flavor at Baskin-Robbins—except that you know once you choose pistachio, that's what you're going to be eating for the next five years! When you're choosing a niche, do as much research as you can first, to see which "flavor" will suit you best.

But once you've chosen, I recommend you create a vision for that business (see Philosophy #2), give yourself a time line for accomplishing your vision, and then go for it. Pour all your energy and focus into making that vision real. Let any other possibilities go; many of them will still be there if you change your mind later. But if you want to make it big, you can't waver between this course and that one. Especially in the early stages of an entrepreneurial career, you have to make up your mind and stick to what you believe is your highest calling (see Philosophy #1).

I had a major "focus waver" during my early days as an entrepreneur. While I was still running the tennis business, I fell in love with a Hollywood actress who was visiting Palm Beach. After hanging out with her for several months, I started to think that maybe I'd like to try acting, too. After all, I was as good looking as a lot of the actors I saw on television; I kept myself in great shape with all the tennis; why not give it a shot? So I took some acting classes down in Miami, and got cast in a few small things. By that point it was summer, and the tennis business was slowing down. (In South Florida, the summers are our slow season. There is a very large seasonal population in this part of the world; people who live farther north come down for the winter months and then go back home in the summer.) I thought, *What a great time to try my luck with this acting thing!* and I headed straight for Los Angeles. Of course, it was no coincidence that the girl I was dating also had moved back to L.A.

Luckily for me as it turned out, neither my acting plans nor the relationship with the girlfriend worked out. But the trip did have two significant benefits. First, after this girl broke up with me, I asked her what kind of man she admired. (I figured if I was getting dumped, at least I might learn something that would help me with the next girl I dated.) She talked enthusiastically about several high-end real estate brokers she had met in Beverly Hills. These men were making a lot of money buying and selling multimillion-dollar estates (sound familiar?). *Maybe if I go into high-end real estate I can be admired by beautiful women, too!* I thought.

The second benefit was the lesson I learned about not getting distracted outside of my niche. I had been building a very nice tennis business in Palm Beach County, and thought I could do the same thing in Los Angeles. But one day I went to the beach in Malibu just to think things through. I had spent two years making a name for myself and my tennis business in Florida. I had a great following and clientele; lots of country clubs knew who I was and were starting to ask about my services. Did I really want to give that up and start all over in California? No. I got up, dusted the sand off my butt, and flew back to Palm Beach shortly thereafter.

Once you've committed to your niche and plunged in, typically during the first years of working you're too darn busy to let yourself get distracted. But when you start to see results and things lighten up a bit, that's when you can be tempted by outside opportunities. "Maybe I ought to get into the stock market." "Maybe I should add a little house-cleaning business on the side to bring in more income." It's one of the biggest mistakes I've seen people make. As soon as you divide your efforts and your focus, you lose some of the forward motion you've been working so hard to build in the niche you've already chosen. Plus, any new venture is going to mean a new learning curve, a new commitment of resources, and the same kind of struggle you've just finished going through with the first business. Does that sound like an intelligent business decision? I don't think so.

Instead of taking on a new venture, I recommend doing what my dad did: Focus on one thing and get great at it. Once I decided to make the move from tennis to distressed real estate, I deliberately chose Palm Beach County as the place where I would develop my marketplace. Whatever segment of the marketplace I concentrated in, I worked hard to be the best; I wanted to get to the point where I could dominate my chosen market. To date, all of my real estate dealings have been in the small part of the world called South Florida. I went from doing single-family homes to entire neighborhoods to ultra-high-end real estate, all within a radius of about 75 square miles. I have concentrated my focus on this particular niche, and it has paid off handsomely.

In addition to concentration and focus, the third element that will allow you to dominate your niche is persistence. There's a lot to be said for concentrated effort over time. If you stick to something long enough you're going to get good at it. When I was in the foreclosure business, there were four or five of us who showed up every week at the auctions. And ultimately, we were the ones who did the best because we stuck with it; we had longevity. But to gain longevity, you have to focus single-mindedly on what you're doing and not be caught in the lure of something new. Remember, whenever you start over you're going to lose whatever edge longevity and experience have given you. And sometimes that edge can mean a lot.

Instead of stepping outside your niche, why not take one segment of your original niche and focus on that for a while? If you're an attorney, study up on a particular kind of case law and become a specialist in it. If you're in real estate, as I am, do the same thing but in a different context. In 1991, after I had been in the distressed real estate market for about five years, I heard through the grapevine that a group of five historic (built in 1925), dilapidated, run-down homes standing in a cluster at the gateway to Delray Beach were going to be sold for taxes. I bought the buildings for a total of $50,000 and decided to turn them into office suites. This was my first foray into commercial property but it was still distressed real estate, a field in which I considered myself an expert by 1991.

I applied everything I already knew about turning around distressed properties to those buildings. We tore down one structure to create more parking (sorely needed) and renovated the other four, turning them into very nice, very distinctive office spaces. I named the complex the Historic Executive Suites of Delray, the first (and only) historic office park in the state of Florida. Within six months of our grand opening, the Suites were 90 percent occupied. I held on to that property for six years, and finally sold it, fully leased, for $800,000. That was as close as I came to a deviation within my niche. In reality, it was more of a reapplication than a deviation, because everything I did at the Suites I had done already with other properties. In a way, the Suites was a perfect transitional project to move my niche away from distressed real estate first-time home-buyer properties and toward oceanfront real estate.

Now, let's suppose you've been working at your business for some time, and you're doing very well. You feel you have mastered the niche you have chosen or created; you're at the top of your game. Well, here's where the *real* temptations start popping up. Once you're successful in one area, it's human nature to assume you'll be successful in another. "I've been a great real estate agent; but I'll bet I could run a carpet cleaning franchise on the side and double my profits." "I've got some money from all the business consulting I've been doing; maybe I'll put it into a duplex or two." Other people also will assume that success in one niche means automatic success in another, and they'll start trying to interest you in all kinds of opportunities outside your field. But I've seen many entrepreneurs lose a lot of money when they try to step too far outside their niches. They're a little bored with what they've been doing for 10, 15, 20 years, and they think they know everything there is to know about success. A fresh start might be just the ticket, they think; it'll be easy and fun. But guess what? Everything you know may or may not apply when it comes to being successful in something new. There's still a learning curve to a new business, and even if your experience can shorten it, remember that you're now 10, 15, 20 years older than you were when you started out. Are you willing to put in the time and energy it will take to build this new business? Are you willing to take that time and energy away from the niche you've worked so hard to dominate? As long as you are, go ahead—but do it with your eyes open.

Notice the wording of this Philosophy. "*Until you are ready*, do not be distracted outside your niche." There does come a time when it might be right for you to look outside your original focus. After I'd been in distressed real estate for five years, I felt I knew enough to start looking outside my original marketplace. I spent quite a lot of time researching the oceanfront market while I was still buying and selling foreclosures. Even when I had made the move and bought that first oceanfront property, I still continued to own and sell several foreclosures for a couple of years afterward.

Over the past few years especially, I've been faced with many temptations to step outside my niche, but I've turned most of them down because they don't fit my needs. This book is the first real step I have taken outside my niche since I started in real estate. However, I feel I am ready. My business is going very well; I'm at the top of my game professionally; I'm leading the marketplace now rather than following it. Plus, this book feels like a natural outgrowth of who I am and what I know how to do. I've done my research and know what's required for this step outside my niche, and I'm willing to put in the time and effort to make it work.

Concentration, focus, persistence, longevity—these are the building blocks of large-scale success. As a real estate entrepreneur for over 15 years, I can tell you the only way to create a solid structure is with a strong foundation, solid walls built straight up and down, and a good roof. Don't build your structure on shaky foundations by scattering your efforts; don't weaken your structure halfway up by taking it in a whole new direction. When you've built your business strong and solid, you can move on to another property or field of endeavor, certain that your original structure will withstand the tests of time even if you're doing only maintenance on it. Don't let yourself be distracted from your niche until your business is solid and strong. Make sure it's something you can be proud of—something that will last.

Actions

1. The best deterrents to distraction are vision and focus. If you have a strong vision of what you want to create in your niche, it's easier to dismiss anything that doesn't help implement that vision. Next, focus on where you want to go. Creating a business is like creating a marriage; you can't be fooling around on the outside and expect it to last!

2. How can you tell you're ready to move outside your niche? It's a combination of strength and opportunity. Is your business strong enough to withstand your disappearance? Are you willing to let it go completely, if needed, to throw yourself into a new venture with uncertain results? If so, look long and hard at the opportunity you wish to pursue. You'll be starting all over, remember; are you willing to put in the enormous time and effort it will take to get to the same level of success you have already experienced in your other endeavors? As long as you go into your new venture with open eyes and a willingness to start over and apply the same kind of focus and concentration that helped you achieve your previous successes, then go for it.

Deal Points

One of the advantages that concentration, focus, persistence, and longevity can give you is an in-depth knowledge of your particular niche. I believe market specialization is one of the fundamental secrets of real estate success. As part of my niche, I have specialized not only in distressed real estate and then the ultra-high-end part of the market, but also in the particular psychology of each segment. I know the psychology of those marketplaces like the back of my hand. This knowledge has allowed me to serve my customers at the highest possible level, anticipating their needs as well as the direction of an entire marketplace.

When you're building or renovating properties for the low end of the market, you need to understand what I call the *psychology of the renter*. Your primary low-end customers aren't home owners; they are people for whom home ownership is a huge step. You need to do everything you can to (1) make that step as attractive and easy as possible and (2) eliminate any barriers that stand in their way.

Renters need to be educated and convinced that they should be (and can be) paying a mortgage instead of renting. That's why I taught all those little seminars on how to buy a home (as described in Philosophy #8). Other realtors will set up credit classes for potential buyers, to show them how to clean up their credit or obtain credit for the first time. Next, you've got to prove to renters that it's possible for them to buy instead of rent on what they're currently earning. You might put together a pamphlet showing potential buyers how much they'd be paying a month for one of your houses, with so much down and such-and-such percent interest. Be thorough: Make sure you cover all the costs of ownership, like property taxes, upkeep, repairs, and so on. The key is to make home ownership seem achievable.

The next thing is to make the potential properties attractive. Even if someone's living in a cramped one-bedroom apartment, if it's an acceptable apartment in a nice part of town they're not going to be eager to trade it in for a mediocre house in a marginal neighborhood. So make sure your house is as nice as you can make it for your price point (and naturally, ensuring an adequate profit for your efforts). Even if the street's not the greatest, if your house is the nicest one around people will be interested in buying it. Remember, this little house will represent the first piece of the American dream for somebody; it'll be a benchmark in the course of someone's life. If you honor the courage it takes to make that step, if you do your best to help your buyer make it psychologically—by showing that it's possible, then offering a property that encourages buyers to go for it—then you are on the way to dominating the all-important, recession-proof market segment of first-time home buyers.

The next segment of the market is the mid-range home, currently selling for anywhere between $300,000 and $1 million in Palm Beach County. (This market is one I have never focused on, so my thoughts about it are based on observation rather than direct experience.) When you're in that middle market where most home buying occurs, you absolutely will need to know something of the psychology of your buyer. But because the market is full of other professionals trying to do the exact same thing you are, it's more important to know the *psychology of your competitors*. What are they doing that you can emulate? What services are they providing that you'd darn well better provide, too, if you want to keep up? What can you do that will set you apart from your competition? When you're in the mid-range market, buyers not only have a wide range of choice as far as property is concerned; they also have an equally wide choice about who they deal with. You'd better figure out a way to do a better job than your competitors, or you'll spend a lot of time fighting over the same customers. The good news is, you don't have to reinvent the wheel; your competitors may have a lot of good ideas you can copy or (better yet) improve upon. The bad news is, they'll do the same to you. Outguessing, outdoing, outimproving your competitors is the way to create a niche in the mid-range market.

When you move into the high-end market, the most important psychology—indeed, the only one that matters—is the *psychology of your likely buyer*. From the very beginning I have done anything and everything I could to understand the minds of wealthy, successful people. I have learned how they think, what they expect, and what will delight them in a home. I work hard on creating appeal on both a conscious and subliminal level when a client tours one of my properties. I know how successful people make decisions, and how they negotiate. When our $30 million estate was on the market, a reporter asked me who I thought would buy it. Instantly I replied, "He'll be around 40 years old, with a young family. He'll be a self-made businessman; he won't have inherited his money. He'll have at least one other home in a more industrial part of the United States, and this will be a second home so he can get away from the winters." I was off by about three years on the age, but other than that, the purchaser of that property fit my description to a T.

Knowing the psychology of the ultra-high-end buyer allows you to (1) build the house to the expectations, desires, and fantasies of such a person; (2) price the house at the appropriate level—appropriate not for the surrounding property necessarily but more for the clientele you wish to attract; and (3) market the property in such a way that will cause them to want to buy. The fact that I understand my likely buyer has allowed me to appear to go against market trends while creating new standards in this particular niche. It's a very small niche; fewer than 50,000 people in the world make up my marketplace. Therefore, knowing their psychology is the difference that has helped me succeed. That knowledge, combined with a sense of market trends based on overall economic factors, allows me to anticipate how and where psychology will shift in a changing market like the one we're in now.

I believe knowing your market's psychology is one of the most important factors in creating and/or dominating your niche. No matter what your focus—real estate or some other profession; low end, high end, or middle range—take the time to discover the psychology of your customers. It'll pay off big.

Have a Passion for What You Do, Both at Work and at Home

To stand out in your marketplace and create an extraordinary life, you must have passion. Passion is the element that turns a plain but nourishing life into something you can't wait to dive into. Passion comes in many forms. You can be passionate about a person. You can be passionate about a cause. You can be passionate about a sports team. But without it, life is gray, dull, and boring. If you lack passion for any significant element of your life—like your job or profession—then you're in trouble.

Have you ever seen all the poor souls on their way to work in their cars, on commuter trains, or in the subways? These people live for the weekend. They leave work mentally on Fridays around noon. At five o'clock (or earlier) they hop in their cars and try to get home as quickly as possible to enjoy their time off. And what do they end up doing? Errands, watching TV—the "same old, same old," weekend after weekend. Sunday afternoon they get into a funk, thinking about all the work facing them back at the office, and Monday morning they're in their cars with sour expressions on their faces.

That is a living hell, in my opinion. Having no passion for what you spend most of your life doing is a tragedy—and so unnecessary. Yes, we all have to make a living, support our families, keep a roof over our heads, and save for retirement and the kids' college tuition. And it's true, we may have to sacrifice passion and do things we do not love while we provide for our families for a while. But security is not worth an entire life—the only one you're going to get—lived without passion. To make a name for yourself, to create a presence in the marketplace, and most of all, to put *life* into your life, you must have passion.

Passion is like a battery: You have to keep recharging and renewing it. Even when you love your job, every day isn't going to be great. Some days you may feel as uninspired as one of those poor passionless souls you see on the freeway, but you can't let that feeling linger. I find it helps to go back to the vision and highest calling that we talked about in Part One. When you connect to why you're going to the job site again, or teaching that rowdy bunch of eighth graders, or taking care of your own kids, or running one more boring meeting—when you put that into the context of "I'm building the most amazing house in the world," or "I can make a difference in the minds of these kids forever," or "I'm shaping the lives of my children by being with them when they're young," or "This meeting will help me lead my company into a profitable new alliance"—somehow it's a little easier to ignite that flame of passion one more time. And the more often you put a match to that flame, the higher it burns.

Most entrepreneurs have enormous passion for what they do. Otherwise, there wouldn't be much reason to put up with the struggle to get started, the endless hours, the living from hand to mouth if a deal doesn't come through, the shouldering full responsibility for both success and failure, and so on. But the challenges and rewards of entrepreneurial business can cause us to neglect the rest of our lives. We ignore our families; we don't take care of ourselves physically, emotionally, or spiritually; we develop tunnel vision and see our lives only in terms of business. To make it big, you need both passion for your work and passion for the rest of your life as well. This Philosophy advocates balance. If you don't balance the amount of energy you put into home and work, you will decrease your chance of success and increase your potential for burnout.

Because I'm passionate about a lot of different areas, it's easy for me to stay juiced. I have as much passion for a homeless project as I do for building my regular homes. Over the past few years, however, I've discovered that passion at home can actually augment my energy and focus at work. For years I never took vacations; I considered them a waste of time, and I couldn't afford them, anyway. Now I treasure the times I can go to our cabin in Colorado or some other destination. I wouldn't want to be out there all the time—that would drive me nuts faster than working 24/7! But as a break from my usual life, it refuels me and reignites my passion for both work and home.

Life is an evolutionary process, and our passions ebb and flow over the years. The business you started as an entrepreneur becomes a large, successful company, but now it's not as flexible, innovative, or fun anymore. Your girlfriend or boyfriend becomes a wife or a husband, and after 10 years and several kids you're not as "hot and bothered" about each other as you used to be. You marched for Greenpeace and joined the Sierra Club 20 years ago, but now that you're in the fifth year of heading up the local fund-raising drive you're tired of begging people for money to save the environment. It's natural for passion to diminish over time; but then, it's also natural to get flabbier each year unless you do something about it. You need to be able to embrace change while still keeping your passion alive. Sometimes that means taking a break, as with the fund-raising; sometimes it means reconnecting to what excited you at the start, like in a marriage. Sometimes it means finding another avenue for your passion: The entrepreneur may prefer to sell his or her company and create a brand-new venture, for example.

When you have passion both at work *and* at home, however, one source can keep you going whenever the other diminishes. For example, if you're in a job you don't really like but you need to support your family, the passion you put into your family life can sometimes rub off on the job. Maybe you could involve your family in your work in some way, or start viewing your coworkers as another "branch" of your family tree. Conversely, if you're the driven, entrepreneurial type who loves what you do, bring some of that passion and energy into your family life and see what happens. I'm fortunate that my wife, Nilsa, does the interior design and decorating on all of my big properties, so we can share in that passion. And I'm already taking my daughter to our project sites so she'll see what Daddy does at work all day.

One thing that fuels my passion is a sense that I have so much more to accomplish. In my weekly introspections and yearly personal retreat, I connect to my vision and my highest calling, see where I've succeeded and where I've fallen short over that time, and then recommit to making my life extraordinary and making a difference. Passion is the natural result of that process—especially since introspection gives me so many things to be passionate about! But the greatest excitement and passion always come from getting out there and making it happen. When I'm working, taking action, living my vision, doing my best to embody the Philosophies that guide my life, then passion isn't just the fuel—it's the by-product. And by the way, it's also a great reward.

Actions

1. Find something to be passionate about at work. Even if you're in the "paying your dues" phase, there must be something you can enjoy. Try doing your best to produce extraordinary results, as we discussed in Philosophy #8. I've found that doing really well at something often ignites passion for the endeavor.
2. What other areas of your life are you passionate about? Make sure you have several different things, people, causes, and so on that fuel your inner fire, and then feed it whenever you can.
3. If the fire of your passion is diminished in some areas, what can you do to reignite it? How can you renew your passion? If you can't, you need to choose between settling for whatever passion you still have and moving on.

Deal Points

Entrepreneurs can't rely on anyone else to keep them passionate about work; they have to renew and reignite their own passions again and again. However, I believe there are three traps that can stifle your entrepreneurial zeal. The first and most obvious is the trap of *failure*. If you're not good at something, or if you can't make something turn out well no matter how hard you try, it's difficult to stay passionate about it. In this case, you have two choices: Either you can find something else to do that will offer you a greater chance of success while it fuels your passion or you can become passionate about doing whatever it takes to turn this situation around (see Philosophy #29, "Be prepared to fail before you succeed").

The second trap is that of *monotony*. This happens when you've been doing the same thing for a while. You construct your sixteenth property of the year, set up your eighth open house in a month, or write yet one more quarterly report, and it starts to feel like the "same old, same old." This common yet devastating trap can devour any passion you might once have had for your work. The best escape I've found for the trap of monotony is challenge. Either you must challenge yourself internally to find new ways of doing the same things (hopefully producing even better results) or you must seek out external challenge by taking on new responsibilities, changing jobs if necessary, even changing professions.

The third trap is one that on the surface wouldn't seem to be all that perilous: It's the trap of *success*. Have you ever known someone who reaches the top of his or her profession and all of a sudden looks around and says, "Is this all there is?" When you get used to success, as with everything else, you can lose your passion for your endeavors. You may also find that your success has produced envy in others; they may even attempt to take what you have worked so hard to produce. As a result, you can start wondering whether all your hard work has been worth it. But I believe passion is best fed (and naysayers thwarted) by challenging yourself, finding new tasks, and achieving something even more extraordinary. Last year my neighbor asked me, "Frank, you're still working after you sold that big house?" I said, "You better believe it. I'm one of the TGIM crowd: Thank God It's Monday. I love what I do, and I have a lot more to accomplish before I'm done." There have been several times in my career when I could have put my profits in the bank and put my feet up for the rest of my life—but who in their right mind would want to do that when there is so much more to accomplish?

Ultimately, passion always comes from within. In your profession, you must find your own ways to create it, renew it, and use it to create the brand that will help you make it big.

Don't Let Others Deter Your Entrepreneurial Passion or Enthusiasm

When I was no older than seven or eight, I remember watching my mom do laundry for the four kids she had at that point. I watched her take the heavy, wet laundry from the washer, carry it over to the dryer, and heave it in. After a moment I asked, "Mom, why doesn't someone invent a washer that sits above the dryer?" (This was before stackable units.) "Then you could put a trapdoor in the bottom of the washer, and when the clothes were done the trapdoor would automatically open up and the clothes could fall out. If you had a matching door on the top of the dryer, they'd fall straight in and you wouldn't have to haul them around." My mom looked at me for a minute, then said, "Mickey, that's a great idea!" (Mickey is my family's nickname for me.) She actually called some people at the local university to see if such a thing was feasible, and they thought it was a great idea, too. Now I'm sure there's a very good reason you don't see that kind of washer/dryer combo on the market today, but what was more important to me was the way I felt when I thought of it. It was my first entrepreneurial inspiration: I had come up with an idea that could be turned into a product people might buy. From that point on, I was an entrepreneur.

I love being an entrepreneur. After I left the job digging sand traps, I've never worked for anyone but myself. I always knew I wanted to be on my own and wouldn't need external motivation to keep me going. Most of whatever talent I have would have been wasted if I had worked for somebody, because no one could ever push me as hard as I push myself. If there's a four-minute mile I've got to run it in 3:59. If I'm twentieth in tennis rankings one year, I've got to come in at least nineteenth the next time. I'm continually raising the bar for myself. I constantly challenge myself from within.

Entrepreneurs aren't necessarily born instead of made, but I do think some us know very early that we have the entrepreneurial "gene." I always felt I would be a good businessman. I started the Professional Tennis Service (PTS) at age 18. However, unlike a lot of the tennis teachers I eventually employed, to me PTS was never about hitting tennis balls or teaching people how to play. It was about coming up with a concept, selling the idea and the service to people, seeing how it worked, and making adjustments. In other words, it was about creating and running a successful business. And PTS was successful. Eventually, however, I realized I could go only so far with tennis (did you ever hear of a Fortune 500 company built around tennis lessons?), but I loved PTS because it was the first business I built on my own.

Even though I never went to college, I feel as if I have a Ph.D. in entrepreneurship. My course of study came from my years founding and running the Young Entrepreneurial Society, or YES, which I've spoken about earlier. Quite honestly, the reason I founded YES was to have people like me to hang out with. In general, YES members were too young to fit in with the usual business crowd, and too interested in success to spend our time drinking beer at keg parties or lounging around at the beach on a Tuesday afternoon like most kids our age.

YES meetings were fantastic. First of all, interacting with young men and women who had the same goals and aspirations was great. At each meeting we'd talk about what we were doing to grow our businesses, and I got a lot of new ideas that way. At the same time we were always comparing ourselves to the next guy: "How'm I doing compared to him? And if he's doing better, what is it that he has that I don't? What characteristics do I need to develop?" The same competitive drive I used in tennis now spurred me to strive to outdo the other YES members.

Second, we invited a wide range of successful, older entrepreneurs to speak. Most of them were flattered by the invitation and delighted to share their experiences with us. I even organized a conference and invited young entrepreneurs from throughout the Southeast to spend two days in the Bahamas. (Where better for a bunch of people age 25 and younger to discuss business success?) The knowledge we gained from speakers who had once been like us was invaluable; of course, we all thought we could do it better than they ever did!

While I was involved in YES, at the age of 23 I composed something I called the Entrepreneur's Creed. I had it written on parchment by a professional calligrapher, and I have the document to this day. (See the page opposite.)

Today, entrepreneurs are everywhere. Entrepreneurship has become a way of approaching any job rather than a description of a particular kind of business. You can be an intrapreneur and be given autonomy within a company. You can have a boss and still be allowed to come up with a project, create a business plan for it, get the funding from within your corporation, gather a team, put the plan into action, and be rewarded based on your results. Corporations are beginning to understand that allowing people to tap into that entrepreneurial spirit will help both the individuals and the company succeed at much higher levels. It gives more flexibility and greater speed in the marketplace. More important, it gives people ownership and a greater say in their own destinies.

Entrepreneurs require only two things to start a business: first, a concept, and second, the passion or drive to put the concept into action. If you have a concept and passion, you'll get the funding; you'll find the backers; you'll put in the long hours to get the job done. But it also helps if you have an unlimited supply of optimism, and occasional deafness to the people who will tell you constantly that they expect you to fail. When you're first getting started, you'll hear things like, "You're too

Entrepreneur's Creed
August 1987

Who are they?

What sets them apart from other business luminaries?

Entrepreneurs, they call themselves.

Risk takers who take pride in being different, in that they make things happen for themselves.

They welcome the initial signs of rejection or failure as a challenge to change the mind of fate itself.

They are born with an innate drive to succeed, to do things their way, and to bring great satisfaction to themselves as well as those they influence. But how short-lived this satisfaction is, for they are off to conceptualize and implement a strategy designed to bring yet another success.

Never to be defeated, these Entrepreneurs know that they will prevail over any situation thrown their way. They are so confident in their attributes that they possess an unfair advantage over their competition. They believe in their cause and in the fact that they are the very best.

The true Entrepreneur is a winner. Could this be you?

young." "You don't have the experience." "You don't look like a [whatever it is you want to be]," "You'll never get the money," "You can't, you can't, you can't." I'm sure some of the naysayers are genuinely concerned about your welfare and don't want to see you fall flat on your face. But I'm also afraid there's a tendency in human nature to discourage anyone who goes out and tries something new. It's the part of us that is threatened by change. It's also the part that looks at an entrepreneur and perhaps feels a little guilty that we don't have the courage to go out on our own, too.

Once you've launched your entrepreneurial venture, the critics and predictors of doom will go right along with you. They'll tell you

you're crazy. They'll tell you that what you're planning will never work. They'll warn you that you're going to lose all your money and then where will you be? What's worse, if you have investors the naysayers will say that you're going to betray the trust of all those people, and how will you live with yourself? Once you get past the people who are telling you this "for your own good," then you're going to run into the inevitable business setbacks: the banks that won't lend you money, the customers who won't do business with you because you're too young or inexperienced, the suppliers who require cash payment instead of billing you, and on and on. I'm sure there are probably hundreds of great entrepreneurs who have great ideas, but once they face enough setbacks, or hear gloom and doom from enough people, they give up.

And even when you've achieved some success with your entrepreneurial enterprise, the naysayers will still call you crazy; they'll tell you you're a one-time wonder and you'll never be able to do it again. (It was only about three years ago that the local real estate community and the media stopped calling me crazy and started calling me expert and visionary. That's because now they know my ideas about the ultra-high-end real estate market have been proven over and over again.) A lot of envy and jealousy arises when you start to produce success and unfortunately, most of it comes from people who were your peers.

If you're going to be faced with these kinds of obstacles during your entrepreneurial career, what's the solution? As I said earlier, selective deafness and unflagging optimism. You can't let the naysayers get to you. Sometimes you will be the only cheerleader amidst a sea of pessimistic predictors. Ignore them—it's the only way you'll be able to keep going. Certainly, be aware of the pitfalls of entrepreneurship, for there are many. But don't let the dire predictions of others scare you away from doing everything you can to make your business succeed. You must believe that you have what it takes to create something from nothing, to take a vision and make it real. You must draw upon traits like courage, confidence, intelligence, and passion to pull you through. You must believe in yourself so much that nothing and no one will deter you from giving your best to your business and to the world. When you do that, whether you succeed at a greater level than anyone else in your field or end up walking away with your head held high, proud of your efforts if not your final results, then you will have honored the entrepreneurial passion in your heart.

Actions

1. Read the Entrepreneur's Creed again. Does it describe you? If not, would you like it to? With a little work and a lot of passion, you can develop each of the traits it describes.
2. If you are currently an entrepreneur or thinking of becoming one, how will you deal with the naysayers you will encounter?

Deal Points

Let's talk about some of the internal pitfalls of entrepreneurship that you should do your best to avoid. *Micromanaging* is a fault of almost all entrepreneurs. We want to be in control of our businesses; usually it's one of the main reasons we go out on our own. But I believe the ultimate compliment entrepreneurs can pay themselves is to empower their employees to be autonomous. I love the fact that I don't have to be at a job site all the time anymore. I still enjoy putting on my work boots and visiting the guys, checking the progress, putting my fingerprints on every square inch of the property; but I know that they're going to do the same great job whether I'm there or not. I can rely on my president of construction to keep track of things for me, and my office staff to keep things running on the administrative side. And I'm freed up to do what I do best: create the vision, provide opportunities, find properties, come up with new marketing strategies, make sure we're following the best path as a company. I can only do that when I trust my team to have the same passion and spirit as I do.

The second pitfall I have observed in myself and seen in other entrepreneurs is *letting drive become obsession*. Entrepreneurs must be driven; otherwise their success is unlikely. But there's a fine line between being driven to accomplish a goal and becoming obsessed with it. It's easy to become intoxicated with the belief that you can do anything, that any risk is worth it, that every opportunity no matter how absurd must be pursued to the end. You see that a lot in business: developers who want to build the tallest building in the world, computer engineers who burn out trying to get one more byte on the latest chip, and so on. I understand the adrenaline rush that comes from the chance to be the best and to go beyond what you've done before. I know how easy it is to get hooked on that feeling. But sometimes making it happen comes at too high a price. And when we can see only the goal and not what we must pay to achieve it, then we've entered the dangerous territory of obsession.

I'm sure there are some who think I have crossed the line from drive into obsession with the oceanfront mansions I have created. I have been pushing the envelope regarding price, style, and quality for ultra-high-end real estate for the past ten years at least. But every purchase I made, every design I approved, every piece of building material I used, and every new price point I set was based on solid research, an appreciation of the fundamentals of good business, and extensive knowledge of the marketplace I wished to reach. I do my best to balance my emotional need for challenge and willingness to embrace risk with the intellectual rigor to make sure the facts and figures back up any chance I take. To prevent drive from stepping over the line into obsession, you must *always* apply the leavening influence of common sense. Otherwise, it isn't business; it's simply gambling on a different kind of slot machine.

When I sold the $30 million Manalapan property, a lot of people came to me and asked, "What's next, Frank? Are you going for $40 million? $50 million? A 100,000-square-foot English castle stretching from the ocean to the Intracoastal Waterway?" But I'm not obsessed with the drive to build bigger and bigger homes, mainly because that's not the direction I see the ultra-high-end market taking. Based on my sense of the times, with economic uncertainty and wealthy clients being less willing to buy ostentatiously large houses, the next property I build from scratch will be a much smaller house (around 10,000 square feet) on a much larger lot in Ocean Ridge, Florida. There will be more landscaping, more use of exterior living spaces as an extension of the interior, more features like gazebos, grottoes, waterfalls, and ponds. The house itself, while smaller in size (with only six bedrooms, and scaling back on some of the grander rooms), will be extremely high quality, better than anything I've done before. (Okay, I have to confess I am pushing the envelope in one way: The house will come in at $9.4 million preconstruction, which will be a record for a house of that size. I think the higher quality of the house, combined with unbelievable privacy found in its beautiful grounds set directly on the Atlantic Ocean, will justify an increase in the asking price above the average per-square-foot price. I also believe that in the ultra-high-end market, the price difference between a well-built $8 million house and a *very* well built $9.4 million house will be insignificant to the buyer.)

The third pitfall of the entrepreneur is *letting common sense overwhelm your drive*. This is actually a much bigger problem than obsession for many business owners. There are a lot of experts in research and business fundamentals, but when it comes to the moment of saying, "I'm gonna do it!" they chicken out. Unless there's little or no downside, they don't want to risk it no matter how great the upside might be. I've devoted an entire section of this book (Part Four) to learning how to manage and embrace risk, so I'm not going to talk about it here. Suffice it to say, I'm more likely to risk something and be confident that I can *make* it work than let an opportunity pass me by. I'm willing to walk away from a deal if we can't come to an agreement that satisfies my profit and upside requirements, but I'll go for greater risk if I can increase my profit and upside substantially by doing so.

To succeed, you need entrepreneurial drive, common sense, a willingness to risk, and good, solid research to back up your decisions. When you have those elements in place, you truly will have reached a golden mean—and I do mean golden!

Learn from Highly Respected, Successful People What Makes Them Tick

Some of the most important learning we can get comes from other people. Experience is the best teacher, but other people's experiences are pretty darn good, too—and often a lot less painful! I want to know what makes successful people tick; not only their deeds, but who they are inside and how they lead their lives. What characteristics, traits, or qualities do they demonstrate? I can learn some of that through books, but frankly I'd rather learn it by talking with successful people directly, watching them, and being sensitive to what they're doing to get and stay ahead.

My formal education stopped after high school, so I've always tried to learn as much as I could from other people. When I was teaching tennis at the clubs and condo complexes, the lessons were usually scheduled to last an hour. But sometimes with the students who I knew were successful in business, I'd push them really hard for 50 minutes so they'd have to sit down for the last few minutes of our time together. Then I'd get them a towel and a drink of water, and pick their brains about what they had accomplished in their lives.

Tennis led me to the person who first mentioned distressed real estate. An older gentleman by the name of Victor took lessons from me, and I got to know both him and his son, Eric. Victor had done very well with foreclosures and distressed real estate, and Eric also knew quite a lot about it. That market seemed perfect for my next business venture, which I was already starting to plan. It didn't require a lot of capital to get started; I could do much of the work myself; it was possible to make good profits pretty quickly; and I believed I could learn enough about foreclosures within six months to make it work. So in 1985 I started to research and study the distressed real estate market while I continued with my tennis business. I bought my first property six months later.

As I mentioned in Philosophy #12, during my time as director of the Young Entrepreneurial Society I was always one of the most riveted members of the audience when other successful entrepreneurs would come in and speak. Those years at YES taught me that if you find someone you want to learn from, ask to spend time with that person. I often think we're afraid to go to someone we respect, like a boss or a CEO or a local celebrity, and ask for a little of their time. I love it when the kids who are part of the Greater Delray Beach Youth Council ask me, "Would you tell me how you got into real estate?" I believe I have an obligation to share what I know, and there's nothing more flattering than others believing you can teach them something valuable.

I continue to seek out successful people to learn from them. I'm honored when I can spend time in the company of people like Rich De Vos, cofounder of Amway; being around him is a humbling and uplifting experience. Occasionally I've also been able to sit down with some of the people I've sold properties to, and I love hearing how they achieved their success. But truthfully, I find successful people everywhere I go. A kid can have traits I want to copy. A mom can have a *lot* of traits I want to adopt (my mom sure does). A janitor can have traits that are admirable. Many of the homeless people I encounter have traits or experiences I can benefit from. While I'm not a great reader, when I do pick up a book it's very likely to be something I feel I can learn from. Early on I read Donald Trump's *The Art of the Deal*, and I appreciated the way he became one of the most widely recognized developers of the twentieth century.

When you look for people you wish to learn from, cast your net wide. There may be someone in a profession totally unrelated to yours who might have the answer to one of your pressing problems; for example, the kid down the block may know something about putting together a great team from his Little League experience. Learn from your peers, absolutely, because they may have found different answers to challenges similar to yours. But to get more creative approaches, go outside your own circle.

When I approach other entrepreneurs, I always treat those who are older with enormous respect and admiration. I want to know their secrets of longevity in our youth-oriented culture. When I approach entrepreneurs who are younger than me (and there are more and more of them all the time!) I look for ways in which they may be more creative and in tune with a younger marketplace than I am. (I also use these younger entrepreneurs to challenge myself to keep a couple of steps ahead of them. For a very long time I was always the most successful person in my peer group; now men and women younger than me are coming up fast. But that's fine with me—I love a challenge.) With my peers, I want to learn as much as I can about how their paths to success have differed from my own.

The one standard I hold myself to is always to keep learning. Sometimes it's hard, not because I don't want to learn but because people don't believe that I'm truly interested. "You're already successful," they say. "You don't need my help; you're doing great." But the only way we keep at the top of our game is always to look to be better. Learning from others is the cheapest education you can get—but ultimately I guarantee it will provide you with the greatest value.

Actions

1. Who are your role models? Who do you know that you can approach and ask about their success? Don't be intimidated if you wish to approach someone like a boss or a CEO or a public figure. There's no harm in asking, and you may find they're delighted to share their experiences with you. You're welcome to contact me on my web site, www.frankmckinney.com. I promise I'll get back to you!
2. Look around and see how many people you can gather experience from. I'll bet almost everyone you know has something to teach you, but it's up to you to approach them. Then enjoy the benefits of this continuing education.

Deal Points

My marketplace is composed of wealthy, successful people, and to learn as much as I can about my marketplace I've done some fairly unusual things. I've hidden in a closet while Bruce Willis and Demi Moore were touring one of my houses. They had requested no one be at the property, but I couldn't pass up the opportunity to hear what they thought about the house. (My wife, Nilsa, also posed as a cleaning lady that day. As I've said before, she's a trouper.) At other showings I've hidden under the bed, or been a limo driver, a construction supervisor, the broker's assistant—anything but the owner. No one's going to talk with any frankness if the owner is listening, but they'll say exactly what they think of a house within earshot of the "pool guy." I regard this as a fairly harmless but invaluable kind of deception when it comes to learning as much as I can about my marketplace.

Because I have studied successful people, spent time with them, and walked through countless showings of my properties watching their every reaction, I now feel I have a very good sense of what affluent people want in a home. I also know within the first two rooms of a showing whether the clients have an interest or are just being polite. How? Body language, eye contact, whispers between the clients; all the little covert signals that even the most poker-faced human beings will demonstrate. There is one great advantage to dealing with successful people: They are usually high-powered, quick decision makers. Don't get me wrong—they'll look at a lot of properties; but when they see what they like, they take action. That's what I'm looking for—and I do my best to be right there to help them!

Once You Are Able to Love Yourself, Don't Hesitate to Let Others Know

I really enjoy being around someone who isn't afraid to express his or her self-love. I don't mean being overly egotistical or talking about yourself all the time; rather, it's being proud of what you've accomplished or what you represent. Rich De Vos is a good example of someone who's proud of the way he's lived his life and who wants to share his experiences with others. I've seen the same attitude in celebrities like Michael Jordan and Oprah Winfrey. I've also seen it in Ellie, the lady who takes care of Nilsa and me and our daughter. Ellie raised three kids and did a fantastic job with them. She's a privilege to be around, because she knows she's really good at what she does. And she's perfectly willing to let you know it, too!

This Philosophy is about developing the essential component of self-esteem. A lot of people think loving yourself is nothing but ego on the rampage, but that's not it at all. I don't think ego is a bad thing when it's kept under control by something we'll talk about in the next Philosophy—humility. Ego to me means you've built your confidence to the point where you're willing to say, "Yes, I am good at this. Yes, I have value as a person. Yes, I deserve the space I occupy on this earth."

Unless they've been abused, young kids rarely have a problem with self-esteem and self-love. They celebrate every single thing they do even halfway well. They are continually asking parents, friends, and teachers to "Look at me! Look at me!" They believe they are the center of the universe, or should be. But unfortunately they learn otherwise very quickly. They do something wrong and get punished or scolded. They're told, "Go away and don't bother me now." They try something new and fail, and perhaps get teased or ridiculed by their peers or (God forbid) by adults. Their healthy self-esteem and self-love disappear, and in their place are fear, self-doubt, and sometimes even self-hatred.

I believe enormously in the power of self-esteem. When I work with teenagers at the Greater Delray Beach Youth Council, I do everything I can to encourage the kids to believe in themselves. I build their self-esteem through the roof because I know all too well that they're not getting much of that kind of encouragement elsewhere.

Entrepreneurs must have ego. It's the only way we would attempt the things we do—going off on our own, going against traditional business wisdom, taking chances that no one else would because we believe *we* can make it work. Self-esteem, self-love, and self-belief are the props that help us get through the rough times (and usually there are plenty). Such traits allow us to take rejection and come back stronger than ever. If I hadn't possessed drive and a belief in my abilities, I never would have had the gall to go up to the manager of the country club where I was digging sand traps and ask him to sponsor me to become a certified tennis instructor. Without good self-esteem, I never would have started my own business at 18, or been able to sell tennis lessons to the affluent people I wanted to become my clients. Without ego, I never would have thought, *Gee, if I can run a successful tennis business, I'll bet I can succeed in another field. What about real estate?* And I certainly never would have made the move from distressed properties to oceanfront estates worth tens of millions of dollars.

Self-love and self-esteem allow you to learn from your mistakes and failures instead of wallowing in them, and then move on. They allow you to be proud of your efforts even when you're just starting out. An essential part of self-esteem is recognizing that even if you haven't made it yet, you can be proud of what you're striving for. You can be proud of the fact that you're in there every day swinging, making it happen, never giving up. You love what you do and who you're becoming in the process, and you're not afraid to let others know it.

It's not easy for most of us to love ourselves. Self-doubt can sneak in at the slightest provocation. We all know those "midnight devils" who ask us if we've taken the best path. Could we have avoided that break in a friendship? Are we taking on that new job because we're excited about the work, or are we settling for security and a steady paycheck? Are we really cut out to be an entrepreneur? A mom? A boss? Did we make the right choice to be a stay-at-home parent and raise the kids instead of focusing on a career? All of these questions can undermine self-esteem very quickly.

On top of that, we're very critical of ourselves and our efforts. It's so sad to hear people tearing themselves down with such frequency. It wrecks their confidence; it makes them unwilling to take risks of any kind. And yet tearing ourselves down is far more usual in our culture than acknowledging our success. It's not considered nice to brag or to take credit for our own honest efforts, so instead we're always looking for ways to denigrate ourselves. "Great round of golf, John." "Are you kidding? I lofted that shot on 17 straight into the rough. Took me four shots just to make the green." "You look so pretty today, Sarah." "Thanks, but I feel like a fat pig—I got on the scale this morning and I'd gained three pounds over the weekend." "Outstanding presentation, Mike." "Well, the client didn't seem that impressed, and I don't think I was clear explaining the numbers." Recognize yourself in any of these? Or do you have your own style of self-loathing? And what the heck do we gain by tearing ourselves down?

Recently I was asked to give a talk to the Business Roundtable, a group composed of two hundred or so of the most successful business-people in the Palm Beach area. I was really nervous; I kept thinking I'd walk in to give this speech and the only people who would have bothered to come would be Nilsa and a couple of my friends. Well, the room was packed, and afterward many of the attendees came up to congratulate me. From their expressions, it was obvious they genuinely liked the speech and thought I had something important to say. I was flabbergasted. I said to Nilsa while we were driving home that night, "I've got to stop doubting myself. All it does is drive me crazy."

It's okay to love yourself. It's okay to have self-esteem. It's okay to believe that you are special, unique, with great talents and unlimited possibilities in front of you. With those kinds of beliefs, and with the drive and commitment to make the most of your opportunities, don't you think you'll stand a much better chance of making it big?

Actions

1. How have you built your self-esteem and self-love? Can you accept a compliment graciously without demur? Do you acknowledge your own efforts even if you haven't quite "arrived" yet? Make a list of all the things you do, have done, or might do that would make you feel great about yourself.
2. Look at the choices in your life and see if they make you feel good about yourself. If you have conflicts, commit to making

the best of your choices in the present moment. Then perhaps you can begin to create something that will enhance your self-love and self-esteem.

3. To build your self-esteem to the point where you'll want to take on challenges, you've got to recognize your successes whenever they occur. Use your introspection time (see Philosophy #3) to learn your lessons, but make sure you compliment yourself for what you've done well, too.

Deal Points

To make it big in most professions you have to be able to generate publicity and deal with media, and self-esteem and self-love can come in useful for both. Especially if you're an entrepreneur, no one's going to generate publicity for your business but you. No one's going to write about you or put you on TV or radio unless you tell them. You've got to be willing to promote yourself and say nice things about your own efforts. You have to be a little kid again, waving your arms and yelling, "Look what I've done!"

I learned this lesson as a neophyte entrepreneur with my tennis business. Remember, the only way I generated income was by recruiting clients myself. How did I do it? Some referrals, certainly, but mostly through publicity. I held free tennis clinics. I played in tournaments. I put flyers in everyone's mailboxes and posted them on the community board. I did everything I could to get my name out there and persuade potential clients I would be the greatest tennis teacher they'd ever had. I got turned down constantly in the beginning, but I had enough self-esteem and self-belief just to keep on going.

When I formed the Young Entrepreneurial Society (YES) in 1985, I used the media to build membership. Before our meetings I'd put a notice in the public service announcement (PSA) section of the newspaper to reach members who otherwise might never have heard of us. I also made sure YES had a monthly newsletter, which was sent to all the members and to the newspaper where we placed our PSAs. After a while, reporters started to notice our group. Here were all these people in their late teens and early twenties, and instead of getting into trouble or hanging out on the beach, they were starting their own businesses! As president of the group, I got the calls from the media, and I found myself giving interviews about YES and its activities. I got really good at talking us up, putting the best possible light on things, making big promises, and then making them come true.

When I got into the distressed real estate market, I was too darn busy to try to garner publicity. (Although there was one time I got into the newspaper inadvertently. At the same auction where I bought my first foreclosure properties, agents for Donald Trump purchased two Palm Beach condominium buildings that are now known as the Trump Towers. Whenever you buy property at auction, you have to put down a $1,000 cash deposit immediately. As I stood there, nervously counting out my $100 bills, the newspaper photographers took a picture of my hands—which were shaking. They then used the photo of my hands with the caption, "Trump buys condo towers in Palm Beach." I took it for a good omen.)

The first real estate project I got any significant publicity on was Banker's Row in 1989. We were renovating five houses in a neighborhood that had been marginal at best, and the press wanted to know why this guy was putting all this money into a bad neighborhood. I took the reporters on tours of our properties and told them what we were hoping—that nice houses would attract solid, middle-class buyers who would upgrade the neighborhood. I gave them some background on what I had done before with other foreclosed properties, and mentioned casually that I liked one of the houses on Banker's Row so much that I was moving in myself. I was very happy to see the article that came out of that interview; more important, I was delighted at the increase in the number of people interested in the houses even before they were finished. Since then, I have consistently used media and promotion for every single project I have undertaken.

People are often amazed when I tell them I have no public relations (PR) firm. I have used one for only two months out of my 15-year career. Right from the beginning, I instinctively understood the need to be appealing to the media, and I learned how to create an interest in what I did so that reporters would want to cover it. I created a complete strategy for getting press for myself and my projects. I discovered that my somewhat outrageous personal style made for a great story lead, so I would emphasize it when I did interviews. After all, reporters are entrepreneurs in a way, too. They're fighting for market share (e.g., column inches or airtime) in their newspapers or on their programs. My job is to give them great material so they're happy, they can make their editors happy, and I can put my own message across at the same time.

Self-promotion is a real art. You have to tread a fine line between tooting your own horn and seeming like a raging egomaniac. (If I've crossed that line at any point in this book, I sincerely apologize.) You've got to get your name out there and still not overstay your welcome or become too exposed. At the same time, if your promotion of yourself and your efforts is too subdued, it might not accomplish what you want—public visibility. And you certainly won't get a shot at the big story, the one piece of coverage that can make a major difference in your business.

For me, that was *Oprah*. I had wanted to increase my national visibility, so I sent media kits (which I prepared myself) to 15 or so television shows like *Good Morning America*, *Today*, *The View*, and so on. I didn't hear anything from anyone, so I figured my homemade media kits were a washout. But six months later Oprah's producers contacted me because they were doing a segment on lifestyles of the ultrawealthy, and they saw in their files the photo of La Marceaux, the $12 million house I was building. Now, when I get someone on the phone I am an expert at telling my story in a compelling way in 60 seconds or less. I managed to persuade Oprah's producers to come down and do a five-minute clip on La Marceaux and on me as the "celebrity developer." What really closed the deal for them was not just the great visuals I provided, but the homeless angle. I was ecstatic at being able to promote both my properties and also my homeless causes on such a quality show. And that's the real goal of any PR—not just to say, "I'm great," but to tell the world, "Here's what I'm doing."

In today's world, with the Internet and cable and satellite TV, the media are content-starved. It's a great opportunity for you to toot your own horn if you do it right. I believe if you have enough self-esteem and self-love to be willing to stand out from the crowd and let others know about the great things you're doing, then your media efforts will only help build your name and your business brand in the marketplace.

Set Yourself Apart and Celebrate Your Individuality, Yet Include Humility

A couple of years ago a South Florida magazine did a cover story on me. I kept the piece, first of all, because I had never seen such a headline: "Golden Boy—Frank McKinney sells record-breaking, million-dollar mansions in Palm Beach County, has heavy-metal hair and helps the homeless. And his mom likes him, too." But it also represented for me the perfect balance between celebrating individuality and expressing humility. It included a lot about my troubled teenage years, and how I can hobnob with rich clients but I'm actually a lot more comfortable feeding the homeless and hanging around my job sites. I made fun of my own reputation and image while expressing gratitude, surprise, and humility about my success.

I think everyone should celebrate his or her individuality. As you might have noticed, I always thought that I was a bit different from the norm. When I was a teenager, in addition to my wild behavior, I used to dress differently than most of my peers. (My mother still comments on a pair of white leather pants I wore constantly when I was 16.) Back then I was just expressing who I was on the outside and who I thought I might become on the inside. Today I still project a unique image, but I try to make it more representative of the brand I wish to create. In the very competitive industry of high-end real estate, anything that sets you and your product apart from the crowd is to your advantage. So that's what I do. I create a very individualistic image that people don't forget very easily. I can drop it when I choose—when I vacation in Colorado I wear jeans and cowboy boots, and hang out with the local ranchers and farmers. But I certainly use my individuality to help strengthen my brand in the marketplace.

We are all unique expressions of humanity, and we deserve to let our talents shine. Yet most of us are so afraid of being labeled egotists that we end up hiding our individuality and doing everything we can to conform. If you do too much conforming, you can vanish into the crowd—which is not what you want if you're trying to establish a brand! You've got to walk that fine line between having confidence in your individuality and having an overbearing ego. I believe you can let yourself shine and acknowledge your own greatness, as long as it's balanced with a healthy dose of humility.

You can take an enormous amount of pride at what you've accomplished or in your own abilities and still be humble. How? First, through gratitude. A couple of years ago we were working on the $30 million property, and as I was walking down the winding staircase and looking out the window, watching the dust flying and people moving around and everything happening, I got goose bumps. All I could think was, *I can't believe I'm doing this.*

Not too long after that, I went over to visit Buster, the guy who rents the Caring House from me. I collected the $1 rent from him after church one morning, and I sat with him for about three-quarters of an hour just talking. Then I drove through the northwest and southwest sections of Delray Beach (the kind of neighborhoods where I used to buy foreclosures) looking for the next potential Caring House property. When I came home, I walked in my front door and saw my wife and my three-year-old daughter, who looked so perfect with her clean little dress, lace socks, and white Mary Janes shoes. I love them so much, and I am so grateful to have them in my life. Then I remembered seeing some of the kids in the neighborhoods I had just driven through, and I was humbled by the thought of all the men and women who had made it big after coming from a lot tougher situations than I did. I am so grateful for the opportunities I've been given. I hope I never get to the point where I take my success for granted.

I am constantly grateful to God. I know I would never have been able to accomplish anything in my life without His help, and I still ask for His support and guidance every day. I'm also grateful to all the people who have been part of my success. From the country club manager who agreed to send me to tennis school, to all the clients who shared their business experience with me, to the girlfriend who told me to get out of acting and into real estate, to the people who bought one of the houses I renovated, to every guy on every single crew who worked for me, to the homeless people I fed, to my beloved wife Nilsa and daughter Laura Katherine, to my mom who never gave up on me even when I was the worst possible juvenile delinquent—the list is endless. I know without a doubt that I would not be where I am today without the help of countless individuals at every stage of my life. Whenever someone praises my success, I see all those faces, and you'd better believe I'm humbled and grateful.

The second way to keep humble is to own up to your own fallibility, including your ego. I'm very aware of both my assets and my liabilities. In my weekly introspection (see Philosophy #3), I go over all of my actions and see where I failed to live up to the principles I wish to embody. I write down all my failures: every time I lost my temper or was thoughtless or let my own ego get in the way of considering others' needs, and so on. Introspection helps me keep my successes in perspective, and continually reminds me of the difference between who I am and who I wish to be.

Humility and acknowledging your ego works especially well with the media, by the way. Reporters are always looking for the tarnish on the shiny image. Perhaps to seem unbiased (or maybe because negativity sells papers), they'll keep digging and doubting and trying to find the chink in the armor. "Frank, you're called the rock 'n' roll developer, but aren't you simply a shameless self-promoter riding a trend of excessive consumption by arrogant people who have more money than they could possibly spend in a hundred years?" That kind of question is tough to swallow, but I do. I'll say, "You know, Mr. Reporter, you're right—I am a shameless self-promoter. And very few people in this world can afford my oceanfront properties. But I'm just doing the same thing I've done all my life: trying to give buyers the absolute best property for their money. I did it with smaller distressed properties for six years, and I've been doing it on the oceanfront for 10. And yes, I tell people about what I do, because I've discovered I can use publicity and the name I create to get attention for the causes I believe in, like building housing for the homeless. I am absolutely shameless when it comes to that. And if my name helps get one more dollar in contributions or one more person to volunteer, then I'm happy."

The third thing that keeps me humble is a concerted effort not to take myself too seriously. I mean really—how could anyone take *my* image seriously? I posed in a loincloth, for heaven's sake. Is this the image of a businessman? While I use my outrageous style to set me apart from my competition, I also want people to know that I'm in on the joke. When I poke fun at myself, people seem to relax, see beyond the long hair and colorful clothing, and realize that my style is a conscious choice and not an ego run amok.

Not taking myself too seriously and remembering to laugh at things also keeps me levelheaded. A lot of public figures run into trouble when they start believing their own image. They think it's who they are, rather than something they've created. If you take any image too seriously, it can consume you and turn you into something you don't want. Or worse: It could be the only thing that you are, and that's pretty empty.

The antidote for "image creep" is never to take yourself, your endeavors, or your life too seriously. Find something absurd in this person you're supposed to be. Enjoy poking fun at yourself. In 2000 I went in front of the Community Redevelopment Agency (CRA) to discuss the next Caring House project I want to do, an 11-room motel that I'll convert to emergency transitional housing units. I began my presentation by saying, "I need to build another place for the homeless because my $30 million house hasn't sold yet and I'm going to run out of money pretty soon. I'll need a place to live, and this proposed Caring House will be a lot nicer than my alternative, which is a Dumpster." (I'll talk a lot more about laughing at yourself in Philosophy #47.)

To create a brand and a presence in the marketplace, you can't be afraid to express your individuality and blow your own horn as often as possible. Create an image, yes—just don't think it's the only thing you are. And never take your image seriously. Remember, whether you're using a toilet with a solid-gold handle in a $30 million house or an outhouse in the backyard of a falling-down shack, the end product is the same for us all.

Actions

1. What elements of your personality have you emphasized, or could you emphasize, to create that individuality which will contribute to your brand? For me, it's being a contrarian—long hair, fashion, and a rock star attitude that seems to say, "Who cares what the world thinks?" What is it for you? And how can you emphasize that in your business?
2. Remember to keep in touch with humility. What are you grateful for? Who has helped you along the way? What are your foibles and failures? What part of your image can you laugh about and perhaps poke fun at?

Deal Points

The one thing you must avoid at all costs is allowing your ego and your image to make you arrogant. In my experience, arrogance leads to carelessness, and carelessness leads to mistakes. It's like a basketball player thinking he can miss a workout because he was so great in the game the night before, or a businessperson reading articles about him- or herself and thinking they've arrived. As soon as you start believing your PR and stop working at what you do, you slide backward. You've got to put in the time and effort to keep succeeding. You can't let yourself be seduced by past successes, because the moment you do, the universe will throw you a curve.

I had a very strong taste of this lesson when I had been buying and selling foreclosures for about a year. I had had enough successes that I started getting cocky. I saw a property listed by the foreclosure service, and instead of following my usual procedure of going to see the house, I simply put a bid in on it based on the paper. However, I was smart enough to drive by the property right after I put the initial deposit down, when I was on the way to the bank to get the cashier's check for the balance. Only one problem: There *was* no house on that lot. The only way I managed to continue my streak of never losing money on a real estate transaction was through sheer luck. I found someone who wanted the lot and was willing to buy my $1,000 option on the property for $1,200. That was a humbling lesson. I learned never to take anything for granted, and to avoid arrogance like the plague.

I believe the best approach to success is to celebrate your efforts and individuality while maintaining a healthy sense of how easy it is to make a mistake that will cost you a great deal. Respect what you've done, and respect what it will take for you to succeed at an even higher level. Don't take anything for granted. The difference between you and the homeless guy who's Dumpster-diving in the alley is a lot smaller than you might think. Be grateful for your successes and celebrate them, but never forget how fortunate you are.

Part Three

Take the "Lunch Pail" Approach
While Answering Your Highest Calling

Once you have a vision you're passionate about, and you've found a niche and a marketplace in which you want to develop a brand for yourself, the next part is often the hardest—getting out there and doing the work, grinding it out day after day, good times and bad, no matter what. I call it the "lunch pail" approach because it's what I see on our construction sites every day. Guys arrive at 6:30 A.M. wearing jeans and work boots, carrying lunch pails, ready to put in a full eight hours or more of backbreaking physical labor. It's the kind of work ethic that shows up in successful businesses everywhere, and it's the kind of approach you must develop if you're ever going to make it big.

But you could just as easily call this section the "Mount Rushmore" approach. Sculptor Gutzon Borglum began with nothing more than a rocky granite outcropping in the Black Hills of South Dakota in 1927. With chisel and hammer, he and a small group of craftsmen began to carve what has been called the eighth wonder of the world. But you can imagine that after the first month there was no visible progress. Heck, after six months you could barely make out even one hair in the eyebrow of George Washington, the first head to be carved! But after 14 years of excruciatingly difficult work, Borglum and his team left a legacy that the world still regards with awe.

I learned about the lunch pail approach as soon as I arrived in Florida. My first job was digging sand traps by hand on a golf course, and most of the guys I worked with were Haitian. They worked harder

109

than anyone I had ever met, and I was proud when I heard one of the managers of the golf course call me "the white Haitian" because I worked just as hard as they did. In every single thing I've done, from teaching tennis, to running the tennis business, to buying and selling foreclosures, to building and marketing multimillion-dollar estates, I have applied that same work ethic. But my approach is no different than that of anyone—busboy or office manager, salesclerk or police officer, homemaker or CEO—who gets up early each day, packs a lunch, then does his or her best on the job. I believe the lunch pail approach is the foundation of any lasting success. Want to know the secret of business longevity? This is it.

The problem is that most people choose not to apply this simple approach. You've no doubt read and heard about endless "instant success" schemes. We live in a society that's obsessed with the attitude of "I want mine and I want it now." But as we've seen all too painfully in the wreck of the dot-com companies and the decline of the stock market, "easy come, easy go" is accurate. I know of no so-called overnight success that was not preceded by years (in my case, 20 years) of unremitting hard work.

And things don't change when you arrive, either! A lot of people seem to think that businesspeople like myself live glamorous and exciting lives; our days must be spent jetting from meeting to meeting in Armani or Ornafarho suits, giving interviews, and attending black-tie functions at night. Well, every morning I still pack my lunch in a plastic bag from Publix supermarket and take it with me to the project site. My days are still long and hard, with many failures and trials. But there is no quitting, stopping, or even slowing down; there's just getting it done no matter what.

I believe success is composed of three elements. First, *vision*. To make it big, your work must be in service to your highest calling (as we discussed in Philosophy #1). Second, *unremitting effort* to make that vision come true. If you have one without the other—vision or hard work—then you are unlikely to achieve your dreams on the level you deserve. The third element is *striving to do a little better or challenge yourself a little more each day*. This is what makes achieving your vision possible and the lunch pail approach enjoyable even on the worst days. Imagine, for a moment, you're a factory worker on an assembly line. You believe your highest calling is to become a plant manager, but you know you'll have to put in a lot more time before you can be considered for the job. Every day you pack your lunch and go to work, like all the other people on the line. But you also look around for ways to do a better job. You develop strategies for streamlining processes. You train your coworkers in some simple techniques for avoiding accidents. You bring ideas to your boss about cost reduction and team building. Who do you think enjoys the work more: you or the person who just puts in eight hours and leaves? Who's more likely to be promoted? And how can you apply this approach to your own highest calling?

My highest calling was entrepreneurship and the creation of a business and marketplace niche in ultra-high-end speculative real estate. But the journey to that business took many years and many small steps. Each step along the way I had to focus on both the task at hand and the greater goal of my highest calling. I had to make sure every day I was getting better and better at what I did, learning lessons and applying them consistently.

In this section you're going to learn nine simple Philosophies that will help you attain and maintain the lunch pail approach while you answer your highest calling. We'll talk about doing the best job you can, paying attention to the details that make the difference between a nice enough house and one that creates the ultimate experience for the buyer. You'll learn the value of perseverance, and how pursuing spiritual fulfillment can help you achieve your highest calling. You'll also understand how proactivity and creativity can make a humdrum virtue like persistence enjoyable while increasing the impact of your efforts. We'll talk about the great vice of pride, and how it can get in the way of your quest for daily improvement.

You'll also master some of the most important secrets for developing customer relationships and negotiating anything successfully, by sitting on the other side of the desk first, thinking win-win, and being fair. You'll learn how easy it can be to close the sale using my system for capitalizing on what I call the "impulse window"—the specific and precious time when the client is ready to buy. I'll talk about something that most success books don't address but which I believe can negate the value of everything in this book: what happens when you indulge in unhealthy vices and temptations. Finally, I'll share with you two traits I believe all truly successful people possess: discipline and organization.

I hope I don't sound like your crotchety grandfather, yammering on and on about the value of discipline and hard work, because I certainly believe in having fun and being outrageous (as you'll see in Part Six). But to make it big, you need both to take the lunch pail approach *and* have a blast. You have to keep that vision of your highest calling in front of you *and* focus on what needs doing in the moment. I believe you can work hard, play hard, and create a great life for yourself in the process. It's not easy; it's not quick—but the results are more long-lasting and the rewards even sweeter, because you know you've earned every moment of your success.

Do Your Job, Do It Well, and Do It Every Day

When you graduate from high school with a 1.8 grade point average and no interest in any more formal education, like I did, the only way you're going to make it in the world is through hard work. You've got to apply yourself every single day, because if you don't you might not eat, let alone succeed. So when I came to Florida, I set out to apply myself daily, with no idea what my career path would be. I just believed that if I worked hard at whatever I was doing and did any job to the best of my ability, I would succeed.

This philosophy has supported me in every single profession I attempted. When I was digging sand traps by hand, I was the best darn digger possible. When I taught tennis, I gave it my all. When I turned the tennis lessons into a business, I worked hard to make that business grow. And when I made the move into real estate, you'd better believe I did everything I could to turn a profit on each and every property I bought and sold.

That meant an awful lot of work. Not just the backbreaking kind you do when you're renovating a property (I can't drive a nail straight, so I'd do manual labor and hire subcontractors to do the skilled work). But before I ever got into the foreclosure markets, I worked hard to learn about real estate. I spent six months going to dozens of foreclosure auctions, sheriff's sales, Internal Revenue Service (IRS) sales, and tax auctions. I researched hundreds of properties so I could find one or two that I could make a profit on. And if I wasn't actually doing the rewiring or reframing or repairs on a property, you'd better believe I was there every single day anyway to make sure things were going right. I'm still at my job sites every single day. It wasn't always fun; in fact, a lot of it was downright tedious. But I knew in order to do the job well, I had to do the research, the work, and the supervision.

Back in those days, I honestly did not think that 12 years later I would be building $30 million dollar spec estates—I simply wanted to buy, renovate, or build little $60,000 to $70,000 homes. I was happy having one or two small homes worth less than $50,000 to pour my life savings into, not to mention my heart and soul. I busted my butt trying to ensure a small profit on those early projects. I drove a 1947 Hudson pickup truck, and had one pair of boots and two pairs of old jeans to wear to work. But I was determined to wake up each day, go off to the job I had created for myself, and do the right thing to the very best of my ability, day in and day out.

Once you've made it to a certain level, however, don't think you can stop doing your job, doing it well, and doing it every day. There is no substitute for your own effort, whether it's pounding nails, canvassing neighborhoods to find the best property, or going over contracts with buyers. In every job I've held, every project I've built, I put in the time (and money) to do things right. And I still work my projects in exactly the same way; you will find my fingerprints on every inch of a 30,000-square-foot project. When La Marceaux, the $12 million property, was on the market, each Monday I walked through every bit of that house. On the second floor was a little closet that held three large, round hot water heaters, and a trickle of dust would accumulate on top of them each week. While you could put on white gloves and check every other inch of the house and find absolutely no dust, I left the dust on top of one hot water heater. Every Monday I put a finger mark there to indicate I'd made my round for the week. When La Marceaux sold, I went to the closet and checked: There were 32 little fingerprints in the dust, going all the way around the top of the unit. For more than seven months, I had inspected each room in the house weekly.

The combination of doing your job, doing it well, and doing it every day creates the kind of quality experience that I believe my clients have come to expect from a Frank McKinney property—and your clients should expect the same from you, too. You've got to hold yourself and your work to the highest possible standards, or set new ones that are even higher than the marketplace expects, because no one else will do it for you.

If you have a team, you're going to have to hold them to the same standards—and that's probably the toughest part of this philosophy. It takes leadership to persuade others to adopt the philosophy of consistent effort and high standards. When asked, most people say they're doing a good job—but are their standards as high as they could be? Are they doing their jobs well every day, or are Mondays and Fridays a little slower and less focused? More important, are *your* Fridays and Mondays that way? My favorite day of the week is Monday, because it is a day of opportunity. If you want to lead a team, the only way is to lead by example. They need to know that your level of commitment, dedication, and hard work exceeds what you're demanding of them.

You've probably heard this story about Mahatma Gandhi, the great leader and proponent of nonviolence. One day a woman brought her son to see Gandhi. "Please, sir, my son is addicted to sugar. He won't stop eating it," she said. "But he reveres you so much that if you tell him never to eat sugar again, he will obey. Can you take one moment to tell him this?"

"Come back in a month," Gandhi replied.

The woman was astounded. "Sir, we have walked two weeks to get here. Can't you please tell him now?"

"Come back in a month," Gandhi repeated.

The woman left, confused and dejected. But a month later, she was back. She and her son were brought into Gandhi's room. Gandhi looked the boy straight in the eye and said sternly, "Don't eat sugar!"

The boy's eyes were huge; he nodded slowly.

"Thank you, master," the woman said gratefully. "I know my son will not eat sugar now. But why couldn't you have told him this a month ago?"

Gandhi smiled. "A month ago, *I* was still eating sugar. I could not tell him to stop eating it until I had done so myself."

If you want your team, your family, or your business to succeed, you must be the model. You must do the job, do it well, and do it every day. Good times and bad, easy days and the days when you have to drag yourself out of bed to get on the freeway one more time, to go to one more property or interview or client meeting, to cook one more meal or pick up one more kid from school, to take one more test or do one more homework assignment—whatever your job is, your own consistent, high-quality effort will make the difference.

I've always believed that I control my own success or failure, and this Philosophy is why. If you do your job, do it well, and do it every single day, there is no way you can fail. You may experience setbacks, and sometimes things might not fall your way; but ultimately you will succeed. And when you make it big you'll know you deserve your success, because you've earned it.

Actions

1. What will it take for you to do your job, do it well, and do it every day? Are you ready to make that kind of commitment to making it big?
2. What does a good job look like for you? If you're a student, how much attention must you pay in class? If you're an entrepreneur, what must you do every day to make your business a success? If you're an intrapreneur working within a large company, how will you know you've done a good job? And do your requirements for a good job at least match, and preferably exceed, what's expected of you?
3. If you're leading a team, what does your team need to see you doing so you can lead by example?

Deal Points

When you do your job, do it well, and do it every day, your efforts will pay off, slowly but surely. This is especially true in real estate, where you're probably going to have to start small and work your way up. When budding entrepreneurs come up and ask me, "How can I get into real estate?" I'll say, "Start with one single property. Do your research and find a distressed building where (1) you'll be able to afford the selling price, (2) you have enough money left over to renovate and make it the nicest home in the neighborhood, and (3) the margins are such that you're guaranteed to make money." Where do you find distressed real estate? In most cities and counties, there are regular sales of properties that have been taken over for one reason or another. *Foreclosure sales* occur when the mortgage hasn't been paid and the bank takes the property back. In *tax sales*, the county or city takes the property for nonpayment of property taxes. Both those kinds of sales usually occur at regular intervals at what's called the "courthouse steps." (This just means in a specific government building.) There are also *IRS sales* (property confiscated for nonpayment of income taxes) and *sheriff's sales* (property seized due to illegal activity), but I did less with those because the property tended to cost more and I couldn't get the margins I wanted.

As you read elsewhere in this book, when I started in distressed real estate in 1985 there was one auction at the Palm Beach County courthouse steps each week, covering approximately 40 properties being sold for foreclosures and taxes. Notice of this auction would appear in the newspaper a week in advance, so I'd have seven days to check out the properties and see if I wanted to bid on anything. I'd drive by the houses, check a little newsletter that detailed all the financials, figure my margins, and then go in prepared with exactly how much I was willing to pay. I averaged around one purchase every three weeks—one deal for every 120 or so properties on the lists. But because I'd done my homework diligently every week, that one property would give me the kind of profit margin (100 percent or more) that I was looking for. After that, of course, would come the renovations, marketing, negotiating, all the other areas where I was also doing the job and doing it every day.

Remember, you make your profit the day you purchase the property, not the day you sell it. Do the job right, restore the house properly, and you'll make your money faster because it'll sell quicker. If you do that over and over again, you'll be surprised at how fast you can build up equity in order to do larger deals.

Persevere toward Your Ideal of Spiritual Fulfillment, Happiness, Dream, or Goal Each Day

It's great to have a vision, but if you're not out there day after day making it happen, it's only a pipe dream. And it's great to have a strong work ethic and get up and go to work every day, but if you're working without a sense of where you're going and why you're working, then you're a drone. You're part of the nine-to-five or eight-to-four masses who work for a paycheck and live only on the weekends if they're lucky. The mission, vision, dream, or goal gives your work a reason; but *persevering* in that work makes your vision or goal real.

Perseverance is actually more than hard work. For me perseverance means to keep going in the face of adversity, challenge, and failure. In real estate (in any business, actually) people tell you "no" all the time. You're constantly faced with clients who don't want your house, bankers who don't want to lend you money, city agencies that won't issue the permits you need fast enough, and on and on. Especially if you're trying to do something that's never been done before, the "no's" come fast and furiously. I can't tell you how many banks have turned me down for financing, how many real estate brokers told me I could never sell my oceanfront properties at the prices I was asking, how many pundits and experts in the media and in the local community said I was crazy and were just waiting for me to crash and burn.

Instead of being discouraged, I regard each "no" as a challenge to change the mind of fate itself, and I persevere. But it's not easy. There was a time in 2000 that I was flying very close to the sun. I had borrowed a lot of money to build up my inventory. Now, the cheapest money for me doesn't come from borrowing against my real estate, because bankers don't consider real estate a very liquid asset. Instead, the lowest-cost funds are money borrowed against securities like stocks. So in 1999 and early 2000, I built up my stock portfolio considerably, and then borrowed money against it. As you remember, in March 2000 the Nasdaq hit 5,000; within a few months, it had dropped by about 50 percent. Guess what happened to the value of my portfolio. At the same time, we completed renovations on our $30 million property and put it on the market. That's a lot of capital to be tied up in one property with no certainty of selling it by any given time. I was also fighting a couple of lawsuits, a contract I had to build a $60 million house for someone was canceled, the banks were ready to call my loans, and on top of everything else, Nilsa was in a car accident. It was probably the lowest point of my life.

What did I do? I persevered. (I also put on a good face about it—nobody knew how close we were to crashing and burning.) I kept doing what I was doing, making deals, finding the money to cover expenses, showing the house, and working on my other projects. I also kept up my charitable work, because I believe giving back must not be contingent on how well or ill you're doing financially. And on November 8, 2000, we sold the $30 million property. I was able to pay off debt and put myself in the position to finance our next project, which was a $15 million oceanfront home in Gulf Stream, Florida. I also went to the bankers who had been ready to call my loans (and who were once again very eager for my business) and said, "Guess what? You're going to lower my rate for future loans, because if you won't, somebody else will."

It's hard enough to be told "no" once; it's even worse when you're told "no" again and again. If you keep at it, if you persevere, sometimes you can turn the "no" into a "yes." I've found this to be true with everything from insurance claims to city permits to getting someone to make a donation to a cause. When I first proposed the idea for this book, at least 15 publishing houses turned it down. But I persevered. I kept talking about the book as if it were going to be published, because I knew someday that it would. I mentioned the book in an interview I had with Greg Zoroya of *USA Today* when the $30 million property was on the market. Michael Hamilton, an editor at John Wiley & Sons, saw the article, phoned my agent, and asked about the book. You hold the result in your hands. If I'd listened to that first round of "no's," my dream of this book would have died. Instead, every "no" fueled my determination to find a "yes" somewhere, somehow. Even during the toughest times (and that was a tough year for me), if your dream, vision, or goal is important enough, you must persevere.

Now, there's something significant in the way this principle is stated. Did you notice the first item on the list of what we're persevering toward? Not success, not a goal, not even a vision—spiritual fulfillment. I believe our dreams, goals, vision, and even our mission are part of the overall picture of our lives. Keeping spiritual fulfillment as the first objective keeps things in perspective. It keeps me focused on true happiness, and gives me the ability to see the big picture. And if I am persevering toward that spiritual fulfillment and being conscientious enough to do it every day, then I believe my chances of making it big are 1,000 percent.

Actions

1. Where have you been told "no" in the past and persevered anyway, managing to turn the situation around? How did you do it?
2. Pick a dream, goal, vision, or mission you want to put into action, and develop at least 10 ideas in advance for dealing with potential "no's."
3. Make sure your dream, goal, vision, or mission is in service to your idea of spiritual fulfillment, what you want your life to be about. Use your perseverance and energy to create a life that means something and has an impact.

Deal Points

In real estate, you spend a lot more time being told "no" than "yes." It only takes one "yes" to sell a property, but there are a certain number of "no's" you have to go through in order to reach that "yes." *Every "no" actually means you're one step closer to "yes."* You can learn from the "no's" and draw strength from them. It takes energy for someone to tell you "no." Take that energy, turn it around, and use it to get the deal you want. Seek out those "no's"; embrace them. They mean you're one "no" closer to a big, fat "yes."

Proactively and Creatively Persist, Day In and Day Out

What's the difference between perseverance and persistence? Perseverance to me means persisting against the odds, facing up to the "no's" that life gives you, staring them down, and turning them into "yes's." But persistence is what makes it happen on the days you're *not* faced with obstacles—and those days are sometimes the hardest to get through. Like we discussed in Philosophy #16, "Do your job, do it well, and do it every day," you have to keep at it no matter whether you're feeling great about your job or not, whether the sun shines or it's raining, whether you've got a cold or you're in excellent health, whether you have a million dollars in the bank or your last dollar in your pocket. Persistence is the centerpiece of the lunch pail approach.

This Philosophy includes two words that I believe make persistence easier and a lot more productive. The first is *proactively*. It's a buzzword that everyone's heard by now, but it's an approach to life and business that I apply religiously. Being proactive means making things happen. It's not reacting to events but anticipating them, creating opportunities rather than waiting for them to come my way. I train everyone who works with me to be proactive. A proactive approach is a cornerstone to successful leadership. I get absolutely crazy if someone brings a problem to me without a solution. One of my people walks in with a worried look on his or her face and I'll ask, "Are you bringing me a problem without a solution?" If the answer is yes, I'll say, "Don't come in until you can identify the problem, tell me what caused it, tell me what your solutions are, and give me your evaluation as to the best one. Then I'll listen." How would you rather live: always a little bit behind the times, reacting to what's already happened, essentially letting yourself be controlled by events, or proactively anticipating and acting to control events before they occur?

I'll give you a great example of proactive persistence. When I was buying foreclosures at auction, I would go through the lists of properties, do all my research, and from 40 or so properties I'd narrow my hit list down to one or two. Now, I knew from my research exactly how much the bank was owed on each property, and I also knew how much I was willing to pay. At the auction, there would usually be a lawyer or someone else to represent the bank's interests on each foreclosed property. This person's job was to bid the price of the property up so the bank would at least get its loan amount out of the auction. Well, a few days before the sale I'd call the bank officer or lawyer who was in charge of the property I wanted and say, "Look, I know you're owed $50,000, but I'm only going to $40,000 and that's it. If you want a guaranteed sale at $40,000, drop out and you'll get most of your money." Some of the banks wouldn't go for it, but after a while they figured out they'd end up spending almost $10,000 on a broker if the property didn't sell at auction, so why not sell it to me? And other smaller banks were just happy to get something out of what had become a liability on their books. By being proactive and persistent, I was able to buy properties at the price points I wanted, allowing me to renovate and still make my profit objectives.

The difference between persistence and banging your head against a wall lies in the second word: *creatively*. Using what I call "creative persistence" I'll try all kinds of different approaches in order to achieve my vision. If this particular bank won't fund my project, I'll go to another one, or to another officer in the same bank. I'll try a different source of funding (like borrowing against my securities). If I can't get permits fast enough through regular channels, I have no problem pulling strings to see if I can expedite the process. I won't do anything illegal, certainly, but I will make use of the contacts I have made through the years to see if they can help me. I'm always looking for other ways I can achieve my vision or goal, and I'm not afraid to try something new that will get me closer to it. (Creative persistence also helps me overcome one of my greatest faults: impatience when something isn't working. As long as I can creatively pursue other ways to achieve my goals, I'm a lot happier.)

When you combine creativity and persistence, you raise your chances for success significantly. Your boss may not like your idea the first time you present it to him or her, but come back in a week with a little more information, and the project may fly. The first client you show a particular house to may hate it. Fine—the next client may be the one who will buy. One bank may not loan you the money, but if you are creative, you can find other sources of funding that may actually be better for you in the long run.

Creative persistence also adds fun and excitement to what could otherwise be a long, hard road. It can take up to a year and a half for one of my oceanfront properties to sell, and I use that time to revise and re-tune the marketing plan for the property. At least every month the marketing director for the property gets a new version of the plan from me, with different elements emphasized and new ideas added. Whenever one of our properties is on the market, I consider that prime experimenting and learning time. I can test new approaches, change them as needed, see the results, and try something new again. Instead of worrying, "When is this albatross going to sell?" I'm happily trying new things to learn more about my marketplace and how to sell to it.

One last point: Always make sure you're persisting in things that are worth pursuing. Have you ever known anyone who is a real pain in the butt, who's made "persisting" their expertise? I've had clients (some of them extremely wealthy) who would call my workpeople 10 times a day in order to get a particular bush moved two feet. I look at that and think, *What a waste of that person's valuable time!* Remember, we're talking about persistence in the service of a bigger goal, not persistence for persistence's sake. It's wiser to choose your battles carefully and put your energy and persistence into things that truly matter.

Actions

1. How can you be proactive in your persistence? What problems can you identify in advance and come up with solutions for?
2. If you're like me, you hate waiting for anything. Where are some areas where you can be creatively persistent during a long-range project? How many different approaches to a goal can you come up with, test, refine, and apply to produce results?

Deal Points

One of the key places where every businessperson needs creative persistence is financing. Banks are very eager to lend you money—on their terms. This usually means that unless you have a significant net worth or great credit record, you're going to have to jump through hoops to get money and spend a lot for it in terms of the interest you're charged. But if you're smart, you'll think long-term right from the beginning.

In 1982, I took out my very first loan from Bank of America. I borrowed $2,500 (the smallest amount the bank would loan, but the largest amount it would loan *me*) at 12 percent interest, and paid off the loan in 18 months. I did nothing with the money; in fact, I put it in a savings account that was earning 6 percent and simply ate the difference. But it was the best and fastest way for me to establish a good credit record. After that, I borrowed small amounts—always what I could afford based on my monthly cash flow—and used the money to finance things like cars and a condominium. (I bought my first home, a condo with views of the ocean, the marina, and the Intracoastal Waterway, at the age of 20. I paid $140,000 for it—$40,000 I had saved from my tennis business and a $100,000 loan from Bank of America.)

When I started buying distressed real estate, however, I used my own savings and money borrowed from a couple of my clients instead of bank loans. (Quite honestly, I believe in putting your own money on the line first before you go out and borrow, because if you fall flat under the heavy burden of bank debt, you're ruined. One foreclosure and you're out of real estate for 7 or 14 years. Plus, when you borrow from a bank, the interest meter starts ticking immediately and keeps right on running until you sell the property and pay the loan back. One delay, one slipup, one downturn in the market or raising of interest rates, and you can see your profits on a sale erode to almost nothing.) I had $30,000 cash saved from my tennis business, and I raised another $70,000 from people I knew. With that $100,000 I bought two houses at auction and renovated them. I sold the first one for a $7,000 profit and the next for a $13,000 profit, and kept doing the same thing over and over. However, I also maintained my relationship with Bank of America, always borrowing small amounts of money and paying them back faithfully. So when I decided to go after my first oceanfront deal, Driftwood Dunes, I had a place to go to arrange the financing.

As you've read elsewhere, the asking price for Driftwood Dunes was $775,000. The house I was living in on Banker's Row was mortgage-free, and I was able to sell it for $225,000. I also had a couple of smaller properties that I was able to finish renovating and sell by the time the Dunes deal closed; those brought in another $150,000. But I had to finance renovations as well as the purchase price, so when I went to Bank of America I requested a loan for $400,000 against the property. Even with my then nine-year relationship with Bank of America, that loan amount was a big leap for them and for me. But I put together a presentation packet that outlined everything clearly, and, God bless 'em, they went for it. Nilsa and I spent the next three years scrimping, saving, and cutting costs to the bone to cover the monthly mortgage payments. Even when the house sat on the market for 19 months, we made those payments on the dot. And our perseverance paid off handsomely. We sold the property for $1.9 million and never looked back.

Banks appreciate persistence. They like customers who pay them back no matter what. When you persist in keeping a strong relationship with your bank, you find it becomes a little more flexible in its approach to loaning you money. In the last large deal I put together for the estate I sold for $30 million, the purchase price on the original property (land and house) was $15 million. My entire investment in the deal would be $15 million plus whatever the renovations cost. I financed over 60 percent of that amount (this time through Bank One) through a stock-secured line of credit; I borrowed against my stock portfolio. The percentage I was able to borrow was much higher than is usually allowed on a land deal—a piece of property you're buying for investment rather than your own personal home. (Usually loan amounts on land come in at 40 percent of the value.) Why did they agree to lend me 60 percent? One, my long-term relationship with the bank's private banking department was in my favor. Two, I had developed enough of a net worth that it was easier to get loans. Three, I had spent a lot of time educating the bank's credit department about the Palm Beach County real estate marketplace. Most banks think within a very small box. They have formulas for everything: the types of loans they'll make, collateral required, loan-to-value ratio (how much a bank will loan based on how valuable the underlying security is), and so on. Because oceanfront land values here increase so quickly—by 2 to 3.5 percent per *month*—the usual loan-to-value ratios for property are too low. Through the years I have taken the entire credit department of Bank of America's Southeast division as well as individuals from Bank One on tours of Palm Beach real estate, to educate them on the impact of supply and demand on property values. As a result of my persistence, I am able to do better on my loan-to-value ratios than anyone else I know.

If you're just starting out in real estate, or if you're making a move into a higher price range of property, persistence can be your biggest friend as far as financing is concerned. So think ahead: If you haven't already, start building a good credit history now. Then use a combination of persistence and creativity to put together the money to finance your deals.

Learn Something New Each Day and Forget the Lure of Pride. Ask Yourself, "What Can I Do Better Today Than Yesterday?"

It's good when you are proud of your work or take pride in what you do. But once you've been at something for a while and achieved a certain level of success, there's a temptation to think that you know everything there is to know about your field—the high-end oceanfront real estate market, in my case. When pride means you think you know it all, then you're in trouble.

I believe narrow-minded pride is a more damaging characteristic than ego. There are a lot of know-it-alls out there who aren't willing to sit back and be taught, to learn lessons for tomorrow from today's experience. I see this with men more than women. We men tend to say, "This is the way I was taught, either in school, by my father, or by my employer, and this is the way it has to be done." Big mistake. In my experience, being too proud to learn usually spells the death of success.

I'll tell you where pride really shows up: in negotiations. Especially with the big-buck power-play guys who are a large part of my marketplace, their pride can keep them from taking even the best possible deal. I've seen people who have the money, want the property, and are completely ready to close the deal; still their pride won't let them move from a certain figure because they would perceive it as a victory for me and a defeat for them. Conversely, I've turned the trait of pride of ownership or pride of having the best to my advantage. If you satisfy the clients' pride by letting them know they've got the finest property in the world, many times that can seal the deal.

I believe the secret to successful negotiation is: *Have no pride of your own while satisfying the customers' pride to the extent you can.* This gives you ultimate flexibility. I simply make sure there's room in the price or terms so the client can always have the last word. It costs me nothing to make clients feel they got the best of the negotiation, and even if they have, it's okay with me. I will never accept a deal I am not satisfied with, so I don't concern myself with who wins or loses the chess match of pride. I have no problem standing there with a check for a large amount in my hand and saying to my triumphant client, "You win."

If you can forget the lure of your own pride, you can approach your business and your life with what Zen masters call "beginner's mind." It's asking every single day, "What can I do better today than yesterday?" It's being willing to admit mistakes and learn from them. It's being willing to hear things you don't particularly want to know about, because you'll become a better businessperson and human being as a result.

I am always doing everything possible to learn what I can do better: to improve the quality of my product beyond even the highest expectations; to exceed my clients' needs; to make myself the best at creating the most luxurious and expensive mansions in the world. I do a lot of different things to get this kind of information. For example, real estate brokers will often bring potential buyers to tour our properties while construction is still going on. I do my best to be there, but if it's appropriate I ask the brokers not to identify me as the owner of the property. I dress in my Investment Equity Construction polo shirt (the one all my guys wear at the sites), khaki pants and work boots, and represent myself as the builder. I've found that when people think you're the owner, they won't speak their minds for fear of hurting your feelings. But with the builder, they'll say exactly what they think about the house, the layout, the design touches, and so on. And that's what I want to hear, even if it's not particularly complimentary.

I'll never forget when the wife of one very well-known CEO came to tour our $12 million property. This woman didn't even go past the front door because she noticed the air-conditioning vents were not either disguised behind a piece of trim or at least painted the color of the wall. "What else is cheap in this house if they didn't paint those?" she snapped, then turned on her heel and walked out. I learned my lesson: Never again will you see another air-conditioning vent, electrical outlet, speaker cover, alarm sensor, or light switch cover in a Frank McKinney property that's not painted or wallpapered to match the color of the wall exactly, or hidden behind a piece of molding.

I'm not too proud to change something that I've done, either, if there's a problem. Normally when first I hear a suggestion or an opinion about one of our properties, I regard it as a personal opinion based on individual taste. However, if I hear the same suggestion two or three times, I'll take it on, even if it costs me money. When we had a $6 million property in Delray Beach on the market, I heard from at least three people that there wasn't enough room in the driveway to maneuver once you pulled out of the garage. Well, I completely redid the driveway: I ripped it up and added parking spaces and a better layout. I wasn't thrilled about having to do it as it put a dent in my profits, but I believed it was important. After that, the property sold within two months.

Part of the reason I'm there almost every single time a broker shows one of our properties is to get the clients' input, so I can make the next estate that much better. About six months after I sold La Marceaux, our French château–inspired property, for $12 million, I went to the buyer and said, "Give me a list of the things we should have done in this house but didn't." The people who live in these houses are accustomed to luxury; their homes usually resemble the top-notch hotels they're used to staying in when they travel. So when the billionaire who bought La Marceaux told us it would be great to have a spigot and a drain in the garage so the chauffeur could wash cars inside, and extra extension rods in the closet so that when you're packing to go on a trip you can hang your clothes on the rods rather than laying them on the bed, I paid close attention. Those kinds of details are like gold to me. You've got to be willing to forget about pride, ask questions like "What can we do better?" and then implement the answers.

I am constantly learning something new about my marketplace. In 1998 I bought a property in Manalapan, Florida, and decided to build a 60,000-square-foot Italianate villa on the land. I put a year of my life into the project—traveling to Italy to study palazzos in Florence and Rome, hiring an architect to make my vision real. I was ready to break ground—until a couple offered to buy the land at a very nice profit and pay me to build the house they wanted instead of my design for the villa. It took me days to make that decision: to take a smaller profit on a sure thing, or to go ahead with my dream. I called the gentleman to whom I had sold the $12 million property for advice. He said, "Don't hang in there for the sake of pride, Frank. If you get a decent offer, turn it over and move on." So I did. I'm very glad I decided to sell; in the amount of time it would have taken to build that house, I have bought and sold several other properties, including the $30 million estate. By going with what the marketplace demanded instead of satisfying my own pride, I came out on top.

To be the best, you've also got to be willing to remake yourself to fit the changing demands of your profession and your life. I greatly admire performers like Madonna and the band Metallica because they have remade themselves again and again. Great companies succeed because they remake themselves to suit the changing marketplace. And, on a personal note, you'd better learn new ways to relate to your children as they grow, or they're going to stop paying attention to you pretty darn quick! Make sure you're not stuck in any one version of yourself. Take a few moments every day to ask, "What did I learn today that will help me do a better job tomorrow?" If you apply what you learn and you're willing to remake yourself consistently, then your potential for success will increase every day, too.

Actions

1. Has pride ever gotten in your way, in business or your personal life?
2. As a part of your daily or weekly routine, ask yourself, "What have I learned today that will help me do better tomorrow? What can I do better tomorrow than I did yesterday?" Don't be afraid to change the way you do things; you might just discover some shortcuts to success.
3. Proactively learn from your clients. Ask them for their opinions regarding what you might change or do better. Often they will be glad to tell you what they think, and happy to know you value their opinions. And whatever they say, don't take it personally. Instead, take it to the bank!

Deal Points

Whenever you sell a property, take the time to talk to the client about the property and the whole buying experience. Some entrepreneurs I know even have a questionnaire to gauge customer satisfaction on both the buying and the selling side. But remember, real estate is a relationship-driven business, so it's better to ask these questions of your clients yourself. Ask them to be honest, and do not react negatively to unfavorable comments. Thank them for their candor.

When it comes to negotiations, set your own priorities and limits, and then leave your pride at the door. I'm not suggesting you let clients walk all over you. You must be firm and command their respect as an equal party in the negotiation. But if you walk in the door knowing exactly what your profit margin must be, as well as which deal points you've got wiggle room on and which you don't, and above all, you're willing to *listen* to what the client wants without letting your own ego get in the way, I guarantee you'll walk out with a deal that satisfies both you and the client.

Sit on the Other Side
of the Desk First

When I am about to enter into a negotiation, before the client arrives I literally sit in one of the two chairs on the other side of my desk. I take everything I have learned from previous meetings—about the client's personality, preferences, even body language—and imagine I am that person. Before I ask, "What's in this deal for Frank?" I ask, "What does the client desire from the deal?" Yes, I think about the client's needs or concerns *before* I consider my own. Once I sit on the other side of the desk, it's clearer to me what I will have to do to get the deal done.

And I sit on the other side of the desk a long time, because what the client really wants may not be obvious right away. In real estate, you'd think it'd be pretty simple: The seller wants to get as much money for the property as possible, and the buyer wants to pay as little as possible. But usually there are many other issues that will make the difference between a happy client and one who leaves feeling like he or she has been sold a bill of goods.

For instance, most of the people who own the oceanfront properties

I acquire are older. They bought their piece of the American dream—a house on the Florida Gold Coast—25, 30, 40 years ago, either when they were at the top of their game or ready to retire. But now they're in their seventies and eighties. The house they bought for $200,000 is worth very little, but the ground it's sitting on is worth $3 to $10 million, and they're getting slapped with tax bills of $80,000 to $200,000 a year. Many of these wonderful older couples are living on pensions or income from investments, and they feel insecure about their futures and their lives. The house they love has become a burden, either because it's too big for them or because it's a drain on their financial resources.

When I approach these elderly clients, I spend a lot of time developing the relationship first. I'm very clear about the fact that I'm interested in buying their home should they ever be interested in selling. But I ask about their kids and their grandkids. I call them every few months. I invite them to openings and other events around town. I'm not just doing this because I want to be the one they call when they're ready to sell; I do it because I genuinely like them! They could be my parents or grandparents—or me in 40 or so years.

When it comes time to close the deal, I have a very clear idea of what's important to this particular kind of client and I do my best to provide it. I've allowed some older couples to stay in their home for a year rent-free. Once I told a woman, "If you sell your house to me, I promise you can stay here for the rest of your life." I'll help clients find a new place to live in the area, and even send guys over to help them move. I do all of this because I've sat where the clients are sitting so I can discover what's truly important to them. As a result, almost every one of the people I've bought property from want to stay in touch with me. And I continue to call them—I remember their birthdays and their anniversaries, and invite them to our events. I treat them as I would like to be treated myself.

Sitting on the other side of the desk first is the most important initial step in any negotiation. When I'm getting ready to sell a property, as soon as potential buyers indicate interest I do my best to put myself in their shoes. What's going to make the difference for them in this deal? Is it a quick close, or time to make up their minds? Is it a discount for cash, or good terms? Is it making sure that every single inspection is signed, sealed, and delivered, or do they want an as-is deal with a warranty that anything not right will be fixed within 90 days?

I learn a lot simply by asking the clients questions and then truly listening—both to their answers and what's behind them. I will study them as individuals, their relationships with their spouses, their brokers, their friends. I'm acutely aware of eye contact and body language. I will go as far as repeating back to them what they tell me: "Do I understand correctly that this is what you want?" Reading and understanding people might be the single most important talent in business and negotiation. But understanding unspoken needs comes from my sitting on their side of the desk for a long time.

I pass this attitude along to the people who work for me. I can't tell you how many times I've said, "Wait a minute—let's take a look at this from the clients' side. From their perspective, it's obvious that we have to do it this way." I remember once we had bought an oceanfront property and found a buyer for it within a few days. She was a working woman who wanted to buy the house and then contract with me separately for renovations. She had scheduled a team of inspectors to come in the middle of the week, so my team and I had just two days to get the house ready for inspection. I called everyone together and said, "Think of yourself as the client, and this is the first house you've ever bought. How would you want it to look? Smell? Feel?" In two days, we replaced garbage disposals, water dispensers, air-conditioning; we cleaned the house from top to bottom; after we cleaned the carpet, I had everyone put on paper booties (the ones you wear in an operating room) to keep it clean. The night before the inspection, I went through every room and anything we hadn't been able to take care of, I wrote on little three-by-five-inch cards and stuck them next to the item: "Top element of oven inspected Aug. 10, replacement to be delivered Aug. 16." "Window rotten, new unit ordered from Pella Windows Aug. 10." When the inspector's report came back, almost everything on it was stuff I had noted and already fixed or replaced. Did I have to do all that? Maybe not. But because I thought like my client, it eased the way for that sale to go through.

Sitting on the other side of the desk first is essential no matter what kind of business you're in. If you're selling ads to small businesspeople, for example, what is it that they want? How tight are their budgets? Is their revenue seasonal, and can you develop a payment plan that will accommodate it? As a salesperson, sitting on the other side of the desk first gives you a completely different perspective. Maybe you're less "hard sell" and more interested in finding out what this customer needs and how your product can help. Sitting on the other side of the desk first builds relationships, and relationships mean better sales in the long run.

What about other kinds of relationships? Can you sit on the other side of the desk with your spouse, your friends, your kids? Of course.

My wife Nilsa is an expert at it; she's one of the best listeners I know. If you want your spouse to do something for you or with you, how much easier would it be to present the idea if you know what's in it for him or her as well as for you? I find this concept works really well with kids. How many times do we grown-ups react to a child's behavior automatically, using our own standards of what's right and what's inappropriate? What if you took a moment to see things from your child's perspective? If nothing else, you might just be able to offer the suggestion or correction in a way so the child can accept it, rather than causing a negative reaction. Of course, sitting on the other side of the desk doesn't eliminate all friction; but it does make it a lot more possible to have relationships that are satisfying to both parties.

Sitting on the other side of the desk is really just a version of the Golden Rule, "Do unto others as you would have them do unto you." Everybody wants things "done unto them" in different ways; it's our job to find out what actions will be "golden" for this person. And the best way to do that is to sit on their side of the desk first.

Actions

1. Where would you benefit from sitting on the other side of the desk first? Your business? Your spouse? Your kids? Extended family? Friends?
2. Pick one relationship or situation in which you want to sit on the other side of the desk. Put two chairs facing each other, and sit in one of them. Picture the other person sitting in the second chair. Once that picture is clear in your mind, go and sit in the other person's spot. What would he or she want?
3. You might wish to develop a series of questions to ask when you sit on the other side of the desk. Some great questions include, "What does this person want? What's important to him or her? What emotions does he or she want to feel at the end of this situation or negotiation? How do I want him or her to view me?" Write the questions down and use them as a guide.

Deal Points

In business, we often think that money is most important in our client's mind, but emotions are often more important when it comes to real estate. As professionals, we need to know how to read the client's emotions—not in a manipulative way, but in order to satisfy the client's true desires.

So put yourself in your client's shoes first. If you have a property you want to sell, think like a client when you're getting it ready. Walk through it as a buyer who is making one of the most important investments of his or her life. What will the person want to see? Hear? Feel? How you can create an environment in which all the buyer's senses are affected positively?

When it comes to the negotiations, I truly do recommend sitting on the other side of your desk. It's a very different perspective when you're looking across at your own chair; the power in the relationship shifts quite dramatically. Before any negotiation, take the time to sit on the other side, and write down what you think the clients will want the outcome of the deal to be. Yes, they want the best possible price, but what else do they want? What's equally if not more important to them? Are they older and perhaps want to know that selling their home to you will mean less dislocation than they fear, and a lot more financial security? If they're busy executives, do they want this deal to go through as easily and smoothly as possible, with minimal contact from you? How can you expedite the paperwork for them so it's a one-contact sale? If they're nervous about the sale for any reason, how can you allay their fears—with professional inspections? Lots of walk-throughs? Talking with other satisfied clients?

To know all of this, you may need to spend time with your clients outside of the showings or meetings in your office. Take them to lunch or dinner. Invite them to your tennis or golf club, or to a cultural event. Find out what they're interested in, and then go with them. Develop a friendship in addition to the business relationship. The time you spend with clients is golden, not just because you're learning about them, but because you are creating a bond that can enrich you both. In the most pragmatic sense, satisfied clients are your best source of referrals and future business. But in the personal, spiritual sense, business based on relationship, on asking what the other guy's going to get from the deal first and then doing your best to give it to him, will make you a lot happier. After all, the Golden Rule has been around for a couple of thousand years; it must have something going for it, right?

Think Win-Win, Be Fair, Then Close the Deal

I'm known as a good negotiator because I follow this Philosophy. Negotiation always involves at least two sides. As you learned in the preceding chapter, it's important to put yourself in the position of the other parties so you can understand what they want. But in the context of negotiation, all parties have to feel they've gotten a fair shake. How do you do that? Simply by *thinking win-win*. Win-win starts by listening to the other side and truly hearing what they're saying. Even though I'm always eager to get my point across, I've learned that I must shut up and listen to other people first. Only when I understand what they want can I construct a deal that will feel like a win for them.

That being said, win-win means both sides have to feel good about the outcome, and that includes you, too. I never enter into a deal that I'm going to regret either because I'm selling too cheap or because I'm paying too much. I've walked away from deals and had people say to me, "You're so close. How could you not take it?" But if the terms or the price aren't a win both for me and for the other person, I'm not interested. Win-win is not about being a doormat and giving the other side everything they want; it's based on the belief that both parties can come out of a negotiation with what's really important to them.

Sometimes win-win can be tough to negotiate. I've been in situations with certain clients or people in organizations where the concept of win-win was completely out of the question as far as they were concerned. "My way or the highway!" is their idea of negotiating. In that case, you have two choices. You can sit on their side of the desk and see what's really important to them. Do they have to feel they've won? If so, as long as you get what's important to you as well, you can swallow your pride and tell them they got the better of you (see Philosophy #19). Your other choice is to walk away. And if you aren't going to feel like you've gotten a win from this particular deal, you may be better off with another client.

That leads to the next part of this Philosophy: *Be fair*. Very seldom will a deal work out if it doesn't pass the "fair" test. It is fine to negotiate a good deal, but not at the expense of the other party. Early in my career I thought the most important thing was to get the lowest price from a seller or a subcontractor, no matter how the other person felt about the deal. Well, I have learned the hard way that you get what you pay for. If you pay a fair price—fair in the eyes of both you *and* the other party—you're likely to get treated fairly in return.

Sometimes fairness means being honest enough to admit when something's perhaps a little bit too much in your favor. There have been deals where the client or subcontractor thought they had a winning deal but I knew they didn't. To be fair to them (and to myself) I told them we needed to renegotiate so both sides would come away with a win. If this seems a little goody-goody, I believe if I'm honest and fair with others, they're more likely to be honest and fair with me.

After you have applied a win-win approach and dealt with the other parties fairly, it's time to *close the deal*. When I'm ready to do a deal I move quickly; I don't place roadblocks in front of a it. I like to deal with the principals and not with lawyers. To my mind, lawyers are there to draft terms, not make them. I believe you succeed when you create a deal that's fair to both sides, keep contingencies to a minimum, and move swiftly.

It surprises me how many businesspeople mess up this part of the process. They either never ask for the sale or keep on talking until they scare the buyer away! The worst thing you can do is oversell someone who's ready to make a decision. Recently I had a handshake deal with a gentleman to purchase a $15 million property. We had agreed on a price, but there were still details to be ironed out on alterations he wanted. So our lawyers were talking, the brokers were calling, we were faxing stuff to England (where the gentleman was), to keep the deal moving. But all these efforts didn't seem to be producing any results. After about a week, I had a funny feeling and told my broker and attorney, "I think our client is feeling pushed. Let's back off for a little while." Unfortunately, it was too late; the man (who was indeed feeling pushed) pulled out of the deal. I had blown it because I was trying too hard.

On the other hand, you can "think win-win" until the cows come home, but at some point you've got to close the deal. If you still need to negotiate, shut yourself in a room with the other party and don't come out until all the details are ironed out. But don't be afraid to ask the question, pull out the contract, or get the deposit check. Whenever we show a house, I have a contract in my pocket that's filled in with everything but the price, date of closing, and the client's name. I have the seller's name, the legal description of the property, the tax folio number—all the stuff that you'd normally have to go back to the office to complete. When the client's ready to buy, I've always got the contract in hand.

The other side to closing the deal is knowing when to stop spending your valuable time. Time is a precious resource, and I'd rather spend it creating new opportunities instead of pursuing deals that won't work for either party in the long run. Besides, I know that as long as I create deals that are win-win and fair, I will always be able to close the sale with someone. It's just a question of how soon that someone is going to arrive.

Actions

1. How can you create a win-win situation in your business? In your intimate relationships? With your kids? With your friends?
2. Have you ever been treated unfairly? What did it feel like? Have you ever taken advantage of someone by negotiating a deal that you knew was unfairly weighted to your side? When the next negotiation comes up, how will you know you are being fair to yourself and the other parties?
3. One of the toughest things to do is to close the sale: It's a leap of faith, and it takes courage. The next time you're faced with one of those "closing" moments—asking a girl (or guy) out on a date, asking for the contract, and so on—how will you know when to go for it? How great will you feel when the deal is closed?

Deal Points

One of the most essential tools of my business is identifying and taking advantage of what I call the buyer's *impulse window*. This is the period of time after the buyer sees the house and that feeling of "this may be the one" arises. At that point, the impulse to buy has been triggered. In that impulse window is your chance to convince the client that it's time to do the deal. The window closes as quickly as it opens, however, and it's never open for very long, so our job is to capitalize on it and to keep it open as long as possible.

Assuming the client is well qualified, after the first showing of the property I ask our brokers to do the following:

- Offer to show the property in a different light—at night, sunset, or sunrise.
- Offer clients access to the house without brokers or owners there. Set up a movie in the theater, turn on the hot tub, and so on. Let them experience the house as if it were theirs. (If they accept, make sure to provide the most inviting ambiance possible, including food, drink, entertainment, sound, lights, candles, smells, etc.)
- Offer to show clients other homes we have built or renovated. This is to show the quality and detail of our work. Because most of our clients are very busy, we make sure these homes are available for showing at a moment's notice.
- Stress scarcity and urgency. Tell clients, "This is one of a very few direct oceanfront properties available in Palm Beach County at this time. It's a brand-new listing, and several other people are looking at it."
- Offer to show the property to anyone associated with the clients who might be involved in the buying decision. Try to determine who might not have been at the first showing. A missing spouse, boyfriend, girlfriend, parent, relative, friend, business associate, or financial adviser may be just what you need to keep the impulse window open. Offering a second showing at any time for any reason may help buyers to make up their minds.
- Invite clients to talk to owners of other Frank McKinney properties. (I make sure there is at least one client-to-prospect testimonial available, by phone or in person, the same day.)
- Have the contract ready, with everything filled in except the buyer's name, the price, and the date of closing. Offer it if the timing is right but never prematurely, as this is a serious turn-off.
- Invite clients to lunch, cocktails, dinner, or breakfast to discuss the local real estate market. Many people are used to discussing business over a meal or drinks. This allows for a more relaxed atmosphere and builds relationships between brokers and clients.

Each of these items helps keep the impulse window open for as long as it takes for clients to make up their minds about the property. I ask my brokers to be flexible and apply only those items they think will enhance the clients' experience. I also ask them to be ready at any time to write the contract after the clients have seen the property. But once the impulse window closes, it's gone. At that point, spending any more time with these clients is usually unproductive. It's smarter to cultivate new opportunities instead.

Avoid Vices and Unhealthy Temptations As They Suck the Life Out of Progress and Success

It may seem strange coming from someone with my background, appearance, and personality, but this is one of the Philosophies I feel very strongly about. I believe violating this Philosophy will destroy all the benefits of the other 48 in this book. That's not to say I don't understand the allure of unhealthy vices. Believe me, I used to enjoy my vices a *lot*. I started them very young and tried them all, and I know the rush they provide. But I also learned what those vices cost me, and it's too darn high a price. I look back on all the time, energy, and health I wasted as a kid—doing drugs, drinking, getting arrested, trashing myself physically—and think, "Where could I be now if I *hadn't* done that?"

The first vice to go was cigarettes. I smoked cigarettes for a year or so when I was 16, probably to be cool. But then one day I read that for every cigarette you smoke, you take three minutes off your life span. I thought, *That's stupid. I want to live a long time*; and I never smoked another cigarette.

But I sure did almost everything else! Between the ages of 13 and 17, I drank. I stole liquor. I experimented with pot (yes, I inhaled) and other drugs; even sold a little to my friends. I was thrown into juvenile detention and eventually jail several times for drugs, speeding, and the like. Two good things came out of those years: First, I got all that out of my system, and second, I realized at a relatively young age how these vices were harming me as well as those I cared about. Today when I talk to parents who are worried about their own teenagers, I tell them, "Look, I'm living proof that there is hope for even the worst kid. This is probably just a painful phase your child's going through. It's not pleasant, but it's not the end of the world, either. In my experience, they'll come back to the way you raised them when they were younger—between birth and age 10. So love 'em, be firm with 'em, and pray they'll learn their lessons quickly."

What turned me around? Moving to Florida and starting my tennis business: I couldn't stay out all night and teach tennis for eight hours the next day. (At least, I couldn't do it very often.) I chose not to indulge in some vices since the consequences of getting caught were a lot worse now that I was on my own. Most of all, I started to notice the people I wanted to emulate: men and women who had achieved a great deal and sustained their success over a long period of time. Invariably, they lived pretty clean lives. They didn't drink or do drugs or speed or do anything else to excess. Even those who were well off enough to have and do anything they wanted didn't fritter away their energy and drive on unhealthy temptations and vices. If I wanted to be like them—and I did—I figured I'd better clean up my act.

The last vice I eliminated was illegal speeding. For several years after I moved to Florida, I couldn't resist taking my motorcycle, Ferrari, or whatever vehicle I was driving, and shattering the speed limit. Eventually, all of those speeding tickets and moving violations landed me in jail as a habitual traffic offender. (In fact, I missed my Dad's remarriage because I was in jail serving time on a speeding charge.) While I was waiting to be transferred from the jail's holding area to a cell, I peered through the bulletproof window into the guards' station, and on the television was a program about Donald Trump. At the time I had already started to buy properties, and when I saw Trump on TV I thought, *Hey, I'm much more like him than I'm like the guys in this jail.* So right then and there I was done breaking the speed laws. Since 1989, I have never had another ticket or a moving violation. Now, I will take my motorcycles to a racetrack or do other things to get my adrenaline rush—legal things, like snowboarding, riding my dirt bike or all-terrain vehicle, running my Jet Ski through eight-foot waves, driving go-carts on my own property, and making bigger and bigger deals in my real estate business. (I'll talk more about adrenaline in Part Four, "Take Risks.")

What unhealthy vices do *you* indulge in? And don't tell me you don't have any. I speak to a lot of groups, and when I mention this Philosophy inevitably it hits a nerve; I watch as people sink a little deeper into their chairs and avoid eye contact. I'm not just talking about the obvious vices like drinking to excess, drugs, infidelity, gambling, and breaking the law. And I'm not talking about one glass of wine with dinner, a weekly poker game among friends, or appreciating a good-looking man or woman walking down the street. I'm talking about anything you do to excess that saps the life out of your life. Overeating or eating poorly can be an unhealthy vice. Sleeping too much can be an unhealthy vice. Reading too much can be an unhealthy vice. Exercising too much can be an unhealthy vice. Watching too much TV can be an unhealthy vice. Spending too much can be an unhealthy vice. Almost anything you overindulge in that drains your energy or stops you from accomplishing what you want is an unhealthy vice, in my opinion.

Some vices can destroy your business just as quickly as they destroy you. Greed. Dishonesty. Laziness. Unethical behavior. Anger. Procrastination. These attitudinal vices can kill your business just as surely as if you'd been caught with another person's spouse or a pound of marijuana in your car. Unfortunately, the more successful you become, do you think the temptations get smaller? No way—they get bigger, and they're easier to obtain. But their cost is also greater. You can work your whole life to build a successful business and yet one slip can bring you tumbling down. Unhealthy vices can ruin your progress and take you back to square one, and who wants to have to start over? That's why you must be vigilant: Don't let your life be sucked dry by unhealthy vices.

How do you handle vices and temptations? You decide what you want your life to be about: Indulgence or accomplishment. Flabbiness or strength. Failure or success. Momentary pleasure or leaving a legacy you and your children can be proud of. And once you've made that decision, you simply say no to the things that weaken or distract you from your true vision and mission.

The great thing is, the more you resist temptation the stronger your resistance becomes. You turn down the referral fee that's nothing but a kickback in disguise. You are honest with a client even if it costs you money. Instead of flying off the handle at an employee or associate, you go for a walk to get your anger under control. You say no to the third martini, the late-night dinner with an attractive client, the latest "toy" you can't afford but really want. You get up early and spend your time productively. (We'll talk more about that in the next chapter.)

Every time you make a decision to stick with your principles instead of indulging your weaknesses, you get stronger spiritually. And eventually this spiritual strength becomes a part of your identity. I don't think of myself as a nonsmoker or "ex"-anything, because smoking and other vices are things I would never do in a million years: They're not tempting anymore. You can reach the same point with your own unhealthy temptations, where they are no longer an issue for you. But until then, it's going to take some willpower and strength on your part.

Unless you can resist unhealthy temptations and vices, you'll never succeed, at least not in the long term. Sure, there are rock stars and businesspeople who make it big while indulging in all sorts of vices, but their success is usually the flash-in-the-pan variety. So whatever you're working toward—being the next Donald Trump or movie star or a valued player on your basketball team—if you indulge in unhealthy temptations, you're never going to make it. You'll find yourself looking at the people who resist temptation and asking, "Why are they doing so well?" They're doing well because they know the cost of indulging in unhealthy vices; and it's a price they're unwilling to pay.

Actions

1. In the past, what unhealthy vices and temptations have you indulged in? What have they cost you? Are you still indulging in them? What are they costing you now?
2. The best defense is a good offense. Come up with a list of ways you can and will refuse unhealthy temptations that are presented to you. Create some very specific responses, and rehearse them in your mind. Then picture yourself having turned down temptation and feeling great about it.
3. Visualize how the energy and strength you gain from this newly healthy life will allow you to fulfill your vision or mission even more quickly.

Deal Points

Your reputation is the most important coin you have in business. It's your entry point in every relationship, yet it can be damaged by the faintest rumor. When you're successful, people are looking for your flaws and faults; they want you to fail so they'll feel better about their own lack of progress. Those are the same people who attend a stock car race to see the crash, not the competition. Don't give others the chance to destroy you because you're destroying yourself through vices like dishonesty, unethical behavior, greed, anger, and procrastination. Safeguard your business, your energy, and your good name by staying away from unhealthy temptations, in both your business and your personal life.

You Must Be Disciplined. Go to Bed Early and Get Up Early

"Oh, boring," I can hear you say. "Discipline? Go to bed early? Come on, Frank—what happened to that daredevil guy who was so wild and crazy when he was a kid?" Hey, I'm still wild and crazy—but once I moved to Florida, I *had* to develop discipline. Nobody was going to bail me out if I got into trouble. Nobody but me was going to save my you-know-what if my tennis business flopped. If one of the properties I bought turned out to be a dud, guess who was going to take the hit? When I went from not caring about tomorrow to realizing I had to be completely self-reliant, I became *very* disciplined. And once I turned that corner, I've never wavered.

There is no more important foundation for making it big than discipline. Discipline underlies most of the secrets in this book. You've got to be disciplined to turn your personal vision into reality. You've got to be disciplined when it comes to creating a consistent brand in your marketplace. (Discipline and consistency are really two sides of the same coin.) The lunch pail approach is completely founded on the discipline to get up every single day, good or bad, and do your job well. Certainly the only way I've been able to handle the enormous amount of risk I take is through emotional discipline. Making sure I take the time to contribute to others and live with integrity (even when temptations appear) takes enormous discipline. And quite honestly, without discipline I wouldn't have the energy to enjoy the ride and make my life rock!

I was lucky to learn one kind of discipline early in life, when I was a champion tennis player in Indiana in my early teens. I also had the example of my dad, who won gold, silver, and bronze medals in the 1956 and 1960 Olympics. He was a world-class swimmer specializing in the backstroke. (Think about how many hours he swam back and forth in a pool, day after day, to be good enough for the Olympics. Talk about discipline!) When I was in boarding school in Colorado with the Benedictine monks, their whole lifestyle was an example of the power of discipline. And when I started my own business, I was grateful to have those models to draw on. It took enormous physical and emotional discipline to teach tennis 10, 12, 14 hours a day. It took enormous discipline to save $30,000 from that business to put into my first piece of real estate. It took incredible discipline to keep going to distressed property auctions and to find properties, renovate them or build them from scratch, sell them, and do it again, week after week.

I'll give you one example of the power of discipline: In 1992, when I decided to purchase my first piece of oceanfront property, it took every dime I had. Literally. I maxed out my credit cards and every other credit line. Nilsa and I sold our cars. We even sold our home. We moved from our 3,500-square-foot mini-estate dream home—a beautiful 1923 Mediterranean compound with guest cottage—into a 600-square-foot efficiency rental apartment. The only furniture we kept was our king-size bed (heck, it was the only thing that would fit). Every night I would wheel my motorcycle in the front door so it wouldn't be stolen.

We lived like that for almost four years, while I kept putting every dime into one oceanfront project after another. For a while, we even saved on rent by moving into the servants' quarters of one of the houses I was building. But we couldn't let people know we were living there, so we kept all our belongings either under the bed or in a locked closet. We ate cold cereal and microwaved food outside so there would be no food odors in the house. I learned to love showering outside because the only shower I would use was the one on the outside pool deck. Even the cat got into the act; every time anyone came to tour the house we locked poor Sewey (I had rescued him from a city sewer drain) in a closet until the people were gone. Living that way took a lot of discipline not just on my part but on Nilsa's as well.

Here's the secret to discipline: It's easier when it's in service to a greater goal. I believed in the goal of creating the most successful tennis business ever. Nilsa and I believed in the goal of moving up to ocean-front real estate. Today I believe in my vision of becoming world-renowned for the properties I build, and contributing to the homeless and young people in significant ways. I believe in taking care of my family and the people who work with me. I believe in leaving a legacy for my daughter to be proud of. All of those goals require discipline to make them possible.

Luckily, over time discipline can become a habit, and then second nature. Monday through Saturday, I get out of bed at five A.M. (Sundays, I sleep in and get up at six.) I love that time between five and seven—it's like I have the world to myself. I go to the gym or run six miles to start my day with a good workout. (Physical discipline in the form of exercise is a vital part of my life.) I take time to pray and align myself for the day. I feel like I'm starting the workday with a leg up on everyone else. Why would I trade that time and that feeling for a few moments more of sleep? Heck, you can sleep when you're dead!

I am equally disciplined about going to bed early; I'm usually asleep by nine o'clock. For many people, this is a lot harder discipline than getting up at five A.M.! But what do most of us do in the evening? We're exhausted from the day so we flop on the couch and turn on the TV. Occasionally we'll spend time with our kids or our spouse, but truthfully, after nine P.M. what kind of quality time is it? Wouldn't your family be better served with more "you" between the hours of six and nine P.M., and less of the person who zones out in front of the 11 o'clock news?

Financial discipline is equally essential for success. Unfortunately, our consumer society doesn't seem to believe it. We're surrounded by temptations to buy things we want rather than need. But you'd be amazed how some of the richest people in the world practice financial discipline. Once a billionaire client of mine asked me to drop some letters in the mailbox on my way home. On top of the stack was a rebate request for something the guy bought. The man could buy and sell the company the product came from, but he was still sending for the rebate!

Nilsa and I use coupons and shop the specials for our daughter's needs and food. I drive a 1974 Cadillac station wagon with 86,000 miles on it. Nilsa isn't off shopping in Palm Beach and Miami for a new wardrobe each year. Our lifestyle is and will continue to be modest, because we believe in being disciplined financially. No matter what your current financial status, remember that a rainy day may be just around the corner. When the showers come (or in my case, if the hurricane ever hits), you'll be glad you practiced financial discipline and put something aside.

I once read that if you do something for three months, it will become a lifetime habit. I challenge you to create the habit of discipline for yourself: Get up early and go to bed early for three months in a row. Once you've established the habit of discipline, you can apply it to other areas of your life. Discipline is one "addiction" that is seriously good for you!

Actions

1. Develop the habit of discipline. Get up at least an hour earlier and go to bed an hour earlier than you usually do for three straight months. No cheating is allowed—you want to establish a habit for yourself.
2. Check your financial discipline. Are you spending money for things you want but don't need? How can you develop more financial discipline in your life? Come up with at least three ways you can practice financial discipline consistently, and do so for three months.
3. If you don't have an exercise program in place, get one. Physical discipline will give you the energy, drive, and strength you need to make your vision for your life come true.

Deal Points

If you're just getting started in real estate, discipline is essential. Take a look at your financial resources, and see how financial discipline can help you put more money aside for your real estate purchases. Become very disciplined in your approach to the real estate market. Start small and stay small until you have mastered real estate on that scale. There is nothing wrong with buying and selling a house or two a year to supplement your income. You will know when it is time to make it a career. And don't give up your current career until you are certain you can succeed.

If you're pursuing foreclosures or distressed properties, you have to go to auctions regularly. The week you miss is sure to be the week the perfect property comes up. You also must be disciplined about your choice of properties and how much you're willing to pay. I always make sure my profit margin is high enough to justify my getting into a particular property. I never fall in love so much with an opportunity that I'm willing to forgo a disciplined approach when it comes to deciding whether to invest. Discipline will save your you-know-what in almost every case, if you apply it regularly and stringently.

Organization Is the Key to Success

This is the one Philosophy that I took verbatim from my dad. He was a highly organized man. He used to say over and over again, "Mickey, organization is the key to success"; in fact, everyone in my family laughed about it. But I never paid attention to it, and certainly never knew the full meaning of it until I started my tennis business at age 18. I quickly became organized. I had to be—I was teaching at three different clubs, scheduling lessons with high-powered people whose time was valuable. They could be late, but God help me if *I* was! So I had all my lessons carefully noted in my date book. I knew exactly how much time it would take me to get from one club to the other, and how soon after one lesson I could schedule another. The best thing about organization is that it allows you to be extremely efficient with your time, and since I was being paid by the hour in the tennis business, time was definitely money.

I have carried my dad's philosophy of organization into the real estate world, and through the years it has been one of his biggest legacies in my life. When I was young, I used organization to compensate for some of the things I didn't know, since I lacked much formal education. I found trial and error a tough teacher, so I figured I'd darn well better stay organized so I could minimize the unpleasant consequences of my mistakes.

When I started buying foreclosed properties at auction, organization was my savior. Since there were auctions every Tuesday, I was investigating upwards of 40 properties at any given time. One mistake on any number of details could mean the difference between nailing a moneymaker and watching it go to someone else. To secure the properties that represented the best opportunities, I had to do tons of research and have endless papers—legal, financial, corporate, government—at my fingertips. Here's what I needed to know on every property I was interested in:

- Location (I'd visit to see whether the neighborhood was at all upgradable and to make sure the house was still standing—those were my only two criteria).
- What the mortgage was and who held it (which bank or loan company).
- What the assessed value was, and all pertinent tax records.
- The foreclosure amount, and if all entities were given notice regarding the foreclosure (if there was a second mortgage holder who wasn't given notice, then the buyer is held responsible for paying that second mortgage—an important point).

On the day of the auction I'd not only have all of that data at my fingertips, but I'd also have my own notes on how much I was willing to pay for which properties. As you can imagine, it took a fearsome amount of organization to keep track of all that information on anywhere from two to ten properties a week! Organization allowed me, a brand-new real estate investor, to find the best deals and pay the least amount for them. It also allowed me to renovate those properties quickly and cost-effectively, so I could get them on the market as quickly as possible. Organization allowed me to manage multiple projects early in my real estate career. Before I switched to oceanfront real estate, I once had 16 different projects (houses) going at the same time. I had to be organized just to visit half those projects in one day, much less keep them moving and get them on the market. (Remember, I was doing all of this on my own, without a partner or anyone but me to manage things.)

As my real estate projects got bigger and my life got more complicated, organization became the cornerstone of my sanity. Today, every element of my life is organized, from my work to my real estate projects to my charitable and civic responsibilities and so forth. Each Saturday, I set aside a couple of hours for introspection (see Philosophy #3) and organization. After I've examined my week's accomplishments, what I haven't completed, and what I've learned, I set clear priorities for the upcoming week. Those priorities include work, family, charity and civic responsibilities, spiritual reflection and prayer, exercise, fun and recreation. (Yes, I schedule in leisure time, and yes, there is room for plenty of spontaneity.) Once my priorities are set, the organizing part is relatively simple. When I get up from my desk, I'm ready to make the most of my week. (That being said, I don't spend a lot of time "organizing to get organized." Some people get caught in the trap of spending hours getting ready to plan, only to run out of time to *do*! Organization for me is a way to do more a lot more efficiently. It keeps me in control, in balance, and in hand.)

My companies and all my projects are organized down to the smallest detail. After we've set the vision or mission statement for a project or the year (see Philosophy #2), we create a list of objectives to fulfill that vision, and then set deadlines. Organization is the only way those objectives can be accomplished, and it's certainly the only way I can manage teams and projects of the magnitude that I take on. Whenever my company undertakes a big project, whether it's building from the ground up or renovating an existing mansion, I start organizing in my head a long time before anyone hammers a nail or puts a shovel in the dirt. I write down who I'm going after with this property, who are my probable buyers, what elements I want to introduce into this design. I outline the design elements and the marketing plan. I schedule the permit process. I organize the improvements, or if I'm building from the ground up, the layout of the house. Only when everything is organized to my satisfaction can the actual physical work start.

Organization makes responsibility and accountability possible. From the moment we put the first shovel in the ground, the superintendents and presidents of construction at each project are very organized. The people who work for me know what our schedule is, what they're supposed to accomplish, when they need to check in. Organization allows me to keep the Holy Trinity—time, quality, and budget—in balance, even when I'm dealing with a $30 million estate.

It's all too easy to spot people who aren't organized; they're usually the ones who are at the starting line while I'm halfway to the finish. Organization makes my life manageable and my success possible. It may not be the only key to success, but it certainly is *a* key. A very small investment of time and energy in organizing your life will produce enormous returns—in peace of mind, if nothing else. So get organized, and then get on with it!

Actions

1. Get organized. Set aside a certain time each week to reflect upon your past week's accomplishments, and to set priorities for the next week. Make sure to include work, family, personal time, spirituality, exercise, fun, and so on. Use organization to create a balanced life.
2. Use organizational tools like handheld organizers, date books, flow charts, goals and objectives lists, and so on. There's a lot of great material and literature to help you, from pocket PCs to time management systems to books by Stephen Covey and others.
3. A system is a shortcut to organization: It's a predetermined series of actions that you or those you work with will follow. My entire company runs on systems that everyone is familiar with and everyone follows. Set up systems for projects you work on repeatedly.

Deal Points

Ever since I started in real estate, I've used some kind of organizational chart or plan to help me implement my vision for success. Remember the chart I showed you in Philosophy #2, the one I use each week to prioritize the different components of my vision? When I was first getting into real estate, I created a version of that chart to keep track of multiple projects. Each project was given a number based on its priority, #1 being the property with the greatest possible upside, risk or exposure, and so on. Projects were listed at the top of the page, and underneath each project were boxes for different goals, listed in order of importance. See the sample chart on the opposite page.

The goal in space "1–1" would be the most important for the week, "5–5" the least important. Anything that I finished I marked in green. Anything that wasn't done I carried over to the next week. This simple organizational tool (which I originally handwrote each week on legal pads) enabled me to keep track of everything that went into buying and selling my properties.

Weekly Organizational Chart and Goals Agenda

Week beginning Monday, _____ ending Sunday, _____.

	Property #1 1620 Ash	Property #2 413 Maple	Property #3 3884 Conch	Property #4 29 Horizon	Property #5 The Suites
#1					
#2					
#3					
#4					
#5					

❑ Nilsa
❑ Cathy
❑ Bob
❑ Ray

I also used this sheet to help me leverage tasks to others. You see the list of names at the bottom of the chart? Those are subcontractors, designers, marketers, and so on. I assigned each of them a color, and any task or goal that I could give to one of them I indicated on the chart in that person's color. I referred to this chart constantly throughout the week, using it as a guide to how much I've accomplished. Then on Saturday I did another chart, reevaluating which property and goals needed to have the highest priority that week.

You can use any tool that works for you to keep your real estate business organized and your priorities straight. But whatever you use, make sure it allows you to keep track of the details while holding on to the big picture. Keep yourself successful and sane: Get organized.

Part Four

Take Risks. They're the Difference between a $30,000 Fixer-Upper and a $30 Million Mansion Built on Speculation

You miss 100 percent of the shots you never take. —Wayne Gretzky

The two weeks between April 1 and 15, 1999, were unique: It was the only time since I moved to Florida that I was completely free from debt and uncertainty. I had sold a huge lot for $27 million; I flipped a contract on another piece of land I owned for a week and made several million more. All my debt was gone; I had one project I was working on and it was proceeding on schedule and on budget. I looked at Nilsa and said, "Wake me, honey, I must be dreaming." It was great—for about five minutes. Then I got itchy. If I have money in the bank and no debt, I'm losing money. For me, uncertainty means I'm doing what I'm supposed to do: take risks. I'm known as the king of speculation, and I sure didn't want to lose that title by any action or inaction of mine. So I immediately started looking around for another property to develop.

I believe the primary difference between success and failure, between living an extraordinary life and enduring a boring one, lies in our willingness to take risks. All progress results from people who have had the courage to push the envelope and see how high they can go. Risk is a part of life. A one-year-old child risks injury with every

151

attempt to walk. We risk rejection every time we approach someone new. Every deal has the potential to go sour; every job has the potential to disappear overnight. Heck, with all the crazy drivers out there, we take our lives in our hands when we get behind the wheel of a car to drive to the supermarket! The question isn't "Are you taking risks?" but rather "How much risk are you willing to take?" If you're unwilling to risk even the smallest amount of time, emotion, effort, or money, you simply cannot succeed. Sure, you can maintain and exist, but you will never really live. The amount of risk you can tolerate and even enjoy will have a significant impact on your success and fulfillment in life. In his book, Donald Trump talked about the "art of the deal"; well, you can't make a deal without risk. This section is about the art of risk.

I've always been an adrenaline junkie. When I was a teenager back in Indiana, in addition to my other rebellious behavior, I used to climb TV towers that were at least 50 stories tall. It was a game; my buddies and I would climb to the top and leave a piece of clothing up there to prove we made it. When I grew up and left my partying days behind, I found different ways to feed my need for a rush. I ride the world's fastest production motorcycle that goes from zero to 60 in 2.2 seconds and has a top speed of 200 miles per hour (not that I'd ever drive it that fast). I once drove from Florida to the Indianapolis 500, a distance of 1,200 miles, in 13 hours, 35 minutes, 5 seconds; and we had to stop for Nilsa to go to the bathroom three times! The only time I'll take my Jet Ski out is when the waves are six or seven feet high so I can get as high out of the water as possible. I've also gone as fast as anybody around the quarter-mile-long go-cart track in my backyard.

I get that same adrenaline rush from being in the ultra-high-end speculative real estate market. I'm grateful I've found a career that satisfies my financial needs, meets my highest calling, and keeps my "need for speed" under control. I love it when someone tells me I can never sell a property for what I'm asking, or that only 50,000 people in the entire world can even afford it, or that no one's ever done this style of house in Palm Beach before, or, "You've made a mistake this time, Frank; no way you're not gonna get burned." Sometimes I feel like I'm back on top of one of those Indiana TV towers and a whole crowd has gathered at the bottom, just waiting to see me go "splat" into a hundred bloody pieces in front of them. That kind of attitude in others only serves to motivate me. Instead of backing away, I draw strength from the criticism and predictions of doom. My ability to conquer risk has enabled me to achieve every success I've ever experienced.

I've built up my risk muscle, little by little, and now it can handle almost anything. While I may risk more than most people, I've seen too many others who are afraid to take even the smallest chance. They don't have the spiritual and emotional muscles to handle the consistent effort and courage in the face of adversity that true success demands. They listen to the naysayers, doubters, and pessimists who tell them how dangerous risk can be. They force themselves to be content with small accomplishments and even smaller dreams, and call it "being realistic." Sadly, all it would take for them to live more abundant, exhilarating lives—where dreams can become reality in a flash, where effort is joyous and adversity welcomed, where spiritual, emotional, and financial rewards flow—is a willingness to take risks.

I am a firm believer that taking risks is a healthy and wholly human thing to do. Life is an adventure, and we all yearn to push ourselves to the limits of our potential. There is nothing else that will help us grow faster, both personally and professionally, than risk taking. It is the "difference that makes the difference" between me and the guy still digging sand traps after 20 years. When you make risk your friend and acclimate yourself to its demands, you'll start to see opportunities where you once saw only brick walls and dead ends. Your vision of who you are and what you're capable of won't just grow; it will expand at an exponential rate. And in my experience, your results and successes will expand just as rapidly.

Most of us can't handle the big risks right away. We need to build up to them, like a kid who goes from a tricycle to a bicycle with training wheels, to two wheels, to dirt bikes, mountain bikes, and motorcycles. I've spent the past 20 years strengthening my risk muscle every day, and by now it can handle almost anything. But I've also learned that the intelligent way to handle risk is to do your homework. Figure out exactly what a risk includes, what both the upside and the downside are, and whether this is a risk you can afford to take. When you've done that, you can forge ahead, confident of your ability to handle whatever this opportunity brings, ready to turn it to your advantage if at all possible.

To handle risk, you also have to believe in your vision and be unmoved by the criticisms of others. You have to have the courage of your convictions, even when you're entering unfamiliar territory. When I moved from distressed real estate to oceanfront property, I had no idea how to present this piece of inventory to the marketplace. After all, I'd never sold a property worth that much. But I did it anyway; I figured I'd been a pretty successful marketer before, and I could do it in this new context. Sometimes the biggest risk you can take is to declare, "Even though I've never done it before, I know what I'm doing." Research and homework can help you prepare, but ultimately a life of risk means attempting things you've never tried, and doing so with confidence.

And you've got to be willing to put it all on the line if necessary. I did that when I bought my first oceanfront property: selling my own house, taking out a sizable bank loan for the first time, and cutting expenses to the bone. We put over a million dollars into Driftwood Dunes, including purchase price and renovations, but I knew we had a potential upside of another million—more money than I had ever made in one year before. We finished renovations pretty quickly, but then the house sat on the market for 19 months. Almost all my capital was tied up in that house; the sensible thing to do would have been to go back to foreclosures and bring in a little money until the Dunes sold.

Well, by now you should be able to guess what I did. Instead of waiting, I used the equity I'd built in the Dunes property to buy another oceanfront lot. And then, instead of letting that second lot sit there and appreciate, I began the planning, designing, and permitting process on the project that became Château d'Amoureaux, a 12,000-square-foot mansion that sold for $5.9 million in 1996. I've continued to operate that way for almost 10 years: seizing opportunities as they were presented to me, and seeking them out if they were not.

It's not a smooth road; upon occasion I've come pretty close to the "crash and burn" that people were looking for. In 1995 when I started work on La Marceaux (the 23,000-square-foot house I designed and built from the ground up), I figured that if Château d'Amoureaux didn't sell I was going to run out of money after about 40 percent of the construction was completed. But I chose to start anyway because I was confident that Château d'Amoureaux would sell. Most of the Palm Beach County locals told me I was crazy, starting a $12 million house when my $5.9 million property hadn't sold. I didn't care; I was willing to take the risk. Managing and handling risk on a daily basis is essential for me, even when it's not easy.

In this section you'll discover the vital secrets of risk taking, within the world of real estate as well as every other area of business and life. You'll learn how to exercise your risk threshold like a muscle until it can withstand any weight. You'll discover the difference between risk taking and gambling, and how you can stack the deck in your favor. You'll learn to check your gut instinct, that inner guidance most of us don't pay enough attention to. You'll understand why it's important to say yes to opportunity as often as possible, and never to hesitate when you make a decision. Risk can bring failure at times, so you'll learn how to use failure to prepare you for even greater success. When you make your decisions based on the future and your imagination instead of past memories, you stand a much better chance of overcoming the fear of risk. And finally, you'll learn to reward yourself for each and every achievement no matter how small, helping you build all-important confidence in yourself and your efforts.

At some point in the process of learning to manage and handle risk, a wonderful transformation can happen: You stop perceiving risk as only risk and instead see it mostly as opportunity. And then you can see opportunity where nobody else can. You start to look forward to risk because of what it brings with it. You relish the challenge of pitting yourself against the odds and the crowd because it makes you strong. The stronger your detractors, the stronger your conviction. When the stakes get higher, you get stronger. The longer the odds, the greater your chance of success because of what you bring to the endeavor. Once you learn to make risk your friend, you can conquer whatever world you choose. You will control your success or failure. When you master risk, I believe you can change the mind of fate itself.

GentlyYet Often ExerciseYour RiskThreshold like a Muscle. Eventually It Will Become Stronger and Able toWithstand Greater Pressure

In June 2000 I stood at the entrance to my latest speculative real estate project, a $30 million mansion, getting ready to welcome five hundred members of Palm Beach society for a grand unveiling gala. Just then a reporter said, "Frank, you have an enormous amount of capital tied up in this house. The carrying costs of the loans, the utilities, the upkeep must be costing a fortune. But only a handful of people in the world can afford a place like this. Won't it be years before you can sell it?"

I smiled. "Possibly . . . although I think it'll sell by the end of the year." (I was right, by the way—it sold within five months, on November 8, 2000.)

"How can you sleep at night, knowing you have this financial albatross around your neck?" the reporter asked.

"Simple," I replied. "I've been building my risk muscle for years, and it's strong enough to withstand the pressure. By the way, it's not an albatross, it's a diamond necklace."

To succeed in life, you must take risks. Those who enjoy success at higher levels tend to risk more than others. My business—the world of speculative real estate—is nothing *but* risk. I undertake these million-dollar projects without a specific buyer. I'm the one who puts up the resources, pays all the subcontractors, buys all the top-grade materials, and supervises every detail of the building. According to the experts, because only 50,000 people in the world can afford the properties I build, I am supposed to have a .000007 percent chance of succeeding. And yet I have never lost money on a real estate deal.

That doesn't mean I've never been scared. I'm scared all the time; I've just gotten used to it. Scared means something different to me: a sensation resulting from the pursuit of an opportunity. That's because for the past 15 years I've been following this Philosophy: Gently yet often exercise your risk threshold like a muscle. Eventually it will become stronger and able to withstand greater pressure.

I built my risk muscle constantly through six years of buying and selling foreclosure properties before I ever moved to the oceanfront. I started by paying between $10,000 and $20,000 for a broken-down house, fixing it up, and selling it for $50,000 or $60,000. Eventually I took bigger risks, doing several properties at the same time. Then I really took a jump when I paid $50,000 for five boarded-up buildings that eventually were known as the Historic Executive Suites of Delray. I had to put another $250,000 into the renovations—more than I'd ever invested at one time in one project.

The jump to that first oceanfront property, Driftwood Dunes, took every bit of capital I had in 1992, and it sold in 1994 for $1.9 million. After that, each property was another big jump: $5.9 million for my next spec estate, Château d'Amoureaux, in 1996; $12 million for La Marceaux in 1998; $26 million for two pieces of property in 1999; and finally, the $30 million estate, which sold in November 2000. (I also had over a dozen smaller projects running at the same time these were.) But I would never have been able to handle the pressure of the multimillion-dollar properties had I not cut my teeth on those $10,000 and $20,000 foreclosures eight years earlier.

I believe there are three factors that make the difference between failure and success: *opportunity*, *fear*, and *risk*. The relationship looks like this.

Life is constantly presenting us with opportunities; unfortunately, many of them create fear because they take us beyond our comfort zone. "What will happen if I put all my savings into a down payment on this property?" "What if I ask that cute girl to the dance and she says no?" "Should I go into that new business?" "What happens if I fail?" All of us have been offered opportunities in our personal and professional lives and been afraid to take them, even if we knew they might bring great rewards.

So, how do we overcome fear? It's simple: *Start small.* I certainly didn't start out building multimillion-dollar homes. I began exercising my risk threshold by purchasing very small homes, sometimes no bigger than a 600-square-foot, one-bedroom crack house. I couldn't afford much, so I was forced to buy properties in some of the roughest drug- and prostitute-infested neighborhoods in Palm Beach County. My first house was so full of cockroaches that when I opened the front door, bugs rained down on my head like a waterfall!

Buying that first house was a huge risk for me because I put up all the money I had. I bought properties that nobody else wanted in neighborhoods others would not even consider entering. I had to believe that I could take these dilapidated properties and not only restore the physical structure but, by having the nicest house on the block, I might be able to turn around the neighborhood a bit, thus making it easier to sell my little house. This took courage and the ability to say yes to opportunity, thereby creating an even bigger opportunity for myself and the neighborhood.

The lesson I learned was, when given an opportunity that involves a certain amount of risk, spend as much time looking *inside* for direction as you do studying external information. I recommend you study as much as you can in as short a period of time as possible, to determine if it is in your best interest to risk. (This helps ensure that you allow your initial gut feeling to guide you. Often it's your best adviser when it comes to risk.) Then ask yourself two simple questions:

1. **What do I stand to gain from pursuing this opportunity?**
2. **What do I stand to lose if I *don't* pursue it?**

I usually find that the answer to the latter question overwhelmingly tells me to go for it! If you find it hard to define what you stand to gain with this opportunity, then perhaps you should abandon the effort. But if forgoing the opportunity leaves you with that "same old, same old" feeling of stagnation, then *the greatest risk may be in not taking one at all.*

Everybody has a different comfort level with risk. I like to represent risk tolerance as a continuum. On one end is the phobic who will not risk getting out of bed for fear the ground's too cold. On the other end is a daredevil like Evel Knievel.

Risk Continuum

Phobic   Daredevil

It is safe to assume that you fall somewhere in between these two extremes. But let me ask you, who do you think has the fuller life: the phobic or the daredevil?

As we evolve into mature adults our tolerance for risk is supposed to erode. While I personally don't believe this has to be true, I have seen it in others. So bulk up your risk muscle now, before you get any older, by taking small steps that might have intimidated you in the past. Have the Tupperware party at your house, even though your kitchen isn't as big as Mrs. Jones's. Ask that cute girl in your English class to the prom. Make an offer on the small duplex down the street. Some might say such small steps are insignificant. However, I have found that every time you exercise your risk muscle, you build confidence. If it is exercised often enough, you'll be able to undertake any feasible risk without hesitation.

Building your risk muscle is an evolutionary process that in time can be quite revolutionary because you will revolt against the "no's" in your life. Exercising your risk muscle will make you feel alive, full of excitement at the prospect of some new experience. Equally important, the advancement you will enjoy in your personal and professional life will astound you.

Remember, you can have fear without risk, but you really can't have risk without fear. When I decided to undertake our $30 million project (the largest, most expensive estate ever built on speculation), I certainly had to look risk and fear square in the eyes. But I was able to do so because I had been consistently exercising my risk muscle for 15 years, buying, building, restoring, and selling small houses, then bigger ones, then bigger ones still. Remember the "opportunity—fear—risk/don't risk" chart? There's one more step in the process: risk can lead to reward, while not risking leads to stagnation. And the more risk you are able to tolerate, the greater the potential rewards.

Exercising your risk tolerance will motivate you to challenge yourself. I am determined to make each project more beautiful, more cost efficient, and more profitable. I still strengthen my risk tolerance by increasing the physical size, financial exposure (upside), and complexity of the projects. But this has happened only because I have been vigilant about exercising my risk threshold for 15 years. It is now resilient and resistant to self-doubt, complacency, and inaction. So I challenge you to get into the gym of opportunity, fear, risk, and reward, and build your own risk muscle up to Mr. Universe size!

Actions

1. Determine where you fall on the risk threshold continuum. If you're closer to phobic than daredevil, it's time to get into the risk threshold gym. Say yes to small opportunities. When you're ready, seek out larger ones. Pursue such opportunities often enough to build your risk muscle.
2. Just like you would in a regular gym, keep pushing beyond your current comfort level. Set new standards for yourself, exceed them, and then set new ones. It's the only way to bulk up your risk biceps.

Deal Points

When I first started acquiring oceanfront properties, most people assumed my greatest risk was from the amount of money I was investing. But I was using the same business model I had been employing successfully for the prior eight years with smaller houses: buy something that was undervalued in the marketplace, fix it up or build it new at a reasonable cost, then sell it at a significant profit. Where's the risk in that? Truthfully, the greatest risk I was taking was in my interpretation of what this new market wanted. I was going to be renovating and building with a new type of buyer in mind. In your business if you continually exercise your risk threshold, you will undoubtedly find yourself in a similar situation. You're moving into a new line of real estate, or a new level of buyer. You're expanding your product line, or adding one to your existing business. You're opening a branch in a new city or country. Exercising your risk threshold means stepping into areas where you have no certainty of success. But I believe if you've built your risk threshold over time by taking small chances, you can get past the fear of not knowing what to do and use the information you have as well as your own instincts to find the best way.

Fear is the great blindfold in those times of uncertainty. When we're fearful, we can't see the clues that are right in front of us, the little things that let us know we're on the right track. But when you've exercised your risk threshold before you're faced with the big choices, fear is less likely to blind you. You have certainty based on past success. Even if it's not necessarily in the same area, you can use it to build your confidence.

When I was working on that very first oceanfront house, not quite knowing what its potential buyer might want, I did what I'd done when figuring out what the buyers of my first houses wanted. I put myself in their shoes and said, "What would I need to see in a house that would make me want to own it?" With the Dunes, I walked the property and thought, *I'm a successful businessman coming to my second or third home, ready to enjoy everything that South Florida has to offer. What do I want my home to look like?* And that's what I built. Sure, I made mistakes; there are things I did in that first house I would never do now. But I risked it, I learned, and more important, I succeeded; and I became a millionaire overnight.

As I said earlier, deciding which risks to take is always a question of research and instinct. You've got to do your homework to make sure the upside potential of the risk is good enough to make the effort worthwhile. But ultimately, you've got to use your instincts as well. I'm always for taking a chance and going for it. Over the years, I believe I have stretched the risk muscle of an entire marketplace here in Palm Beach County. The properties I have built (and the values they have commanded) are setting new standards for ultra-high-end real estate. It's an exciting feeling when you can create your marketplace rather than following it; and it entails nothing *but* taking risks. I'm a passionate believer in trusting my instincts and pushing the marketplace to accept my vision, because that's where legacies are built. I am most comfortable on the edge, leading the pack, going where no one has ventured before me because I have built that muscle over the years. If you can overcome your fear of risk and learn to make it your friend, you, too, can conquer whatever world you choose.

Never Gamble. Calculate the Maximum Amount of Risk You Feel You Can Afford to Take

I don't gamble. If I go to Las Vegas or the Bahamas and bet $100 (my absolute limit) and lose it, I'm likely to be in a bad mood for the rest of the night because I hate throwing away my hard-earned money. Yet when it comes to a business proposition (like some of the spec homes I build), what everybody else sees as an unbelievable gamble I view as simply a calculated risk. I believe if I can have some control over the risk, the project's worth doing. Otherwise, it's gambling and a waste of my time and capital.

This Philosophy is what allows me to harness my need for adrenaline and pushing the envelope and turn it into a business asset. I'm a fiend for doing my homework on every deal. Let's assume I'm looking to acquire a particular piece of oceanfront property. I know what the seller is asking for it, and I know what I'm willing to pay based on the property itself and the current condition of the marketplace. From there, I start calculating my risk. I always start with the upside, how much I can potentially make when I sell. What's the most I can make in this market I am creating? How high can I price this property and be able to justify the asking price? That figure is determined by what other properties in the area are selling for, how much oceanfront footage there is, the amount of land, the size of the house, and so on. I factor in scarcity (a finite supply of oceanfront property versus ever-increasing demand) and time. Oceanfront land values in Palm Beach County have been rising between 2 and 3.5 percent a month for quite a while. That means even if I do nothing but hold on to the real estate for a year, its value will have increased by approximately 24 to 42 percent. I also have to be able to forecast where the economy will be when I finish a project, not when I begin it. I price my homes for 18 to 24 months after I begin a project, as that's how long it will take to complete. (I also have to be able to set or recognize trends in styles, sizes, and finishes. A few years ago the biggest house on a large piece of land was the norm in ultra-high-end real estate. By the time this book comes out, however, I think the trend will be toward smaller houses on larger plots of land, with lots of outdoor amenities. That's what I'm building even as I write this.)

So the basics of pricing are (1) acquisition price, (2) appreciation of land, and (3) how long it will be before the property goes on the market. Then I start adding other factors. Any improvements I make to the property, whether I'm building new or doing renovations, are going to add significant value and get me closer to that ceiling price I want to establish. Keeping in mind that we use only the absolute best materials and craftsmanship, how much money is it going to take for me to improve it to the point I want? What will it cost me to build from the ground up? All of those are important calculations when it comes to my final net profit.

Now comes the part that's more indeterminate. How long will the property be on the market? What will the monthly carrying costs be? How much am I going to have to pay on bank loans, caretaker fees, upkeep, and so on? How long will I have to cover this monthly amount? (That last answer has to be as long as it takes. No house has been on the market forever. If I need to, I can always lower the price. I don't do it very often, but I could. And I'm banking on my ability to create a marketing plan—to be able to expose that property through word of mouth, publicity, advertising, and so on—to make the sale in a reasonable amount of time.) I calculate the risks, make sure I've taken into account every possible contingency and accounted for the consequences of every worst-case scenario. Then I start adding up the numbers, figuring out exactly what my risk level is for this particular deal. The entire process usually takes me less than a day. Once I feel certain I know what both my upside and potential downside are, then I check my gut instinct (see Philosophy #27). Often the deciding factor for me is, what if I *didn't* pursue this? What's the risk in the lost opportunity? After I've considered all of that, I usually find I can make my decision quickly.

When I was buying foreclosures, there was never a house I wouldn't take on. If it was standing, then I'd buy it and fix it up. But in the late 1980s/early 1990s there were some neighborhoods where I feared for my life. I considered them too big a risk because I knew I could get only so much for any house in those areas. There were also some neighborhoods nearby that weren't great but could go either way, up or down. By buying houses in those "verge" neighborhoods, I could get a little bit more for the house and also help turn an entire neighborhood around. Sure, it was a risk, but one with a great personal and professional upside.

In the late 1980s I did several houses in a neighborhood called Banker's Row in Delray Beach, Florida. At the time the neighborhood was definitely what you would call marginal at best. The properties were boarded up, with broken windows; there were prostitutes and drug dealers hanging out in them. I had actually started out looking at single properties, but quickly discovered it was more convenient for my small operation and its crew to work on houses that were close together. So I bought five foreclosed houses for anywhere from $20,000 to $70,000. Within the year not only had those five houses sold for prices in the $100,000 to $130,000 range, but we had turned the entire neighborhood around. (This was done with absolutely no government or Community Redevelopment Agency funding; I wasn't going to wait around for it.) I liked one of those Banker's Row houses so much that Nilsa and I moved into it ourselves. That was the house we sold for $225,000 to raise the money for my first oceanfront property deal.

I calculated the risk on the Banker's Row houses to the penny. I knew I could make money; I knew that if I improved these houses enough, they would attract the kind of buyers who would turn the neighborhood around. I also knew that by doing so many projects in such close proximity, I'd reduce my overhead and make more efficient use of my time and money. To me, whatever risk there was was far outweighed by the potential benefits.

With one project in particular I took an enormous but calculated risk and had it work out well. When I bought the five buildings that I turned into the Historic Executive Suites of Delray, I paid so little for them ($50,000) because there were $212,000 worth of city liens on the properties. Now, those buildings were in a prominent location, almost the gateway to Delray Beach. I had a feeling that the city commission might be willing to forgive at least a portion of the liens in exchange for us turning those buildings into something nice. I had no guarantee, though. They could have said, "Sorry, you're stuck with it. You owe us $212,000." Well, we ended up getting the liens negotiated down to a total of $7,000. It was the ultimate win-win: They ended up with nice buildings instead of flophouses; we ended up with a profit. But it was still a rather large, if calculated, risk.

Have I turned things down? Sure, when the margins aren't there. I've negotiated on properties on the buy side for quite a period of time, and finally walked away because I just couldn't get the price down to where I needed it to be. (Remember how often I've said that in real estate you make your money on the buy side.) I'm also not afraid to limit my upside if I don't think the market will support me. I'd rather hit a few singles and doubles, take a little bit lesser profit and move on, than hold out for a home run that may or may not happen. I don't need to hang on for the last dime in the margin. I'll give that up and find a new opportunity.

I am sure you can think of many instances when taking a risk proved to be a smart choice for you. You took a new job, changed the way your company does business, bought a house in an up-and-coming area, asked the girl (or guy) to marry you. Why did you succeed? I'll bet you researched your choices and spent time thinking about the risks at hand, both the upside and the downside. Once you figured the odds were in your favor, you probably went for it. In my book, that's the basis of sound, not risky, decision making.

The real key for me, however, is in the wording of this Philosophy: "Calculate the maximum amount of risk you feel you can afford to *take*," not "Calculate how much you can afford to *lose*." There's a big difference. Most people go into real estate or any other investment or business venture with the question, "How much can I afford to lose?" If you think you're going to lose, why are you doing it? As I said in the preceding chapter, build your risk threshold by taking small risks consistently, and then judge any new opportunity by how much risk you can carry given your current psychology, financial resources, and business acumen. That's the way to calculate whether you should take something on.

Being able to calculate risk helps me feel that I have control over my success and failure. It's also one of the reasons I've never lost money on a real estate transaction. I know what my upside and downside potentials are; with this knowledge, I believe I can make the right decisions every step along the way to keep myself on the positive side of the equation. When you calculate the amount of risk you can afford to take, keeping in mind both the upside and the downside, you aren't gambling; you're simply making the most intelligent choice for where to put your time, money, and efforts.

Actions

1. Where have you taken a risk and had it work out to your bene-fit? How did you make the decision to go for it? What were your calculations? Have you taken a risk and it didn't work out? Did you calculate your risks beforehand? If so, where did you go wrong, and how can you learn from that choice? If you didn't calculate your risks, what would have happened if you had?
2. When faced with an opportunity, don't automatically say yes or no. Instead, calculate just how much risk you can afford to take in this particular area. Then make your decision and don't look back.

Deal Points

Let me talk a little here about a couple of places where I *don't* believe that taking a lot of risk is to your benefit. The first is financing. I used to have a complete aversion for high levels of debt. I worked very hard from the time I first became an entrepreneur to establish excellent credit, and I've done everything in my power never to risk my credit rating unnecessarily. When I began buying and selling distressed real estate, I did it almost entirely with my own money. I had a few in-vestors, but very quickly I was using my equity alone to finance my business. When I speak with people who want to get into the real estate business, I tell them, "While it may work for some, I do not subscribe to the 'no money down' concept. What if there's a downturn in the economy or the real estate market slows for any reason, and you're stuck with property that's not selling? The interest meter on your loans doesn't slow down when the market does; it just keeps running and you keep getting farther and farther behind. Put your own money on the line first. Save to start with, then use your savings. Borrow from friends and family before you go to the bank, and borrow as little as possible. Then make sure to keep your credit good by faithfully paying back any loans on time. That's the best way I know to get into real estate with as little risk as possible."

Another place I have learned to avoid taking risks is in curb appeal. I built two of my spec properties, Château d'Amoureaux and La Marceaux, in the style of a French château, a very unusual choice for the Palm Beach marketplace. Most of the houses down here are more influenced by Mediterranean, Spanish, and Italian architecture, so my two properties really stood out. I knew at the time they were going to attract a very specific kind of client, but I believed the buyers were out there. Luckily, I was proved right. Since then, however, I have gotten a little more conservative about the outward appearance of my properties, letting the gates and walls and the entryways reflect a more refined yet luxurious style. Where I take my risks now are on interior elements. I'll have deep azure, quartz-granite countertops in a kitchen, for example, or a study that is be a scaled-down replica of the Oval Office. As long as I believe I am tapping into the taste of the would-be buyer, I feel I can create as much "wow" factor as I want inside. People either love or hate my houses, and that's fine with me. After touring a $15 million home of mine, I wouldn't expect a buyer to say, "Gee, that was kind of nice." They must love it to make the decision to purchase. If they don't, I quickly move on to the next prospect. That's the kind of calculated risk I'm happy to take.

The one place I will *never* take a risk is in making a decision without doing my homework first. I learned to do my homework in the foreclosure market, when I was faced with 40 properties a week to choose from and each choice meant a large chunk of my capital. I also discovered that by doing your homework well, you could find some absolutely astounding values that might represent a year's worth of profits in just one transaction. Once, I remember, a very nice oceanfront condominium in Jupiter, Florida, was in foreclosure. Now, in a foreclosure sale the county clerk has to receive a certificate of service, showing that the property had been advertised in the newspaper on consecutive dates. Usually the lawyer or representative of the bank brings the certificate to the auction, then bids on the property himself or herself to ensure the bank gets at least the amount of its loan out of the sale. Well, in this case the lawyer mailed the certificate in and didn't show up for the sale. No one from the bank was there to bid on the property and run the price up! Three of us at the auction realized this and went in on the condo together. I think we ended up paying $4,000 total for the property. Of course, the lawyer realized his mistake and tried to get the sale set aside, but the judge told him no dice. We sold the condo for $125,000, and split the profits three ways. You can see why I will *never* risk not doing my homework!

There are all kinds of risks in real estate: declining market values, economic downturns, changing tastes, neighborhoods deteriorating, fires, floods, and hurricanes. The key to success is to be like a bank. In the same way a bank calculates how much money it can afford to lend you, you should calculate how much risk you can afford to take on any given venture, based on past experience, market conditions, willingness to work, and so on. Once you've decided to take the risk, however, it's up to you to make it happen. Almost any external factor can be overcome with our own grit and determination. I believe that with enough commitment we can turn anything around—especially if we've been smart enough to know what our risks are to begin with.

Trust in, and Act on, Your Initial Gut Feeling

When I tell people how much I rely on my intuition—that initial gut instinct telling me whether the deal is one I want to go for or not—they're amazed. "You mean you risk millions, sometimes tens of millions of dollars, based on something as fluffy as *intuition*?" they ask. Yep. If a deal doesn't feel right to me, no matter how great it may look on paper I'm probably going to pass. And conversely, if there's a significant risk involved but my gut tells me, "Go for it," as long as the possibility for profit is there, I'll say yes.

We all have that intuitive little voice inside us, but very few of us act on it. We don't listen to the feeling inside that urges us to give it a shot, whether it's a logical choice or not. Then often we find ourselves saying afterward, "I knew I should have done that—I felt so all along!" Gut instinct is not just the result of the bean burrito you ate for lunch; it's a valid voice in the decision-making process.

I'm not saying you should rely *only* on intuition. As should be clear by now, I'm a fanatic about doing the research, checking out the deal, reading the contracts, dotting the "i's" and crossing the "t's." I apply logic and common sense to every opportunity presented to me. But I've never found that following my intuition ran counter to what my common sense was telling me, too. (Quite honestly, without much educational background, and with only the experience I could gain through my own hard work, I had to learn to observe *and* sense *and* check my gut whenever I broke new ground in my business.)

I tend to make decisions very quickly. The time between the stimulus (the offer to buy or sell) and my response is always as short as I can make it and still cover my bases. I always run the numbers and throw in a few worst-case scenarios, but then I check inside. Was my first response to this deal favorable or otherwise? What's the feeling I'm getting now—to go for it or not? If the choice isn't clear-cut and I'm not quite sure what to do, I trust in and act upon that initial gut feeling.

I learned to trust my gut early on when I was looking at upwards of 40 distressed properties every week. Sure, I'd always research them thoroughly, but I'd drive by the properties, too. Not only to make sure the house was still standing; not only to eyeball the extent of work I might be called to do; not even just to check out the condition of the neighborhood, even though I did all those things. I would look at a house and get a hunch on whether this particular property in this specific neighborhood would be something I'd be able to make money on. A favorable hunch was a subliminal feeling that I started calling "Midas," because whenever I had it, I knew the deal would work out.

While I think some people are born with more intuition than others, I absolutely believe this feeling can be honed and cultivated. The more you listen to that voice or heed that feeling, the clearer it becomes. Let's use the $30 million house as an example. That property, which included beautiful grounds and a large existing house that I would need to renovate completely, came my way just as I had had to give up my dream of building a $40 million house from scratch on a huge piece of oceanfront land in Manalapan, Florida. I had spent a lot of time creating the vision for that $40 million house—architects' designs, full models to scale, and so on. I was so excited about that property, but then I received a fantastic offer for the land alone. After a lot a painful soul-searching I had decided to let my 60,000-square-foot dream house go. But at almost the same time this other property appeared. As soon as I saw it, there was this overwhelming rush of feeling inside me. I knew the only way I'd lose would be if I *didn't* pursue this opportunity. I couldn't build my dream house? This was the next best thing. I could renovate instead of build while creating a new standard of luxury and taste for the marketplace, and it would take around a year to do instead of the two-and-a-half-year process of building from scratch. Even though it was a fearsome amount of capital to lay out at the time

(I had several other smaller properties going, too), I followed my gut and went for the new deal. And that property set new records for both me and my business.

Another time, my instinct told me to take the money and move on. (I hate when it does that; I prefer getting in there and doing my thing.) A few years ago I bought a property in Gulf Stream, Florida, consisting of a house built in the 1960s on a 100-foot oceanfront lot. I was going to renovate the house and ask $6.4 million, a record for the area. (The property next door had just sold for $4.2 million.) But right then, someone offered me $3.5 million for the house and property as is. That represented a significant profit to me. I was ready to go ahead on the house and forge a new market high in Gulf Stream, but I thought, "Hey, this is a message. I want to get back to Manalapan, where I've got that big job, and there are a couple of other things up there, too. Let's take the cash and move on." That turned out to be a very wise decision, as it allowed me to pour all my focus into our big property and get it on the market even faster.

I also rely on my gut instinct a lot when it comes to people. In some cases, my feeling may be based on observation. I'm a keen observer and listener; I'm always trying to figure out what's going on in the other guy's head. (See Philosophy #20, "Sit on the other side of the desk first.") When I meet people, interview them for jobs, choose subcontractors, and so on, I rely on my gut instinct, and it's very rarely off. In fact, I rely on it so much that I often hire people for jobs they've never done, simply based on my instincts about them. I've gone up to guys who are banging nails on somebody else's job site and said, "You know, even though you're not the greatest carpenter now, I'll bet you could turn into one. Come see me if you're interested." I did the same thing when I hired a new assistant not too long ago. There was this great lady who's married to a longtime friend of mine on the local police force. She worked in a bank for 20-odd years and had never done any kind of administrative assistant work, but I knew her and knew she would be great at the job. And she is.

One place I almost always go with my gut is with design elements on the multimillion-dollar houses I build or renovate. One of the jobs of my president of construction is to ask about some of my more outlandish decisions, "Frank, are you sure you want to do this?" And often I'm tempted to change my mind, because nobody likes to be doubted. But after I look at the space or the design, I'll usually go back to my original gut instinct to put a sunken bar in the corner of the living room, for example, or a koi pond inside a $15 million house, or double doors leading from the master bathroom to an outdoor balcony. I don't know how much of my intuition is based on instinct and how much on knowing my marketplace, but following it has certainly helped establish my estates as unique in the industry.

Too many of us have a tendency to talk ourselves out of great decisions. We ponder; we equivocate; we second-guess ourselves out of what turns out to have been the right course. And I think that if more people would stick with their true initial gut feelings and commit themselves quickly, they'd make better decisions overall. I tell the superintendents and managers on our jobs, "I would rather you act on a hundred decisions in a day and be wrong on five than act on a dozen and be right on all of them. I'll never jump on you for making a decision even if it costs me a little bit of money, as long as I know you were trying to move things forward."

The toughest time for me is when a deal isn't logical *and* my intuition says no. It's very hard for me to pass on an opportunity. I'd rather have my plate overflowing than be comfortable with what's on it. But when something's not meant to be, it's pretty clear: Either logic and intuition say no, or I go after the deal and give it my best shot but it feels like I'm swimming upstream. At that point, I figure maybe God is looking out for me and keeping me from doing something stupid. I'll say, "It's not meant to be," and move on. You've got to stay tuned in to that gut instinct and make the decision without too much pondering— then work like heck to make sure it turns out the way your intuition says it will!

Actions

When faced with a decision, apply logic and common sense, and then check your intuition. Take a moment to see what your initial gut instinct is about the deal, or the job, or the relationship, or whatever. Then decide, and start making your intuition come true.

Deal Points

When it comes to negotiating, you have to do your homework and know your figures backward and forward, but you've also got to have an intuitive sense about two things. First, the marketplace. If the market for ultra-high-end property is hot and getting hotter, you can hold out for more money. However, if you think the market has hit a peak and is on the way down, perhaps it's time to take a little less and do the deal. As I've said elsewhere, I think my marketplace is moving toward smaller houses on bigger lots, with extensive outdoor elements like pools, grottoes, gazebos, and so on. I'm building a new 10,000-square-foot ultra-luxurious house based on my intuition; we'll see if I'm right.

The second thing to use your intuition for is in knowing when the other guy is willing to go higher or lower and when he or she is out of wiggle room on a particular deal. In 1998 I sold La Marceaux, a 23,000-square-foot home I built from scratch, before the season started here in Palm Beach. (The season lasts from October to May; that's when all the seasonal people come down for the good weather, and the average wealth per capita in Palm Beach County triples overnight.) If I had waited, I could perhaps have gotten a million more than I ended up with, but something told me, "Sell now." I followed my instincts and sold. Was I right? I don't know. But one thing I learned from my dad was never to look back and regret a decision you have made. You made it, it's over, move on. And I did—within a year after selling La Marceaux I had sold three other pieces of property.

On the other hand, if you get the impression that the person across the table from you really wants what you have, hold out for all you're worth. Especially when you're dealing with the high-end market, another million dollars might be nothing to your buyer who's worth a half a billion; but a million dollars more profit is a big thing to me. You have to ride that intuition train carefully, though, because if you hold out too long even a high-end buyer can walk away. Tune in to your customer and see how much you can pick up of his or her bottom line. Then trust your instincts, be flexible, and do the deal.

Make a Commitment to Yourself to Say Yes More Than No. Don't Hesitate.

We spend approximately the first five years of our lives being told "no" constantly. "Don't touch that." "Don't put that in your mouth." "Don't climb that—it's too dangerous." In order to protect our children, we surround them with a fence of "no's." Is it any wonder that a lot of us grow up reluctant to try things, to put it on the line, to risk? "No, I can't buy that property." "I'll never get that job, so why should I apply for it?" "I'm not asking her out—she's too pretty." We've become our own parents, trying to protect ourselves from hurts that are, for the most part, completely imaginary! And we close ourselves off from the possibilities of a more successful life.

I do my best to limit the number of times I tell my daughter "no." She's three years old now, and believe me, she gets into a lot! She's also growing so fast she can be a little clumsy, so it's possible she'll hurt herself if she tries things. I'll say, "Be careful," and I may try to direct her away from something that's not good for her, but I really want to get her used to hearing "yes"—because that's what I want her to say whenever she's faced with a challenge or an opportunity.

There are two stories in my family that I always remember when I contemplate this Philosophy. One is about my grandfather and Walt Disney (see Part One). But the second happened with my dad. As you might remember, he was an Olympic swimmer in the 1956 and 1960 Games, and the swim teams were training on the island of Hawaii, on the Kona coast. Back then, Kona was a dumpy part of a dumpy island. It took forever to get there, and there was nothing but cattle and the occasional coffee plantation on the island; so it was the perfect place for the swim teams to get away and train. Now, somebody found out my dad's family background, and they knew my grandfather was interested in all kinds of investment opportunities. So they offered my dad the chance to buy a huge chunk of the Kona coast for almost no money. My dad talked it over with my grandfather and they both decided to pass. After all, who would spend all the time it took to get out to Hawaii in the first place, then bypass Oahu and the other islands to come out to the rat- and bug-infested Kona coast? Of course, today the parcel of land they could have bought is covered with luxurious megahotels, golf courses, condos, and resorts, and is worth hundreds of millions of dollars.

Those were both very expensive "no's" for the McKinneys—and I vowed very early on that I wouldn't add a similar story to the list. I'd much rather say yes to an opportunity and be proved wrong than say no and regret what I passed up. (I think I also feel that way because I believe I can always turn an opportunity to my advantage, even if it turns out other than the way I planned.)

The hardest opportunities to say yes to are the ones that take us out of our comfort zone—you know, that little patch of ourselves that we've fenced in with our "no's" all these years. To tell the truth, my business comfort zone is a lot bigger than my personal one, maybe because I've focused so consistently on business when I've stretched my risk muscle. I'm much more likely to hang around with my family and a few close buddies than expand my circle of friends very much. This is a trait I need to work on, and I've started to reach out to more people. Recently I asked a good friend and his wife to come to Colorado with my family for a Super Bowl weekend. We had a great time and got a lot closer as a group. I was delighted I had stepped out of my comfort zone and extended the invitation.

Another area where I am continually expanding my comfort zone is with public speaking. I'm frequently asked to speak to groups, but it's never something I can do off the cuff. I also can't use a written speech without it sounding canned, so I always speak from a few notes. I'm getting better at it, but it's still a conscious decision on my part to say yes. It'd be easy for me to say, "I'm busy that day," and avoid the anxiety, preparation, and effort. But somehow the rewards when I say yes always outweigh everything else.

What's especially sad to me are all the opportunities we turn down that never come around again. You say no to asking out the woman of your dreams and you never have another chance. You stay safe by remaining in your dead-end job instead of submitting your great invention to the Patent Office, only to see someone else bring out a similar design two years later and strike it rich. That perfect house you've always wanted comes up for sale, but you're afraid you can't make the payments or your credit isn't good enough to get the kind of loan you need, so you don't even call to find out about it. At the end of your life you're living in a teeny-weeny comfort zone, which hasn't expanded for the last 50 years. The fence of "no's" surrounding you is now a cement wall 12 feet high. You're safe, all right—but are you really living?

We each need to push past our comfort zones. We need to get in the habit of saying yes as our first reaction rather than our second. Like this Philosophy says, don't hesitate. In that moment of consideration, it's all too easy to talk yourself out of things. When you are faced with a decision, make it, and don't ponder about it too long. Pondering is usually nothing but putting off a decision out of fear. After a certain point (and it comes pretty quickly, in my opinion), pondering becomes shilly-shallying. Decide "yes" or "no," but get on with it.

I'm not talking about being stupid, however; you've got to make educated decisions. And there are times when "no" is the appropriate answer. Last year I saw that Buckskin Joe's, a tourist attraction "frontier town" near Cañon City, Colorado, where we have our vacation home, was being sold. It's an Old West town composed of 25 historic buildings, some standing on their original sites and others brought in from all over the state, and a railroad. I spent almost a year negotiating to buy the town, but recently I sent a letter saying no. We just couldn't come to an agreement on terms, and even though I know I could make a success of running it and have a lot of fun doing so, I'm not going to go against my common sense.

When I'm faced with an offer to buy or sell a piece of property, I'm not going to just say yes and to heck with common sense. I do a lot of figuring and weighing of options and alternatives and scenarios before I'll accept a deal; but once I see the numbers are what I want, then I say yes without hesitation. You want to get to the point where it's natural for you to say yes more than no, because no matter what the results, saying yes will bring more possibilities and opportunities. It'll not only open things up for you, it'll open *you* up. And that's always a good thing.

Remember the Reagan-era drug prevention slogan, "Just say no"? When it comes to stretching your comfort zone, accepting opportunities when they're presented, attempting new things that may have enormous benefits for you, your business, and your life, I believe you should "just say yes." Any regret you might feel if things don't pan out or if the road is a little bumpy for a while is going to be a lot less than the regret you'll experience when you look back over a lifetime of "no's" and hundreds of missed opportunities that could have brought you so much, or even worse—the contributions you never made to the world because you were too afraid to jump in with both feet. Practice saying yes—it's your ticket to a more abundant, expanded world, a world where it's easy to make it big.

Actions

1. Commit to saying yes more than no for a week. Whenever you're faced with a decision, make your automatic response "yes." See how much richer your life is as a result.
2. See if you can reduce the amount of time it takes you to make a decision, especially if you've been a ponderer in the past. Weigh your options and get the facts, but educate yourself and then decide quickly, without hesitation. Even if you're wrong, it doesn't matter. You can almost always fix things or handle the consequences. But I'll bet more of your decisions will work out than won't.

Deal Points

When you say yes, you have to be willing to handle the risks and back up your decision with good, hard cash. When Driftwood Dunes was still on the market, the opportunity came up to buy another piece of oceanfront property for $1.325 million. I had very little cash because almost everything was tied up until the Dunes sold. Remember, this was my first foray into oceanfront real estate, and I had no idea how long the Dunes would be on the market. Remember also, I had sold everything and moved into an efficiency apartment to buy the Dunes; buying this second piece of property would mean Nilsa and I would have to continue living close to the bone. But I knew what a good deal that property was, I had a sense that the oceanfront market was only beginning to get hot, and I felt I could do something really great with this opportunity. So I called my broker and said, "Make the offer." I said yes even though it would be a major stretch financially and with no certainty when or how it would pay off. But that property was where I built my first "from the ground up" spec house, Château d'Amoureaux, which sold for $5.9 million.

Saying yes takes *cojones*, but as long as you can back up your decisions with good, solid research and the commitment to make them work, then you'll almost always come out ahead. In fact, I believe it's the only way to create any kind of success.

Be Prepared to Fail Before You Succeed

I am a perfect example of this Philosophy. As I've said before, I was a massive screw-up as a teenager. From being an altar boy and great tennis player, the son of a respectable Indiana family, I became a wrecking ball. I was a complete loser. I did drugs. I sold drugs. I drank like a fish. I vandalized. I stole a lot of things, like cars in which I went joyriding. I was arrested and remanded to juvenile detention several times, and was even in jail a few times as a teenager. (Fitting, because I was voted "most likely jail candidate" at my high school.) I was the type of kid who would throw a brick through a car window and laugh. You would not want your son to hang around with me for fear of my corrupting influence, much less your daughter (for obvious reasons). I had friends whose families would not permit me even to set foot on their property. If you've ever been inside a Catholic church, you may have seen the offering boxes where you put money to pay for candles you can light at a shrine. Well, this ex-altar boy broke into those boxes and stole the pitiful amounts of cash they contained. I was sent to various reform schools and boarding schools (four in four years) because I kept screwing up. I turned my back on all the opportunities I was presented with and caused my family and the community I lived in untold misery. I wouldn't let anybody help me or even get near me; I was on my way to being a drain on society. One of the reasons I left Indiana and moved to Florida was the fact that I was such a massive, public failure at home.

The only good thing about all these failures is that I got them out of my system early, and stopped by the time I was 18. What changed for me? I looked at where I was headed and decided I wanted to make something of my life. I began to take responsibility for my actions and vowed to be accountable for the decisions I was making. I began to study how successful people lived, and I added discipline to my life. I listened intently to my conscience. No more late nights, no more vices. Within a year of my moving to Florida, I had my tennis business going. My rebellious side was still showing up every so often, particularly in a desire to break the speed limit, but basically I was committed to changing my ways. Instead of being the most spectacular loser ever, I was going to leave a legacy I would be proud of.

Many of the great people you and I look up to have experienced a great deal of failure in their lives. Michael Jordan was cut from his high school basketball team; during his professional career he missed 55 percent of the shots he took. The best baseball players command $10 million and more a season if they can hit over .300—which means they fail 70 percent of the time they come to the plate. Abraham Lincoln lost far more elections than he won. Thomas Edison tried 996 times to invent the lightbulb before he succeeded. In business there are countless stories of men and women who have come back from bankruptcy to run billion-dollar companies.

I actually believe we learn more from our failures than from our successes. Success can breed arrogance, complacency, laziness, a sense of being invincible. Failure will shock you. It will cause you to become acutely aware of where you went wrong and if analyzed objectively can prevent you from making the same mistake again. You must look at failure as a celebrity teacher, a mentor who might make random and infrequent appearances, but when he or she does you must make certain to pay close attention and learn the lesson as quickly as possible.

In truth, failure is one of the most important parts of each and every life. Hard words? Not really. When you try something new, you'd *better* be prepared to fail before you succeed. How many kids do you know who walk on their first try? Or ride a two-wheeler bicycle down the driveway without taking at least one header? And if you mastered fractions the first time someone taught them to you in school, you're better than I am. Learning is nothing but the process of using our failures to teach us how to do it right.

One of the best lessons I ever learned came when I bought my first oceanfront property. I completed the renovation in just four months and put it on the market at the price I thought it would sell for, $2.2 million.

Within the first month, a buyer offered me $1.9 million. That amount would absolutely meet my required profit margin, but remember, I was new to this marketplace. So I turned down the offer. Eighteen months and a lot of carrying costs later, I sold for very close to that same $1.9 million. The lesson I learned on that first house has made me a lot of money on the multimillion-dollar deals I do now. In that case, and many others, I was determined to learn from my mistakes and never make the same one twice if I could help it.

All of us are fallible. We're all going to make mistakes, and sometimes the most difficult thing is to admit them—or to have them pointed out to us. Failure is the best indication I know that you need to pay attention to something, either an area of your business or a part of your personality. For example, along with many other entrepreneurs I can be a little bit of a control freak. (Okay, a *lot* of a control freak.) I tend to micromanage, yet I have an absolutely great team of people who work with me. I know I can rely on them, and I want to encourage them to think for themselves and grow in their jobs. Well, this past January, as always, we had a company meeting where we set our objectives for the year. As a group we came up with 25 different objectives, everything from selling specific properties to having a company picnic. I told my team about some plans I had to help make all of us more autonomous, interactive, and efficient—things like personal digital assistants (PDAs), walkie-talkies, and so on. And someone said, "Well, if you want us to be autonomous, you have to back off. You're going to have to let us do our jobs." That to me was a failing, and something I needed to take a look at. I'm working very hard now to make sure my team has the autonomy they want while they take responsibility for producing the results we need.

Most failures are compounded with the feeling of regret, and that's not a bad thing—as long as you use the feelings to motivate you. Things like regret, inadequacy, and failure can keep us humble and show us the perils that might lie on a particular path of action or a particular way of being. One of the ways you can use failure is during your weekly introspection (see Philosophy #3). Every Saturday I sit down and ask myself, "Where have I failed to live up to my vision? Where have I failed in accomplishing my goals?" I usually find several areas in which I have failed to live by the Philosophies contained in this book. But here's the secret to using failure rather than being overcome by it: *Don't take failure personally.* Failure is not a sentence handed to us by fate, and it is not who we are. *You* are not a failure; you just failed at something. Failure is nothing but a sign to try again. Get up, dust yourself off, learn what you can, and then steamroll those failures right out of your life.

Today I embrace failure as a challenge and chance to change the mind of fate itself. Like Rocky Balboa, or Michael Jordan, or Thomas Edison, I will not let a little thing like failure keep me from my ultimate vision. I will learn from fate but remain unbowed. As the great football coach Vince Lombardi put it, "It's not whether you get knocked down. It's whether you get up again." And, I might add, whether you learn from the knocks you get along the way.

Actions

1. Use your weekly introspection time to examine your successes and failures. Pay particular attention to the areas in which you didn't meet your own expectations. Were they due to deficiencies in your approach? Challenges with your personality? Bad choices? Systems that don't work? Learn from what's not working, and then move on.
2. If you're starting anything new, expect to have some failures along the way. You'll learn more from them than you will from your successes.

Deal Points

If you are a manager or a team leader or the president of your little entrepreneurial company, sometimes the hardest but best thing you can do is admit your mistakes. Internally, when something goes wrong in my company, 95 percent of the time I'll let it sit on my shoulders. Not too long ago, a gentleman contracted my company to do some work on his house. He asked for a "cost plus" estimate, which means I charge whatever our costs are plus a percentage. He was in a hurry and so was I, so I guesstimated that the total for the job would be $150,000, and faxed the written estimate over to him.

Well, the gentleman called me back and said, "I need more detail on this. Can you send me a breakdown of the costs?" Of course I didn't have one. I apologized to the client and said I would send it over within a day or two. Then I had to call my president of construction and tell him what had happened, and ask him to put together the real numbers for me. "This is my fault," I told him. "I should have done it myself or asked you to do it from the beginning."

Often our failures in business come when we apply our strengths inappropriately. I have a reputation for getting things done quickly, but in the above example doing it quickly created a sticky situation with a client. I'm great at getting publicity for my brand and my products, but I can tread a fine line between good publicity and being viewed as an overbearing egotist out to get his name in the papers no matter what. I'm meticulous when it comes to every detail of the properties I build, yet if I try to control my people in the same way I will drive them insane. The key, as I said earlier, is continually to look at your failures and mistakes and learn from them. In my view, only if you repeat a mistake again and again does it become the kind of failure that can derail your progress and undermine your success. But above all, never let failure get in the way of trying again. Failing to try is the most devastating failure of all. And like Thomas Edison, you never know whether the next attempt to invent the lightbulb will be the one that succeeds.

Live in the Future instead of the Past—Use Imagination, Not Memory, When Making Decisions

You wouldn't think that we'd already be calling the 1990s the "good old days," would you? Yet with the decline in the stock market that started in 2000, a lot of people are looking back on the hot economy when their jobs were safe and their stock portfolios were worth a lot of money. (Heck, by the time you're reading this book the economy could be hot again, who knows.) It seems the older we get or the worse times become, the more we yearn for days gone by rather than focusing on the future. But in business and in life, I think that's one of the worst mistakes you can make. As someone once said, it's like trying to drive using only your rearview mirror. I recommend focusing on where you want to go (i.e., the future) and using imagination rather than memory when making important decisions.

This Philosophy has contributed greatly to my life. After all, if I had used the past as my reference instead of focusing on the future, I'd still be running a tennis business, or even worse, I could have been a significant drain on society. At the very least, I'd still be buying and selling foreclosures at $100,000 a pop, rather than multimillion-dollar estates. That was a huge leap for me, personally and professionally, and one I would never have had the confidence to make if I based the decision on what I had been doing up to that point. I went from spending $20,000 to buy a property to $775,000, an increase of 3,875 percent in my investment. And that didn't include the $350,000 I figured I would need to put into additions and renovations. I had been doing very well with buying and selling distressed properties, yet here I was, putting everything I had on one throw of the dice, changing the direction of my business significantly for a very uncertain return. If I had used the past for my reference point, it never would have happened.

But I didn't. Rather than saying, "What have I done like this before?" I asked, "How will this affect my future? How might I change my future by making this choice?" Then I went to Nilsa and told her, "We're knocking our heads against the wall trying to do 20 houses a year. I think we can make the same amount of money on one or two, if we focus on oceanfront property. There's such a limited supply out there that if we do it right, apply the same approach to renovating or building that we're doing, I honestly think we could really do well. Let's mortgage it all and give it a shot." Luckily, Nilsa's a future thinker, too, and she agreed that we should go for it.

When you're just getting started in any field, you've got to rely on the future rather than the past, because you don't have any past to speak of. I learned quickly throughout the years to be able to sell myself based on my future results rather than what I had done in the past. Not too long after I moved to Florida and was working at the country club maintaining the tennis courts and digging sand traps, I watched the tennis pros giving lessons and thought, *I can do that!* But I needed professional certification before I could teach. So I went to the club's general manager and sold him on my future. I said, "I want to teach tennis for you. Here's the accreditation I want to get. I don't have the money, but if you front me the fees necessary for tuition, I'll pay you back from my lessons." The general manager admired my guts, and underwrote my tuition. I went to the school and graduated with the highest rating you could get from the United States Professional Tennis Registry. And eventually I turned that certification into my first business, the Professional Tennis Service.

Being a real estate developer is all about the future. It's about your vision for a property, and how you are realizing it; it's about the next job rather than the previous one. I often refer to it as having a keen sense of the big picture. I start by seeing my desired result, and work back from there. Every successful businessperson I know has this kind of future focus. You can't ever rest on your laurels. You always have to be looking ahead at what you will do next, the results for the next quarter, the next year, the next five years. I've heard there are Japanese companies that even have hundred-year plans. (Now that's a future focus!)

You can't base your future success on your past efforts, either. With the speed of change in business today, your entire profession can take off in a new direction and leave you gasping in the dust. How much has changed in real estate in the past five years? Clients tour properties by clicking a mouse and viewing 3-D projections on their computers. (By the way, an entire industry has arisen to make those films and put them on web sites for realtors.) Prospective home owners shop for loans on web sites instead of at their local banks. Deals can close in hours instead of days through the use of e-mail, faxes, cell phones, PDAs, and so on. If you're doing business the same way you were even five years ago, you're losing the competitive race by a very wide margin.

Making decisions based on the future instead of the past isn't always easy, for me or anyone else. We find our security in our memory, in what has worked for us in the past. But I've seen far too many people become trapped by relying solely on their past experiences when it comes to charting their future courses. These people get to a certain point and then just stop growing. They stagnate at the level where they believe they deserve to be. They lose any sense of vision because they are looking to the past instead of the future.

I'm not advocating forgetting the past entirely, because I believe there are lessons to be learned from it. In some ways, I tend to let the past go almost too quickly. Once a deal is done, I'm on to the next challenge. When I make a choice on whether to pursue something, of course I consider factors like commitment of time and resources, benefits to my business or life, and so on. But one of the first and last questions is always, "Will this take me where I want to go, as a businessperson and a man?" I don't ask, "Have I succeeded at this before?" If I had asked those kinds of questions, I would never have gotten into real estate, started buying oceanfront properties, or written this book. Most of my success has come from a willingness to focus on the future and take chances based on my vision of who I want to be.

You can't let your life be dictated by what has happened to you before. You've got to learn your lessons from the past and move on. Use imagination rather than memory when making decisions that affect the course of your life or business, and you'll always be ready for your next new success.

Actions

1. What's your vision for your future? When you make decisions, are you basing them on what you've done before or on what you want to accomplish and believe you can become?
2. Are you holding on to the past because you're afraid? Learn your lessons and move on. Every day is a new opportunity to create a new future.

Deal Points

You would think that banks would be focused almost completely on past results, but as a developer I can tell you that your biggest job is to get them to focus on the future. When a developer goes into a bank to apply for a loan, what is he or she selling? The future. You're selling the bankers your ability to create something that will allow you to pay back the money they're loaning you. Yes, they'll look at your past results and your collateral and all that; that may affect how much they loan you, or the terms. But I believe your vision of the future is just as important.

I had been buying and selling foreclosure real estate for almost six years before I applied for a loan to help me with the first oceanfront property. In that presentation, I focused completely on making my vision of the future of that project as real and vivid to the bank officers as it was to me. I went to a community bank so the loan committee would know the property and be able to visualize what I was talking about. I put together a presentation package that included every kind of picture and chart I could come up with. Then I invited the bank's local board of directors out to see the property. I tried to think like the bankers would (see Philosophy #20), so I could anticipate all the questions they might ask and have the answers already in the proposal. And I ended up getting a loan for $400,000, which was just enough to cover the renovation expenses and carrying costs on the project.

Were those bankers looking at the past or the future when they loaned me that money? Certainly I could show them a solid track record of making money on real estate; but there's a big difference between a $20,000 house and a $775,000 property. I had no background in high-end real estate; I certainly didn't have $400,000 worth of collateral to cover the loan unless I could renovate and sell the oceanfront property. The only reason—the *only* reason—for them to risk the bank's money on me was because they used their imagination rather than memory to make their decision.

You, too, can adopt this attitude when it comes to your own business. If you go in with a strong enough vision, backed up with the lessons you've learned from the past, then you're far more likely to be able to take others along with you into the future of your own choosing, rather than one dictated by others. See a big future for yourself, then create it. It's the only way to make it big.

Celebrate Each Humble Victory as a Triumphant Achievement—Build Confidence

The first house I ever bought was in 1986. It was a Department of Housing and Urban Development (HUD) repossession at 1423 West Hardy Street in Lantana, Florida. I had to submit a written bid for the property and I hadn't honed my skills in evaluating and bidding at that point, so I probably paid more than I should have—$36,000. I renovated the house and replaced the crummy pool in back with a nicer one. (I can't drive a nail straight, so I ended up doing the grunt work. I'd lay sod, I'd tear the roof off; anything that was unskilled, I did.) The renovations took two months, and then the property was on the market for another two. I sold it to a chef at Bush's Seafood, a local restaurant. I made all of a $7,000 profit, but it was some of the most exciting money I ever made because I had proved that my concept worked! I could buy properties in distressed neighborhoods, and with a lot of hard work on my part, make money. I'll never forget the feeling the day that first house sold. I went out and bought a bottle of Dom Perignon, the finest champagne in the world. On the bottle, I wrote the address of the house and the date I had sold it, and then I popped the cork and drank the champagne with some of my friends. Even after I decided to stop drinking I continued that "champagne bottle" tradition for many years with many other houses.

That humble victory and the others that followed have gotten me to where I am today. I believe more of us should reflect on how each of our little steps, those humble victories, leads to another and then another, until we're at the top of our profession and a long way from where we started. (The great thing about starting from the bottom is that the only place to go is up!) We not only need to recognize those humble victories, however; we need to *celebrate* them. Turning each humble victory into a celebration is how children learn to walk and talk. The first time my daughter spit out a few sounds that approximated the word "Mama," did we tell her, "Peeker, you need to speak more clearly for us to understand you"? Of course not. As soon as there's even the hint of a first word or a first step, every parent in the world is telling the child, "You're the most wonderful kid that was ever born!" When children are praised like that for their efforts, they develop the confidence to keep on trying.

Us "big kids" aren't all that different when we grow up; only all too often we're surrounded by a world that tries to discourage rather than encourage us (see Philosophy #28). And then our confidence can turn into debilitating self-doubt. You and I are inherently hard on ourselves. We're usually our own worst critics. We think, *My grades aren't good enough to get into that school,* or *I'm not pretty enough to make the cheerleading team,* or *Why was I so stupid and clumsy as to blow that double play?* or *Why couldn't I meet my sales objectives this month?* or *Why am I such a bad parent?* or *How could I lose that account?* Such subliminal sentiments begin to erode what little confidence we have.

As a teenager, I had so much self-doubt that I rebelled against almost everything and everyone. I acted tough and wild and crazy so I could differentiate myself from my family, since I thought I could never be successful like they were. Some teens rebel; others turn timid. Still others do what's within their comfort zone but go no further. All of it is due to a lack of self-confidence in ourselves and our endeavors. And just as many adults continue to punish themselves with harsh feelings of falling short of expectations. Let me be clear: There is nothing wrong with self-criticism if undertaken with a positive approach. To be a successful entrepreneur you must push yourself harder than any boss ever will. But you must be constructive with your self-evaluation. And you must focus just as much on what you've done right instead of always looking for how you failed.

Celebrating your successes, however small, helps you build confidence in yourself. You have to be your own cheerleading squad, do your own awarding of medals, be your own parent on the sidelines telling you you are amazing just for making the effort. Every single time I sold a house, for example, I bought that champagne. I also looked in the mirror and took pride in my efforts no matter what I was doing. Whether it was washing a car, giving tennis lessons, or buying and fixing up dilapidated crack houses, when the project was complete I celebrated the fact that I did the best that I could.

Remember a circumstance when you put something—your time, emotions, reputation, money, or a combination of those—at risk and came out ahead. Did you take the time to celebrate what you had done? Did you pat yourself on the back? When we say to ourselves, "I did a good job on that test," or "I'm proud I decided to stay home while my children are small," or "I really nailed that presentation," or "I can make money at this," we find we can take on bigger and bigger challenges. Building your confidence muscle is an essential part of making it big.

April 1999 was quite a month for me. On March 29 I signed a contract to buy 150 feet of oceanfront property in Manalapan, the deal to close on April 16. But within a few days of March 29, I had sold an option on the property for $1.5 million. That option allowed the property to be purchased from me for $4.2 million, or about $37,000 a front foot. I was receiving $1.5 million for a property I had owned for a few days! The day I came home from closing that deal, I also sold another piece of property for $27 million, my largest sale up to that point. It was an unbelievable high, two huge deals coming to fruition so quickly. I sat down on the sofa in my house, and you know what I thought about? All the years and months I spent researching foreclosures, putting all I had in the world (which was $20,000 or maybe $30,000) into a couple of properties, working in the hot Florida sun toting sod and taking tile off roofs because I wasn't skilled enough to do any of the real building work. I remembered the Sundays I would head over to an open house, vacuum cleaner and cleaning cloth in hand, hours before the first people arrived, to make sure everything was sparkling. The humble victories are the ones you cherish as you go through life. If you create and celebrate enough of them, I guarantee you will make it big.

Actions

1. What are some of the humble victories that have gotten you where you are today? You might want to make a list of the things you've been proud of. If the list seems scanty, think back to times where you might not have had the level of success you wanted, but you were proud of your efforts nonetheless.
2. How will you celebrate your humble victories in the future? Create something that will be meaningful and fun for you. It will help build confidence and get you ready for the next opportunity.

Deal Points

When it comes to celebrating, I actually celebrate the buy date more than the sell date. The date you purchase the property is when you make your profit. It all comes down to spending the right amount for the land or the house or whatever, so you can either turn it around immediately at a profit, or put money into improving the property and sell it for a profit, or build a house from scratch and—you guessed it—sell it for a profit. One of the reasons why I have never lost money on a real estate transaction (and I'm at around 102 and 0 now) is because I have always paid very close attention to the buy side.

Most real estate books will tell you that a profit of 30 percent is quite good when you buy and sell on spec, but when I first started I tried to build in at least 100 percent profit potential. I bought houses in the most inexpensive way possible, through foreclosure sales. I renovated them and made them the nicest houses on their blocks; at the same time I watched the pennies and made sure what I did was suitable for the house and the neighborhood. (You don't need cut-glass chandeliers on a street where most houses sell for under $100,000.) If I bought at the right number and renovated at the right price, then I could get the sale price that would represent that 100 percent profit. And it gave me a huge advantage when it came to negotiation because I had a lot of wiggle room if the house stayed on the market too long.

The buy date still represents opportunity to me, a huge what-if.

I'm anticipating the whole process of designing and building or renovating and marketing and negotiating and putting my thumbprint on every square inch and turning my vision for this property into something real and concrete, something that will hopefully make the world's ultra-wealthy have to own it. *That's* the feeling I love to celebrate. After that, it's the lunch pail approach for as long as it takes to realize the vision and find that perfect buyer.

Yes, we celebrate the sale date, too. Most people will make a big deal out of taking the check to the bank and paying off the loans and such. But what matters much more to me than the money is the validation of my concept. I've seen it, I've created it, and people have liked my vision enough to make it their home. But deep down, I'm just itching to get back in the game again, to create another vision and turn it into reality. That's a real victory in my mind, and not a humble one.

Part Five

Make a Difference:
Live a Life That Matters

When you have a vision for your passion, you've created a unique brand for yourself and developed your niche in the marketplace, you've applied the lunch pail approach day in and day out to make that vision come true, and you've exercised your risk muscle consistently yet intelligently, you will have fulfilled every requirement to create what the world considers "success." But will you be happy? Not necessarily. I've had some very rich, very miserable people tour my properties. They can buy everything they could possibly want and then some, yet they are exceedingly unhappy. These people may have enough money for several lifetimes, but they've sacrificed *this* lifetime to accumulate it. They are missing the part of success that makes all the difference: sharing what you have with others, giving back some of what you yourself have received.

   Why do you want to make it big? After a certain point (and sometimes very quickly) you've covered your basic needs. Soon after that if you keep working you'll have more than enough to take care of any contingency. Eventually, you might even have so much money you'll never have to worry about working another day if you don't want to. Great! Now what? Do you go out and blow everything on more houses, toys, parties, trips? Do you put everything in investments so you can have the biggest net worth around? When you die, what'll all that money mean to you? Is that really the way you want to make it big—just in terms of money?

Maybe you're like me, and you're driven to make it big at ever-higher levels. First you're competing with people who are more successful than you, then with your peers, then with yourself, and finally, with your own reputation. Great! You're number one in your field. Now what? Keep fighting to stay on top? Put your drive into another field just because you have to be the best at something? Again, how does your being the best developer or media mogul or movie star or politician help any other person on the planet? And how do you feel about the life you've been living while you've been clawing your way to the top?

The single-minded pursuit of wealth and success is not what we were put on this earth to do. True success has nothing to do with money or achievement. True success includes happiness, peace, contentment, serenity, and clarity; and it happens when you put some of your focus on giving back, on lighting the paths of others who are less fortunate than you. I've seen that kind of success in boardrooms and homeless shelters, in high-rises and churches. To me, it's the essence of spirituality.

While I've seen miserable millionaires, I've also been privileged to meet several very successful people who know the secret of contributing to others and using their success to make a difference. It almost seems as if there's a force field around the ones who make a difference. Even though they may experience ups and downs professionally or financially, it's like they're okay no matter what. (Or maybe they just know what's really important in life.) People who focus on making a difference are creating a legacy that will live on after they've gone, after their money has been spent or transferred to others, after everything they've built has crumbled or merged or been torn down.

I was fortunate enough to discover the secret of giving back almost 10 years ago, when I started feeding the homeless every Monday night. Making a difference in the lives of others quickly became an essential and important part of my week, and it still is. I set aside 15 percent of my time for charitable and spiritual contribution. Even when things are crazy and it's a struggle to take the time to go to a Youth Council meeting, or hold a fund-raiser for building houses in Third World countries, or visit the tenants of one of my Caring Houses, I do it. Giving back to others keeps my feet planted firmly on the ground. It keeps me in touch with what really matters, which is the betterment of our world. As a result of my focus on making a difference, I am not only a better, more compassionate businessman, but I'm also a better father, husband, son, friend, and man.

Without that focus on making a difference in the lives of others, success may seem sweet, but ultimately it will be empty. And in my observation, it has a much greater chance of vanishing, too. Conversely, if you are connected to making a difference and your success does disappear, what are you left with? A coin that no one can take away from you, because it is the coin of improving the lives of others. It is the only kind of coin that will have value and keep you warm for the rest of your life, and it's the only kind of coin that will be your true legacy to the world. If I had to choose between being a miserable millionaire or just a guy who cooks at the homeless shelter, brightening the days of others less fortunate, no question who I'd be.

The best of all possible worlds, of course, is when you can have both, and you use your success to make a difference in the lives of others. I believe spiritual fulfillment and material success complement each other. In fact, the first can augment and support the second, as you'll see in Philosophy #33. When they do, you stand the chance of living a truly happy, extraordinary life, a life filled with wealth of every kind.

In this section I'm sticking my neck out a bit, because there aren't a lot of books that speak of spirituality as something you need in order to be successful. But I think you'll find as you explore these seven Philosophies that they will enrich your life far more than another marketing secret or team-building suggestion could ever do. In this section you're going to discover why you've succeeded (and it's not for the reason you might think). You'll learn how to add a new kind of brightness to your life. You'll be reminded of the timeless values of honesty and compassion, and how they can actually make you more successful. That inner voice of conscience will weigh in, and you'll discover how to tap into the universal principles of abundance and generosity. Finally, you'll put your life in the context not of what you do or acquire, but what kind of legacy you will leave.

Once two men were standing outside the Pearly Gates, waiting for St. Peter to admit them to heaven. "Welcome!" St. Peter smiled at them. "Give me your names and we'll make this as quick as possible."

The first man stepped up. "I am John Curtis Brown III," he said importantly. "I was the wealthiest man in my entire state. I left over a billion dollars in assets, plus 12 flourishing businesses, a horse farm with a stable of Thoroughbreds, seven houses all over the world, a fleet of cars, a corporate jet—"

"Yes, yes, yes," St. Peter interrupted. "Be quiet a moment, and let me listen." The man shut his mouth, flustered. St. Peter cocked his ear toward earth—but there was nothing. It was completely quiet down below. St. Peter sighed. "I'm sorry, I can't admit you. Wait over there for a moment, please."

The first man was dumbfounded. He moved to the side, sputtering in anger and confusion while the second man stepped forward hesitantly.

"And who are you?" St. Peter asked.

"My name is Thomas Johnson, sir. I had a small business in Minnesota. It was pretty successful; nothing to write home about, though. Nothing like this other gentleman."

"Let me listen for a moment." Once again, St. Peter tilted his head toward earth. Only this time, you could hear dozens of voices drifting upward on the wind. "Thank you, Mr. Johnson. . . ." "You saved my son's life, sir. . . ." "You gave me a handout when no one else would. . . ." "You visited me in the hospital. . . ." "You took the time to mentor me when I was just getting started. . . ." "You always put something in the collection plate. . . ." "You treated your employees like family. . . ." "Thank you. . . ." "Thank you. . . ." "Thank you. . . ."

"What was that?" Mr. Johnson asked, puzzled.

St. Peter smiled. "It's the sound of every occasion you helped someone, were kind to someone, made a difference in someone's life. Those voices rise up to heaven when you die, and each 'thank you' becomes a feather in your angelic wings. Come on in, Mr. Johnson—it's a pleasure to welcome you."

Welcome the opportunities to make a difference. They will be your most enduring legacy, and the proof that you truly have made it big.

Many of Us Are Fortunate to Be Blessed with the Ability to Succeed— Not for Our Sole Benefit, but So We May Apply the Result of Our Success to Assist Others

Not too long after I bought my first oceanfront property in 1992, there was an article and photo of me in the local newspaper—"McKinney Plans $6 Million Home on the Oceanfront" or something like that. I was happy when I saw the article because it was good publicity, but then a life-altering sensation swept over me. On one side of the page was the article about me; on the other side I noticed an article about a bunch of homeless guys being fed out of the back of a rundown van by a group called the Caring Kitchen. The article had a photo of one of the men hunched over a plate of food. I looked at the picture and it hit me: If I hadn't turned my life around when I came to South Florida, that homeless guy could be *me*. In that instant, I knew the meaning of the observation, "There but for the grace of God go I." I felt an overwhelming rush of wanting to give something back. I wasn't put on earth just to build multimillion-dollar homes; I was here to make a difference.

I went down to Caring Kitchen and volunteered. Every Monday for the next four years, I served meals to the homeless in the alleyways of Delray Beach out of the back of an old white van. I did so anonymously, because it wasn't about getting recognized—it was about how I felt when I did it. Those Monday nights, and my subsequent efforts on behalf of the homeless and young people, have made a bigger difference in the quality of my life than any property I have sold or financial success I have had.

Why do some people sustain their success? Why do friends and strangers alike admire them? Which of your heroes have created a legacy that combines longevity with doing the right thing? My heroes are people who have used their gifts and then given back to those who may not have been blessed with the same good fortune. One of my living heroes, Rich De Vos, the cofounder of Amway, is an exceptional example of this. In his book, *Hope from My Heart*, one of my favorite passages reads:

> *When God blesses us materially, he does so for a reason greater than merely our personal comfort. Those who have money must accept responsibility for that higher purpose. We can never escape the responsibility of God's requirement that we use our wealth in a manner consistent with our faith.*

I believe God has put all of us on this earth to do great things, but I think He has a special plan for people who take care of those who need it. We are not the end product of our success, merely the conduit for it: We are given the ability to succeed not just for ourselves, but for what we will do for others. Sharing your success is not just writing a check or dropping five dollars in the collection basket (although sharing your wealth is important). It is making a commitment to share whatever resources you have been blessed with. And for many of us, our two most valuable resources are time and personal attention.

One of the most encouraging signs for the future of our world is the way so many of our young people contribute to others. I see this every time I go to a Greater Delray Beach Youth Council meeting. These teenagers make a point of giving their time for civic projects, charity work, and making a difference. When I was in my teens, I'll admit (with some shame) I was completely self-centered. But once I reached even a small level of success, something started to press on my heart. It was only when I started giving back to others that I felt a release of that pressure; it was like my life had come into balance. This Philosophy has allowed me to continue to create balance in a life that could otherwise be pretty crazy.

Contributing to others doesn't have to take the form of regulated, regimented charity work. How many times are you presented with opportunities to do something kind for someone else? These opportunities don't just happen before or following the time we spend in temple or church, or during the holidays when we decide to go to a soup kitchen for an hour at Thanksgiving. Opportunities to offer sincere compassion appear every day—at work, at play, with our friends, family, and strangers. No matter how small, such acts of kindness are very important. They are a chance for us to fulfill our obligation to our Creator. We can't answer them all, but we can say yes to a few.

Through the years my passion for the homeless has only increased. I moved from feeding the homeless every Monday night to using my professional abilities in service of others. I began a program I call the Caring House project, in which I buy rundown properties, fix them up nicely, furnish them, and rent them to homeless families for $1 a month. (Most homeless people have pride and dignity; they want to pay something for their housing, even if it's a token amount.) As I mentioned earlier, the first gentleman I rented to was Buster. Buster was 80 years old and rode around on a three-wheeled bike because he had had a stroke five years earlier. He lived on Social Security and the money he made collecting aluminum cans. (He would spend hours each day in the hot Florida sun searching for those cans; on a good day he could make $20 by turning in 1,500 of them.) Buster was independent and determined to take care of himself, but in 1999 he was kicked out of his rat- and roach-infested room when the landlord wanted the space to expand his business. When I helped Buster move into the first Caring House, he was so happy. Every month I made it a point to go down and collect the rent personally from Buster; we'd sit down and I'd listen to him talk. His stories of his life were amazing, enlightening, sad, funny, wonderful. Buster was a blessing in my life. He passed away in 2000, but I treasure our friendship. Today another gentleman, David, lives in Buster's house. David and his dog had been living under the I-95 overpass; now he pays me the same $1 monthly rent, which I continue to collect in person.

I truly believe God wouldn't have continued to bless me with success if I didn't make a frequent effort to give back to others. Successes are to be shared, not hoarded. We are given success so that we may help others, not so we can buy another toy or throw another party or blow a bundle in Vegas. I've noticed that the people who have what I call "flash in the pan" success are usually those who focus only on themselves. The ones whose success lasts the longest put a large part of their time and energy into giving back. They use their success to benefit others, and that energy comes back to them a thousandfold.

So acknowledge the blessings of success you've been given by giving back to others. Do it on your own or with an established group. Do it anonymously or let others know what you are doing. Put aside selfish interests and invest your time in something that benefits those less fortunate. If you do so, I can confidently say that you will be repaid more than you could ever expect.

Actions

1. Start giving back! It doesn't have to be anything formal, although with our busy lives it's almost easier to have something you can schedule. But the main thing is to acknowledge your success by sharing it with others. Pick one charity or civic activity, a sick person you're going to visit on a regular basis, a child you're going to tutor—whatever works for you. I think you'll find giving back as addictive as I do.

2. I believe that giving of our wealth is an essential part of keeping ourselves and our priorities equally balanced. It also keeps us tied into the Philosophy of abundance (#38). Whether it's through tithing at your church or synagogue, contributing to the Sierra Club or a foundation that builds houses for the homeless in poor countries, setting up a scholarship fund for local kids, and so on, use your money to make a difference rather than just buying another TV or car or house. I admire the way Ted Turner approaches money. He gave $1 billion to the United Nations and challenged other rich people to do likewise. "Give something that's going to hurt a little," he said. For you, that may mean giving $100 to the church building fund, but the principle is the same.

Deal Points

One of the best things about succeeding in business is being able to apply what you are good at in the service of others. That's one of the reasons I moved from feeding the homeless to providing housing for them. I'm good at finding and renovating properties; I love doing it; why not do it to give back? When you're good at what you do, there will always be causes and charities out there that need your skills. If you're an accountant, you can help a local church straighten out its books. If you're an entrepreneur, you might find a nonprofit that's struggling to get off the ground and could use your advice, energy, drive, and start-up knowledge. If you're in real estate, you can help a community group find space or you might do title research or permitting for a shelter that wants to build a new facility.

I am frequently asked to lend one of my properties or my home for charity functions. Many of us can throw a party in our houses or backyards to raise money for a good cause. If you're in real estate and have properties on the market, maybe you could offer the house or commercial space to a local organization for a night's fund-raising event. Sure, you have to take care of cleaning and make sure there is no damage, but I'll bet the favorable publicity you can generate from such an event will more than offset any possible expense.

Remember that giving back to others is a way we keep our successes in perspective. It keeps us attuned to why we've been allowed to succeed, and provides some very needed balance for most of us. When we're trying to make it big, we spend most of our time with our eyes focused ahead, on our vision of what we want to create and have. Take a few moments to look back at those who either aren't as fortunate or haven't had the same chances we've had. Reach back and give them a hand up. When you take others along with you, making it big is all the sweeter.

You Cannot Brighten Another's Path without Lighting Your Own

I really admire my sister Madeleine. She spent a year in Peru working at a place called the Center for the Working Child. This particular section of Peru is so poor even the youngest children have to work. It breaks your heart to see four- and five-year-olds bringing water to graves, cleaning shoes, or washing windshields, and doing it for hours at a time. But the Center provides children with a place where for a little time each day they can play and learn and have fun. In the year my sister worked there, she made a five-figure salary: $900.52. But she was happy, and she came back with a lot more than money. She probably has her head screwed on the best of anyone I know.

This is one of the great secrets that people like Mother Teresa, Albert Schweitzer, and Martin Luther King, Jr. knew: *You can't brighten the paths of others without lighting your own.* Just as we have a survival instinct that directs us to take care of number one, I believe we have an instinct to help others. The survival instinct is what keeps us alive, but the altruistic instinct is what makes life worth living. It connects us to our family, community, and spiritual side in a way our survival instinct can't.

The only way the altruistic instinct has lasted throughout the long history of humankind is because it gives us an advantage. (According to many scientists, evolution's like that: It keeps only the things that make us stronger and more likely to stick around.) The instinct for altruism continues to exist because there are such enormous benefits to the greater community whenever we help others. But nature is a very practical mother and she knows helping others sometimes isn't quite motivating enough, so she makes sure that altruism makes us feel good as well.

First, it makes us feel good about ourselves. Don't you feel good when you open a door for an older person, or teach a child a new word, or write out a check for a cause you believe in? Second, it makes the community stronger. It links us to something bigger than our own selfish interests. And third, it links us to a bigger plan for human beings. I read somewhere that man was a little more than the animals and a little less than the angels—well, I believe helping others moves us farther up that ladder.

Unfortunately, a lot of people are stuck in the survival instinct. They're the ones who talk about "looking out for number one" and are ready to cheat you in a business deal if they think they can. But by focusing only on "What's in it for me?" these people automatically cut themselves off from the rest of the world emotionally and spiritually. "What's in it for me?" turns into "Me against the world." Can you think of a more terrible way to live: isolated, unloved and unloving, worrying about how someone is going to take advantage of you, or planning how you'll do it to others first? To me that sounds like a classic definition of hell. On the other hand, individuals who help others are connected not just by their actions but by their hearts to the heart of humanity. The survival instinct gives us life; the instinct for altruism makes life worthwhile.

When you give to others, many times you feel good immediately. You might even see the effects in your life—your heart may be more open, you may feel more balanced, and you may be happier because you know you've done something that supports your vision of who you are. Sometimes, however, you give and the benefits don't show up right away. You tutor a kid in reading and he or she is less than grateful. You put in your efforts week after week helping out at a shelter, and it seems there are always more people to help no matter how hard you work. You put on a big fund-raiser and somebody else gets all the recognition. I won't lie to you: Giving to others doesn't mean you'll automatically and instantly get back. (If it did, there'd be a lot more people out there doing it.) But have you ever heard the expression "What goes around comes around"? I'm a firm believer that when you keep giving, you'll get back. The returns might not come from where you expect them to, but they will absolutely be there.

A few years ago, at the same time I was renovating the first Caring House, supporting the Caring Kitchen, and deeply involved in the Greater Delray Beach Youth Council, I agreed to head up a fund-raising drive for my church, St. Vincent's. Our goal was to raise $3 million to renovate the building, and I had pledged $100,000 as my personal contribution, with only one catch: In order for me to pay the $100,000, one of the multimillion-dollar properties I had on the market had to sell first. So when Father Skehan came to me and said, "Frank, whatever I can do to help you with the fund-raising drive, just let me know," I answered, "Do me a favor: Pray that my project sells."

Do you think that it was a coincidence that I sold a property for $2.7 million within a couple of weeks of my making that pledge? I don't. I believe that everything I was doing to help others at that time was a signal to the universe that it was okay to give Frank a hand, too. The fact that I was using my wealth to help others let God know I was a responsible steward. And I was rewarded, not just financially, but by the fact that I was able to make good on my promise of that $100,000. And yes, we raised over $3.5 million for St. Vincent's.

When you help others, you help yourself. It's one of those cosmic laws. It's like the scene from the movie *Ghostbusters 2*, when New York is being inundated with the slime of negativity and hate. A few people on the streets begin laughing and being nice to each other, and all of a sudden the slime starts to disappear. As the love spreads from one person to another, the entire city is transformed. Giving to others can change how you view yourself and how you relate to others. It can turn you into a saint if you let it. At the very least, it will clear the way for the universe to support your success.

Actions

Sometimes in the "busy-ness" of helping others we don't take the time to appreciate what we are receiving in the process. We focus so much on accomplishing the task of making a meal, building a shelter, teaching a kid, visiting a sick person, and so on, that we don't realize how our altruism is contributing to our own lives. However you choose to give to others (and I hope you came up with at least one way while reading this chapter), always take a few moments to ask yourself, "What did I gain from this? How was my life brightened by this person or this action?" And cultivate gratitude. Be grateful for being given the opportunity to make a difference, to touch someone else's life. It's a real privilege.

Deal Points

Let's be brutally honest here: Contribution is a great business builder. If you aren't seizing the opportunities that come your way to help out in your community, you're passing up great publicity, connections, marketing, and positioning. I'm not saying that this should be the only reason you help others, because the inner rewards will always far outweigh any external benefits. But the outer rewards are definitely there.

I believe every business should make altruism a conscious part of its marketing plan. Can you sponsor a Little League team or a Girl Scout troop? Can you get good publicity for helping out with a shelter? Even something as minor as adopting a section of the highway and being responsible for keeping the roadside clean can get your name out there. (Have you ever seen those highway signs: "This mile of highway adopted by Such-and-such"?) Why do many national and multinational companies have entire departments focused on corporate giving? Just for the tax breaks? No way. They know what an advantage corporate altruism can give them. Becoming a good corporate citizen can enhance your business, too.

Altruism is also great for building teams and employee morale.

People love to give back and help others, but when life gets busy (as it does for all of us) it's hard to find the time to find a project. What if you were to organize a food drive at Christmas or Thanksgiving? Or put together a team to spend a weekend building houses with Habitat for Humanity? Or find a project or cause one of your employees is already involved with and expand the involvement company-wide? When your team comes together for these kinds of activities, they become a stronger team at the office, too.

Ultimately, however, when you make altruism part of your business, your path will be brightened not by the publicity, nor by the recognition of your good corporate citizenship, nor by the increased strength and cooperation of your team at work; it will be brightened inside your own head and heart. It will keep you and your success connected to something much bigger. It will allow you to feel good about making it big because you're making it big for others, too.

Be Honest and Truthful with Others As Well As Yourself

Have you ever known someone who says one thing and does another? How do you feel about such a person? More important, how do you feel about yourself if you ever end up in that position? I hate the phrase "Do as I say, not as I do" more than anything. Saying one thing and doing another is like trying to drive a car with one foot on the accelerator and one on the brake at the same time. You're not going to go anywhere, you'll cause a lot of friction, and you'll burn out the engine in no time.

Honesty and truth are the social contract we make with the world. People expect us to keep our word, to be who we say we are, to live by the values we say we believe in. What kind of a relationship is based on lies? I'm not talking about the little social fibs that help us to get by; I'm talking about misrepresenting ourselves as something we're not. Sure, you can get the contract by lying to the customer; you can get the date with the girl by driving up in your buddy's Porsche and telling her you're a big-time lawyer when you're really working as a temp in a law office. But eventually—unless you can turn the lie into truth through your own hard work—it will come back to bite you.

In my business, hyperbole is our stock in trade. Our job is to present each property in the finest light possible. But if I say something is one way and the client finds out it's another, in that instant my credibility is gone and I may never be able to get it back. Being honest and truthful in business is sometimes tough. You don't want to give away your negotiating position to the other guy. If your cash dries up, you can't let the media or possible clients know how close to the sun you're flying. I have to admit (somewhat shamefacedly) I haven't always been completely truthful. I've certainly been known to put the best spin on things. But I will not misrepresent a property or change the elements of a deal once they've been agreed upon. And my word is my bond. Once I say something is so, that's it. I will do whatever it takes to fulfill my commitment, even if it means financial pain.

Trust is the foundation of any partnership, relationship, friendship, business deal, or contract. And trust is built on an assumption of a certain level of truthfulness between partners. You have to trust that your spouse will be faithful to you. You have to trust your subcontractors will do the work they promised. You have to trust your employees will take care of your interests. You have to trust the other side in a business deal will fulfill their side of the bargain. And all of those people have to be able to trust you to do the same thing. With a foundation of lies instead of truth, no deal or relationship will hold. Your life will be built on sand instead of bedrock.

Where the rubber meets the road isn't really the lies you tell other people, however: It's the lies you tell yourself. That's where the most damage is done, when you don't face the truth head-on about what you do versus what you say, how you're acting versus what you believe. And we're all so good at this kind of lying. We tell ourselves, "It's not that bad. . . ." "I just did it once. . . ." "It's not like I do this all the time. . . ." "Sure, I cheat people in my business, but I'd never cheat on my wife. . . ." "Everybody else does it. . . ." We're really good at rationalizing and making ourselves comfortable with our lapses in conduct. Stephen Covey calls this "to rationalize—tell rational lies." Our minds are making us comfortable with the difference between who we are and who we say we are.

But we *need* to be uncomfortable when we step out of our integrity. We need to get uncomfortable enough to make a change, to take a stand, to stop taking the wide and easy way and put our feet back on the straight and narrow path of honor and honesty. Lying to yourself is like a cancer, because it'll spread throughout your entire life and kill your sense of integrity. Little by little, lie by lie, your beliefs and strength and commitment will vanish, until the only thing left is a compulsive liar, unable to tell the truth to yourself or anyone else, because there is no truth left inside.

On the other hand, how do we describe people who are honest and truthful? Upright. Upstanding. Honorable. There's a reason every schoolkid in the United States is taught that story about George Washington and the cherry tree: That's the kind of guy who we want for the father of our country, and who we wish we were as well. It starts with being honest and truthful with ourselves. I don't read a lot, and certainly not a lot of Shakespeare, but there's one line from *Hamlet* I remember hearing: "This above all—to thine own self be true,/And it must follow as the night the day,/Thou canst not then be false to any man." It's good advice. Make your word your bond. You'll feel better, and your reputation will be founded on the bedrock of honesty and truth. Be honest with yourself and honest with others, and you'll not only make it big but you'll also deserve your success.

Actions

1. In this world of hyperbole, overstatement, and misrepresentation, sometimes it seems nobody expects you to tell the truth. How many times each day are you tempted to lie or to shade the truth in your favor? How often do you tell the truth regardless of whether it's painful?

2. Are there any areas of your life where you lie to yourself on a regular basis? A good way to tell is if you find yourself rationalizing, telling yourself those "rational lies." If you use phrases such as, "It's not that bad" or "It's not like I . . . " or "Everybody does it," you're probably rationalizing about something. Give yourself the gift of looking at this area, this problem, straight in the eye and telling the truth about it. Then, if you need to, tell the truth to any others involved and make the situation right.

Deal Points

Early in my career I violated this rule and it cost me dearly. I bought an old house (built in 1923) in a rough part of West Palm Beach. It was a Spanish/Mediterranean-style house that I felt had great curb appeal. I paid $12,000 for it. I was just coming off a string of a few small successes and I was feeling the impact a little financial freedom could have on my life. Maybe I was getting a little too cocky.

This particular house was built of wood lath and plaster, and when houses like these were originally built, builders utilized very good plaster. Well, once renovations got underway we tore open a few walls and found that nearly all the wood lath framing had been eaten by termites. The *only* reason that house was still standing was the good plaster. I chose to close up the wall and "not deal" with the significant repair costs. I repaired all the walls, painted them, added decorative crown molding and other ornate trim, and was able to get a clear termite inspection. I knew what I was doing was wrong, and it ate at me just like the termites ate through the property.

After we sold the house for over $70,000, the buyer tried to nail a picture to the wall and nearly the entire east side of the home came tumbling down! The buyer called me, very upset and scared. I couldn't live with myself unless I fixed it. I apologized to the owner, and repaired and replaced all the wood lath and walls. I had to redo all the molding, repaint, re-everything. I ended up paying for the renovations twice, and I had ruined my relationship with this first-time home buyer. While this happened over 15 years ago, I will never forget what violating the Philosophy of being honest and truthful with others as well as yourself did to me. I vowed never to let this happen again, and it never has.

When Your Conscience Speaks, You'd Better Listen

There's a moment between stimulus and response, between being presented with a situation and deciding what to do about it. That's the moment when your conscience speaks up. And from hard experience I can tell you that if your conscience says something, you'd better listen.

In Philosophy #4 we talked about integrity and living up to your own idea of who you are. Conscience is the voice of your integrity. It lets you know if you're getting ready to step out of line. It's the mom or dad or priest or mentor inside your head saying, "No, that's not right." It also is the inner voice that holds you to your vision and mission statement. Each item on my personal vision statement is an opportunity for my conscience to check in with me and make sure I'm staying on track.

Even when I was a teenager, doing drugs, drinking, and acting wild, I had a conscience—I just didn't listen to it very often! But it was still there; it had been planted in my brain by my mother, my church, my dad, and all the other influences that help you know right from wrong. Every time I did something crazy, I would have to stifle that voice of conscience telling me to stop, think, choose another path. But I caused myself and my family a lot of pain because I wasn't listening to that inner voice. I guess it just took some growing up for me to realize that my conscience wasn't there simply to make me feel bad or to represent good, old-fashioned Catholic guilt. In truth, conscience is the voice of the part of us that wants the best for us. It's asking us to live up to our own highest standards of conduct.

Conscience isn't something that makes us comfortable. In fact, it usually makes us do stuff we'd rather not, because it often asks us to go against what on the surface seems to be in our own self-interest. Conscience never tells us to take the easy path; it points us to the path that will do us the most good. Its job is to induce that one moment of hesitation in which we can change course. But it's up to us to decide whether to do so.

Conscience can be one of your best friends when it comes to your reputation. If there's ever a moment when I'm tempted to cut corners on a job, or to use less than the best materials because I want to get it finished, between the idea and action is that little voice saying, "Is this going to look like a Frank McKinney job when you're done? Are you providing the best qualities for your clients the way you claim?" I've learned to listen to that voice and follow its direction, because I know it has the best interests of the Frank McKinney brand at heart.

Sometimes, however, my conscience has led me to do things that aren't exactly popular. For example, I've gotten some good publicity for renovating single-family homes and renting them to the homeless for $1 a month. But as soon as I wanted to buy an old hotel (which currently rents by the hour, if you know what I mean) and convert its 16 rooms into "temporary emergency housing" (which is a fancy way of saying homeless shelter), the town and the neighbors and the local newspapers were all over me. They had a severe case of the NIMBYs—"not in my back yard." I've had to go in front of the city commission and other agencies to get the zoning changed, and all of them are dragging their feet. It's generating a lot of negative publicity, which is something I usually do my best to avoid or counter. But I'm not going to back down on this, because my conscience tells me it's the right thing to do. While I can understand the city's reluctance to create a homeless shelter within the community, this hotel is the closest space, it's available, and the need is right here. This is one case where I'm willing to take the heat and the negative publicity. And I'm going to persevere and make this happen, either here or in another location. By the time it's done, this project will have taken at least as much drive and energy as one of my multimillion-dollar estates, but my commitment to the homeless and my conscience won't let me back down.

Ultimately, listening to your conscience has a lot more to do with how you feel about yourself than how you appear in the world. One of the best stories I've heard about conscience was told to me by George Valassis, who has made billions printing coupon inserts for newspapers. One time many years ago, George took a coupon printing job without giving the customer a quote for the work. He had done other work for this company before, and he just figured the client would pay him what the job was worth. Well, when the check arrived, it was quite a bit over the figure George had in his mind for the job. Most people I know would think, *Glad my client thinks this job's that valuable!* and pocket the extra. But George went to the client and returned $75,000 to him. He told the client his conscience wouldn't let him keep the money. From then on, almost every time the client saw George, he would mention the check. And the jobs this company has given George's firm since then have generated millions of dollars in revenues.

Someone once wrote, "A good conscience never costs as much as it's worth." I'm not saying that every time you listen to your conscience you're going to benefit financially. But you *will* benefit in terms of your integrity, because you will be standing by your idea of who you truly are at your best.

Actions

1. Have you ever been in a business situation where you were faced with a decision where your conscience weighed in? Did you listen? Were you able to make a decision that kept you in line with the voice of integrity?
2. Notice those moments between stimulus and response, between an opportunity being presented and your acting upon it or not. Make an effort to listen to the voice of conscience when it arises. The more you listen, the stronger that voice becomes—and the easier it becomes to follow it.

Deal Points

Sometimes following your conscience in business means being willing to admit you were wrong and take a hit. After we sold our $30 million property last year, the new owner had about $2 million in renovations and changes he wanted made, and he asked us to do them as quickly as possible. We submitted a bid based on what Nilsa and I call "combat pay": We're perfectly willing to work 24/7 to get the job done fast, but it's going to cost more, and we make sure clients know that.

The bid I gave the client started with one phase and 20 items. By the time he had finished requesting additional work, the bid had grown to four phases with 62 separate little projects, all of which were subcontracted. The client wanted the job priced at a flat rate rather than cost plus (where I bill for my costs plus a percentage). This put me at a disadvantage; in order to estimate a flat-rate job completely accurately, I would have needed to get prices from subcontractors on all 62 items. If I had done that, by the time I got the bid to the client we already could have completed 15 items. So what did I do? I priced the individual projects based on my previous experience from other jobs. I gave him a flat-rate bid for each phase based on what I thought the work would cost, with a little extra built in to ensure we could do the job at the speed he wanted it done. The bid was accepted and we started work in January.

By March, we had completed almost all of the work, but in the meantime the client's mind-set had changed. Now he was looking at the bid and questioning some of the line items as being too high. It was affecting our relationship; there was even talk about canceling the rest of the work. It was tough to hear that, because I felt I had done the best job I could, both in the bidding process and in the renovations themselves. But I sat on the other side of the desk (see Philosophy #20) and agreed to review all the bills we had submitted and the overall bid for the job.

We worked all weekend on that self-audit and discovered there were a few items we estimated too high for what the work ended up costing. At that point, there were three things I could have done. I could have said to the client, "Sorry you feel we were too high, but you agreed to the flat rate for the job." That's the stupid response in my business; my clients are wealthy enough to pay for the work they get, but the minute they feel you're taking advantage of them, you're gone. The second response could have been, "Sorry you feel some of the line items were too much. Because we value you as a customer, we are deducting X amount off your bill." That's an adequate if not forthcoming response to keep a client satisfied.

I went the third way: I opened my books to the client. I sent him a detailed response, showed him our costs, how much we billed, and what we were crediting him on certain line items. We ended up refunding $26,000 to the client. (That may not sound like a lot on a $2 million job, but it did represent a healthy chunk of my profits.) Then I visited the client and apologized. I told him why the job had been bid high originally, and explained exactly what we were doing to ensure he was clear on our costs and our profits.

I didn't have to take the third course, but even though it cost me money, I believed it was the right thing to do. It was part of my commitment to maintain a reputation of professional integrity. Conscience kept me honest with the client and myself, and it enabled me to handle a potentially sticky situation from a position of strength rather than defensiveness. For that reason alone, I recommend conscience as a valuable tool in achieving business success.

Truly Feel What Compassion Is

The words *compassion* and *business* are not usually juxtaposed. But I believe the trait of compassion not only makes me a better man but a better businessman as well. Compassion to me means putting yourself in the other guy's shoes and responding accordingly. When I'm buying a property from an older couple (as I talked about in Philosophy #20), I go the extra mile to make sure these people are taken care of. I have compassion for what it's like to sell the home you've lived in for 30 years. I put myself in the shoes of people who perhaps are afraid of change but are facing an uncertain future because of health or reduced financial circumstances. I walk a while in their shoes, then I do what I can to make their decision easy.

Compassion also means considering the consequences of your own decisions in the light of how they will affect other people. As the head of a company with dozens of employees and many more subcontractors, I'm not out to make friends with my decisions; you can't be, if you want to run a successful business. But I know that when I make a decision I've considered all elements, used compassion, and done my best to mitigate whatever negative impact the decision may have on others.

My knowledge of what compassion truly is comes straight from my mom, Katie McKinney—she's the most compassionate person I know. At the same time, she's not a pushover. She knew all about "tough love" when I was growing up. Now that I have a daughter myself, I can't imagine my mom having to watch her child act the way I did when I was a teenager and coming to pick me up from juvenile detention not once but several times. (We joke now that most of my mom's gray hairs are due to me.) My mom taught me how to feel compassion while still making the difficult choices. I always knew she loved me and only wanted the best for me, and that's the same principle I follow when I exercise my compassion now.

On some things, it's easy to put myself in the other guy's shoes and be compassionate. If someone who works for me is having financial difficulties and asks for an advance on his or her paycheck, I'm likely to say, "Okay, sure." But I'll also add, "Don't make a habit of it." Compassion shouldn't make you a patsy; I'm not interested in becoming known as an easy touch or supporting people in behaviors (financial or otherwise) that are going to hurt them in the long run. But I will always take that moment to put myself in the other person's shoes before I make the decision.

Compassion doesn't always make life easier. It's hardest to exercise compassion in situations where you have to be tough—laying someone off or firing an employee, for example. In those situations, I exercise my compassion by giving the person the news myself. A couple of years ago, I bought a large piece of property and was planning to build a $40 million house on it, but then someone came along and offered me a great deal on the property. Since I wasn't going to be building the house, I had to lay off one of my top carpenters. Sure, I could have had my president of construction do it, but I didn't. I sat down with the guy and put it to him straight. "This is why I have to let you go. We're going to give you two weeks' salary and any kind of referrals or references you want." I hated doing it, but it was my job, and the guy appreciated hearing it from me. And I knew that a tough situation had been handled as compassionately as possible.

Far too many people, in my opinion, act like there's a complete and total separation between business and any form of emotion, especially compassion. One phrase I cannot abide is "Hey, it's business." It's one of the biggest cop-outs I know. "But my family has no food." "Hey, nothing personal—it's business." You can't separate your business and personal lives like that. Eventually the heartlessness with which you practice business is going to affect the rest of your life. If that's the way you want to live, fine; but I'll keep using a more compassionate approach, and we'll see whose life is happier.

Take a moment to think about a time you felt compassion. Maybe you helped a friend; maybe you gave $10 to a panhandler. How did you feel? I pray to be given those opportunities because they make me feel so good. Recently I went to a convenience store to get some Gatorade. I was standing in the checkout line and I saw this old gentleman pull into the handicapped parking spot in front of the door. He was extremely frail; he managed to get out of the car and onto his walker, but he didn't even have the strength to close his car door all the way. As he started shuffling toward the store, I put my stuff down, went over and held the door open for him. (I held it a long time—the guy was *slow*.) He thanked me, went up to the counter, and ordered a bag of ice. I knew there was no way he could carry the ice even the short distance to his car, so I asked the clerk where the ice machine was, got the bag of ice, and took it outside. I waited for the gentleman to come back out, put the ice in his car, and helped him in. He looked at me with such gratitude and said, "Thank you, young man." That same day we received a very good offer on one of our multimillion-dollar properties, accompanied by a $1 million deposit check and a two-week cash closing deal with no contingencies. But you know what I told Nilsa about when I got home? Helping the guy at the 7-Eleven. Talk about a return on investment—for the tiny amount of time, effort, and energy it took for me to help that old gentleman, I received an enormous reward.

Every opportunity for compassion is an opportunity for you to be a hero or heroine in someone's life. You don't have to leap tall buildings or defeat armies; you just have to exercise a little common human decency. But if more of us did it, what a great world this would be!

Actions

1. How can you exercise your compassion? There are organized outlets, like feeding the homeless, working with kids or hospital patients, and so on, or maybe you just want to take the opportunities that life brings your way. Whatever you choose, find ways to be a hero for others.
2. How you can be compassionate within your business? Put yourself in the other person's shoes. Remember that old Golden Rule: Do unto others as you would have them do unto you.

Deal Points

I actually believe that real estate is one business in which it's relatively easy to stay connected to your feelings. We're dealing with the stuff of people's lives when we help them buy and sell their homes. One of the ways we can set ourselves apart from the competition is to make sure we stay connected to the emotional side of the transaction, and keep the other side connected to it as well.

Sometimes it's tough to be compassionate and to stay in touch with the emotion of the deal. People get weird when a lot of money is involved, and in real estate we're dealing with a lot of money proportionate to someone's resources. Even when I was buying and selling renovated foreclosures for $40,000 to $60,000, they still represented an enormous financial commitment for the people who bought them, many of whom were first-time home owners.

Every time I was smart enough to stay connected to the emotion of the deal and was able to help the other side do the same, I have not only felt good about myself, I also have benefited greatly. It helps keep the client's impulse window open (see Philosophy #21) and allows me to create long-lasting relationships with my clients. Allowing emotion to enter your business life means you are not just dealing with figures and numbers, you're dealing with human beings who have the potential to become your friends. And when that happens, your business can enrich your life in so many other ways than just the financial one.

Give More Than You Receive

This sounds like something you'd read in a book on religion or volunteerism, doesn't it? But in truth, it's a principle that business has been applying for the past several years, only there it's called "added value."

To stand out from the crowd, your product has to be perceived as having value over and above your competitor's. I actually prefer the term "exceptional value," because I believe the estates I build provide an exceptional experience that makes them worth their (admittedly) high prices in the marketplace. And if you provide exceptional value in every area of your life, giving your best efforts to your business, your family, your community, and your own personal development, then your life will reflect that high level of quality across the board. I guess my attitude isn't truly "Give more than you receive," but rather "Give your best and let the receiving take care of itself"—because in my experience, it always has.

My reputation as a developer of ultra-high-end estates is built on giving exceptional value and service that go far beyond what the clients could expect. Our properties are known for their impeccable construction using the finest materials available. The homes are decorated with fabrics, furniture, artwork, linens, and objets d'art drawn from all over the world and tastefully combined to produce a showplace that also provides every comfort the ultrawealthy can want. Everything is the very best, from the plantings by the entrance to the estates to the Jacuzzi on the top floor overlooking the ocean, and every square foot in between.

I work hard to make sure that in every interaction—from first showing to final closing to the umpteenth call on a warranty—our clients feel that we are providing them with more value than they could ever expect to receive. In the Deal Points section of this chapter I'll talk about some of the particulars of how we provide that value. But our attention to detail and service creates a corporate identity of going beyond expectations, satisfying not just needs and desires but even the smallest wishes the client can dream up. My clients are wealthy people, accustomed to being surrounded by only the best. To stand out in *their* minds, it takes quite a lot, but I am willing to give it because of what I receive in return: the most important coin in any businessperson's pocket, reputation.

Giving more than you receive is a good approach in any business. What's the easiest, quickest way to stand out at work? Do a better job than anyone expects. Give more than the job demands. Take on additional responsibility. Make your boss's or your coworkers' lives easier. If you provide that kind of exceptional value, who do you think the boss is likely to remember when raise and/or promotion time rolls around?

This Philosophy is equally important in your other relationships. I've seen a lot of marriages falter when one partner or the other starts to keep score: "I've given, so now it's your turn." After that, the relationship usually deteriorates into resentment, accusation, arguments, and upset. When you first fall in love, do you concentrate on who gives what, and how much? Or are you so happy to be with this person that all you want to do is give him or her everything you possibly can? When you become a parent, do you say to your baby, "Listen, I'm spending a lot of time feeding and changing and taking care of you; you'd better get on the stick and start giving back to me soon"? Of course not. Scorekeeping only diminishes relationships, whether they be business, intimate, familial, or friendship. We get so much more when we come to them focused on what we have to *give* rather than what we want to receive.

Now, I'm not saying your relationships should be completely one-sided. If you feel you're giving and not receiving anything, you're not going to be happy, either. This Philosophy doesn't say, "Just give." It says, "Give more than you receive." But you've got to be willing to give and receive and not worry about whether you're getting back as much as you put in. When you enter a relationship willing to come from a place of generosity—ready to give from your heart, not worrying about how much you're receiving yet open to receiving what's being offered—then you can create strong, loving, vital partnerships where both people can bring the best of themselves together and offer it gladly.

Think about those times where you have given with no concern about whether you were going to receive. Spending time with a baby; volunteering in a shelter or visiting a sick friend; teaching a young person to ride a bicycle; mentoring a new hire in your office; giving advice to someone who's going through a bad patch; or referring someone to a competitor if you don't have what that client wants. Didn't you feel good? Were you thinking in those moments, "I wonder if this will come back to me? I wonder if I'll receive anything from doing this?" Or were you absorbed in the experience of making someone else's life happier and easier? Even if you never got anything back from your actions, didn't you feel good about yourself simply because you were able to give?

In all honesty, I believe giving is the easier and stronger position in any relationship, business or otherwise. Giving is active; it allows you to take the initiative and get things started. And when you give more than you expect to receive, you are coming from a place of strength within yourself. You stop being a bookkeeper always trying to keep score, and instead become a philanthropist, knowing there is enough for you to be generous. And ultimately, with this attitude you do receive just as much—but don't let that secret get around!

Actions

1. Check out your business. Are you providing exceptional value for your clients, coworkers, or boss? What more can you do to create your own brand identity of impeccable service?
2. Are you keeping score in your intimate relationships of how much each of you is giving? That's a guaranteed road to disaster. Try focusing on giving rather than receiving. If you feel you're not receiving enough, talk to your partner and let him or her know, and then start giving again.
3. Find a place where you can give with no thought of reward, whether it be some kind of civic or charitable activity, taking care of a child, counseling or mentoring others, or other area. Allow yourself to experience the position of giving from strength. See how good it feels.

Deal Points

In real estate, whether you're marketing starter homes or ultra-high-end estates, reputation is critical. And the best kind of reputation you can have is providing exceptional value for the client. This value obviously comes from the construction and finishing touches of the homes, but I believe it's vital to provide exceptional value every step of the way, to make the experience of buying the home as memorable as the home itself.

One of the best ways to do this is to create showings that titillate all of the clients' five senses, beginning with sight. When we have an estate on the market, I'll go through each week to do what my brother Bob and I call "tweaking" the property. I make sure everything looks absolutely perfect, and the visual appeal of the entire estate is impeccable, even down to the screws in the lighting fixtures lining up with each other. If the showing's in the day, the drapes are drawn and the windows are sparkling. (One of the main reasons people are interested in one of my properties is the magnificence of the ocean views—so I'm not going to let that impression be dimmed by even the smallest amount of salt spray.) If it's at night, the right lamps will be lit, the bulbs will have exactly the right wattage, and the clients will be able to go through the entire house without once having to flip a switch to illuminate a room. The grounds are immaculate, the pool is inviting, and everything looks as though the client could move in that day.

Throughout the house there's soothing music playing in the background, emanating from the speakers in every room. Outside, the clients will hear music coming from speakers concealed in rocks in the gardens or disguised as coconuts and hidden in palm trees. Some of our swimming pools even have sound that plays while you are *under* water! I'll also make sure the clients have time to listen to the sound of the waves breaking on the beach. (Even my web site has the sound of waves in the background.)

For smell, there are fresh flowers providing delicate fragrance in many rooms. In the kitchen, there'll be the smell of apple pie or chocolate chip cookies. And every room has that indefinable aroma that says it's sparkling clean. For touch, I encourage clients to feel the luxurious fabrics, like heavy silk or velvet, used to cover walls and upholster furniture. I'll have them sink into an armchair beside a fireplace (with a fire burning brightly, if the season allows) and feel how comfortable it would be to read or have conversations there. I'll ask them to walk barefoot on the $100-a-yard carpeting in the master bedroom—it's as soft and as comfortable as a mattress. Every part of the house provides for the client a truly heightened experience of the ultimate in luxury.

For taste, at many showings (especially at night) we'll provide champagne and caviar, and a full wait staff to serve it. We've served afternoon tea to ladies and poolside lunches for families. And throughout the house you'll find dishes of Godiva chocolates and Ferro-Rocher confectionery. It's been scientifically proven that eating chocolate creates feelings of euphoria and puts you in a great frame of mind—just the way I want our clients to be!

Do I need to do all of this for every single qualified client? Yes, I do, because I want them to remember how great an experience they've had when they've toured one of our properties. They may not be aware of everything we've done to make it a fantastic showing, but every single item that heightens their senses can be the one thing that opens the impulse window and makes them want to buy. And if this property isn't what they're looking for, they'll remember the great experience if nothing else, and that will make them more likely to consider a Frank McKinney property in the future.

I apply this Philosophy of giving far more than the client expects to receive even after the sale. The clients I deal with are people who are extremely busy, and they love anything and anyone who can make their lives easier. With the last property I sold (which came completely furnished), I helped the new owner hire a house manager, housekeeper, grounds people, masseur, even someone to come in and take care of his fish. Since he moved in, he has contracted with Nilsa and my company for eight figures' worth of custom work on the house. Do you think he would have been as open to giving us his business if we hadn't already provided him with enormous value ?

Added value is very important when it comes to warranties. My custom-built properties come with a year's warranty, meaning that I will repair anything that's defective to the customer's satisfaction at my own cost for a full year. Other renovated properties (or as a negotiation point on some deals) I sometimes sell as is. But when you're operating at the $12 million, $15 million, and $30 million level, and you want to maintain your reputation for impeccable quality, there really is no such thing as "as is." On one as-is property, the owner found a leak by one of his chimneys a few months after the sale. We weren't legally bound to do anything about the leak, but I sent a roofer over to repair it immediately because it was the right thing to do. Repairing a roof that's not under warranty is a small cost compared to the potential damage that leak could cause my reputation. In another instance, I continue to cover small repairs for an estate I sold almost three and a half years ago, even though the warranty expired over a year and a half ago. Why? Reputation. I want my brand to stand for the highest level of quality, service, and taste, and I will do almost anything to keep that brand strong. This client is someone who can sell a multimillion-dollar property for me just by picking up the phone and calling a friend. That's enormously valuable to me, so I provide him with enormous value in return.

Giving more than you receive in real estate comes down to one basic question: Which kind of client would you rather have—dissatisfied, satisfied, or delighted? Most businesspeople know enough to keep their clients satisfied, but the ones who truly make it big know that the little extra effort it takes to delight a customer can make all the difference when it comes to the scale of your success.

Approach Life Knowing There Will Always Be Plenty to Go Around. Be Generous

Isn't it amazing that we can live in the most prosperous country in the world and still worry that we might not get our share? We think if we don't close a particular deal, we'll die. If we lose a contract to a competitor, it's disaster. If our child gets a smaller piece of birthday cake than his or her cousin, we're furious. We don't get our full asking price for a property, and we think we've failed. We're envious of other people's successes and jealously guard our own. When we feel our share is being threatened, it's like there's a contraction at the core of our being. Does that sound like the kind of attitude that leads to making it big?

I'm afraid it's human instinct to protect what we have and be afraid someone will come to steal it. One of the reasons this philosophy is on my list is that I fight this instinct myself. But I realize how important it is to believe *there's always more than enough to go around.* Even in the business of oceanfront real estate—where there is (1) a finite amount of land available and (2) an even smaller amount on the market at any given time—I know that if one opportunity isn't right for me, there'll be another one that is. And as long as I don't tie myself up in knots about "the one that got away," the right one will show up very soon. I make a conscious effort not to look back after I have chosen to pass on an opportunity. An attitude of abundance is critical if you're going to take advantage of the chances life throws your way. Whatever time and energy you spend obsessing about what you don't have or missed out on you aren't using to find and seize the next opportunity.

In the same way you can't move ahead if you're focusing on what you missed, you can't welcome even more abundance if you're not generous with what you've already received. By giving to others, I believe we open the door for God to be generous with us. I have participated in this "circle of generosity" throughout my life. Many teachers and adults were generous with me when I was going through my "wild and crazy" years in Indiana. They watched out for me and believed in me even when I was getting busted. When I came to Florida, I found myself giving the same support to others. I founded the Youth Entrepreneurial Society (YES) so young men and women like myself could get together and learn from each other, as well as be mentored by older businesspeople. In the past few years a wonderful woman, Lula Butler, and I have created and supported the Greater Delray Beach Youth Council, which teaches teens about life and gives them a voice and a vote on youth-related issues in our city. I'm grateful I can make a difference in these kids' lives the way certain adults made a difference in mine.

Keeping the circle of generosity going in business is even more critical, but sometimes it's a lot harder to do in the win-lose climate of commerce. When I was buying and selling foreclosures, after the first year or so it was obvious that I was doing well. I was clearing a profit on every single property, and since the number of people dealing with foreclosures was pretty small in those days, I was making a name for myself. Guys started coming up to me and asking, "How do you do it? How do you go to the courthouse? Where do you get your information? How do you decide which property to go for?" I have to admit that I thought, *If I teach these people the tricks of the trade, they'll show up at the courthouse with a bunch of money and outbid me. I'll lose my competitive advantage.* Luckily, I had a second thought, which came from a more generous place: *I'm going to teach this guy what I know. There are plenty of properties out there, and even if we end up competing I'll still be able to do well.* So I shared what I knew, and somehow I did even better than before. Amazing, isn't it?

"But I'm just getting started," you might be saying. "Every deal could mean life or death right now. I'll be generous when I can afford it—when I'm really successful." But if you don't start with an abundant mind and a generous heart now, you won't develop it even when you're rolling in dough. I've met some tightfisted billionaires who won't let go of a dime's worth of cash or a minute's worth of time to help others. And without exception, they're the most miserable people you'd ever (not) want to meet. Think about Ebenezer Scrooge before the visits of the three ghosts: Is that how you want to end up? Then think about Andrew Carnegie, the nineteenth-century businessman who made millions in steel and railroads and then spent the last 20 years of his life giving almost all of it—$350 million—away. Among his many charities, he established 2,500 free libraries all over the country. Isn't that the kind of legacy you'd like to leave?

Being generous doesn't mean giving away the store and making your family suffer in poverty. But it does mean extending a helping hand to others. It means believing there are enough clients, business, and opportunity to go around. And it means doing something with your money other than buying stuff for yourself—tithing to your church, for example, or contributing to a local charity. Do you remember the story from the New Testament about the widow's mite? This woman had almost nothing, yet she offered what she could—the smallest coin of the land—to Jesus. But just the gesture of giving made all the difference.

Whenever you're faced with those moments of contraction when you think, "I can't afford to give this away!" take a look at what you're afraid of. Are you coming from an abundant mind and a generous heart? Will giving this time, money, or opportunity decrease your prosperity, or simply allow you to step into the great universal circle of abundance? Use your common sense, of course, but let your generous heart have a vote in the decision.

Actions

1. Find some systematic way of reminding yourself there's always enough to go around and to be generous. Many people like to contribute regularly to a charity or offer their time at a community center, for example. Simply making the gesture will help you develop an abundance mentality.
2. When someone places a demand on your time or money, notice if you experience a moment of contraction and fear. Take a moment to examine the request from the perspective of an abundant mind and a generous heart. Can you satisfy the request? What will happen if you do? Whatever your decision, make sure it arises not from fear and contraction but from common sense and a desire to be generous.

Deal Points

Remember Philosophy #21, "Think win-win, be fair, then close the deal"? It's a lot easier to think win-win when you're coming from an abundant mind and generous heart. There's a serious competitive advantage when you come from an abundance mentality—it means there's always another deal. I'll be as generous as I can when negotiating, but I also know my requirements for a deal that works for me. If those requirements aren't met, I'm perfectly happy to walk away, because I know that if this deal doesn't work out, there will be another one that will.

An abundance mentality gives you an incredible amount of confidence and certainty when it comes to your business. It also helps create a powerful brand within the marketplace. Generous people are seen as well off and more successful; you will automatically have an advantage over your competitors just because people will want to do business with you. Giving of your time and money is also one of the best ways to create powerful connections with your clients and your community. Who do you think John Doe will go to when it comes time to buy or sell his house: a stranger, or the guy who helped his daughter's Girl Scout troop sell cookies? A name from the Yellow Pages, or the lady he sees at his kids' soccer practice? A big, well-known realty company, or the local brokerage that's gotten great press for cleaning up the area beaches every week?

I want to be very clear, I'm not advocating giving just to get your name in the paper. That's not the reason I do it, and certainly not the reason you should, either. But in a world where setting yourself apart from your competition is absolutely critical, wouldn't you rather be known for generosity than for greed? For helping others rather than for cutting deals that only you benefit from? Wouldn't you rather be Andrew Carnegie than Ebenezer Scrooge? And who would your customers prefer to do business with?

Leave an
Enduring Legacy

We all want to make our mark. We want to create something that will endure after we're gone, something that will make a difference. For some people, it's constructing the tallest building on the planet. For others, it's a business they can pass down to their children. For still others, it's being the absolute best at something, whether it be business, sports, art, or science. But I believe everyone can leave a legacy. In fact, you're building your legacy every day of your life. The question is, what's yours going to be?

I used to dream of taking a helicopter ride over Palm Beach County. As we swooped and soared over the oceanfront, I imagined the other people in the copter saying, "Look, there's a Frank McKinney house. . . . And another . . . and another. . . . " In my dream, someone turned to me and said, "Frank, you've changed the look and the value of oceanfront estate on the entire South Florida coast. That's quite a legacy." I'm committed to leaving my mark in the world of business. When I'm done, I'd like people to see the brand I've built, the market identity, and see how it's lasted for my entire career, how I've gotten better with each and every project I've undertaken. At the same time, I know that a few hurricanes and a recession or two would wipe the physical evidence of my legacy from the face of the earth. Even if there are no disasters, the mansions I build will be gone in 50, 100, 200 years. But the legacy of who we were, how we lived, and most important, the impact we have on the lives of others can last forever.

Think about those individuals whose legacies have outlasted the years. Thomas Jefferson—his vision for the United States as articulated in the Declaration of Independence shaped an entire nation. Andrew Carnegie—he's not remembered for his business deals, but for establishing libraries and charitable foundations all over the country. Mahatma Gandhi—he altered the course of history with his use of nonviolence to create social change. Martin Luther King, Jr.—he changed the mind-set of millions of people, black and white, when it came to race relations. Mother

Teresa—the poor, dying, and abandoned in cities all over the world have benefited from her compassion. Nelson Mandela—will he be remembered more as the first president of the postapartheid South Africa or as the man whose vision, commitment, and leadership changed his country while he was imprisoned for so many years? Enduring legacies are not built on a piece of earth or business success, but in the minds and hearts of others.

You or I may not be able to build a legacy that will compare with Gandhi or King or Mandela, but we can always build an enduring legacy in the hearts and minds of those within our own family and community. It doesn't have to be high profile. My mom, for example, is building a legacy as an incredible mother, a devoted friend, a tireless supporter of many philanthropic causes, and a selfless giver of her time and energy to all who need a hand. Your legacy may be raising a son or daughter who grows up to be president of the United States or simply an outstanding human being. It may be to create a beautiful garden, saving the rain forest, or planting a tree that will shade your grandchildren. Whenever you leave the world a little bit better than it was before, you are creating a legacy that will last beyond your lifetime.

Building a legacy is no different than building a house: You do it one post, one brick, one nail at a time, until the house is finished. You build your own legacy one day, one choice at a time. And like building a house, it's better if you have a vision of what you want to build, then apply conscious effort to creating that vision. But to create an enduring legacy, you can't build one area while ignoring another. As we discussed in Philosophy #8, an enduring legacy requires an extraordinary life. Do you want people to say at your funeral, "Yeah, he was an amazing businessman and gave a lot to charity, but he drank like a fish!" or "She was at the top of the recording charts until she started doing drugs"? Or even, "I know he helped the homeless, but he was married five times and was a real bastard when it came to closing deals"? Every choice you make in your life will be part of your legacy. It's up to you what kind of "house" you want to build.

When I think about my own legacy, certainly I see the big properties, the magnificent homes I create and the manner in which I am able to do it. But I believe my *real* legacy is in the Caring Houses I build, or in the lives of the teens involved with the Greater Delray Beach Youth Council, or in the homeless people I feed through the Caring Kitchen. I also hope that part of my legacy is this book. I feel obligated to pass these Philosophies on; it's my way of saying "thank you" for everything they have given me. By sharing them with readers like you, my faith is that they—and their impact—will live on long after my multimillion-dollar homes are forgotten.

An enduring legacy requires that you live up to what you have done so far, and then build upon it. You can't just spend a few years working on your legacy and then say, "Whew! Glad that's done." What if Mother Teresa had stopped after she helped the first dying beggar on the streets of Calcutta? Or if Martin Luther King had done one march and then said, "Okay, that's enough. I'm going back to my church in Atlanta now"? Enduring legacies are built on a lifetime of consistent effort. This is especially true in the world of business. What kind of legacy would Bill Gates have if he left Microsoft after MS-DOS? Steve Jobs is a great example of what can happen if you stop working on your legacy. After several years Jobs retired from Apple Computer, but without his vision the company got into trouble. Eventually Jobs came back, and he has managed to revitalize the vision and the company again.

An enduring legacy has five characteristics: (1) it's usually built throughout the course of a lifetime; (2) it's built one day, one choice at a time; (3) it includes all of your life, not just one area; (4) it grows through the years as you learn and grow; and, most important, (5) it makes a difference in the lives of others. One of the surest ways I know to evaluate your legacy is what I call the "funeral test." What will your eulogy be? What will the people who knew you say about you after you're gone? Will they come to your funeral out of a desire to honor a life well lived, a life that has made a difference? Or will they come to your funeral for the very worst possible reason, in my opinion—out of a sense of obligation rather than love?

You are building your legacy every single day. It's up to you whether you build it on the sand of transitory successes or you place it firmly on the bedrock of making a difference.

Actions

1. If you died tomorrow, what would your legacy be? What impact would your life have had on your family? Community? Business associates? The world at large? Are you happy with the legacy you have created? Would you like to change or augment your legacy? What do you need to do to ensure your legacy will endure? How will you create a legacy that is built upon making a difference in the lives of others?

2. Imagine your funeral again, only this time it's occurring when you're 90. Who's there? Who's delivering your eulogy? What will they say? Are people attending because they want to honor a life well lived, or out of a sense of obligation? What can you do between now and your (hopefully) distant funeral that will create the legacy you want? Don't put it off. Start now creating the legacy you wish to leave.

Deal Points

In business, the brand you create can be a fundamental part of your legacy. Think of Hewlett-Packard, Wal-Mart, Harley-Davidson, Disney: All these companies have well-known brands that have lasted long after the company founders retired or passed on. You can use the five characteristics described here to create an enduring legacy for your business.

First, your professional legacy is built throughout a lifetime. Walt Disney didn't have much of a legacy after his first cartoon; Sam Walton's legacy encompasses a lot more than one store in operation for a couple of years. You have to be willing to put in the time and effort to create your brand and expand its impact. As I said earlier, most "overnight success" is the result of many years' work. Once you have success, you must maintain and expand upon it to build a legacy that will endure.

Second, your legacy is built one day, one choice at a time. Every single time I choose a building material, a subcontractor, a plant for a garden or design for a kitchen cabinet, I am deciding whether to maintain my reputation and legacy of the finest work and the highest quality available. Every phone call you do or don't return and every client who walks out of your office happy or dissatisfied is part of your legacy. The choices you make, day in and day out, will determine how your business is run and what its impact will be. To create an enduring legacy, you don't have to be perfect, thank goodness, but you do have to be consistent. You have to choose to do whatever will create the reputation and legacy you desire, and then do it over and over again.

Third, and this is a little harder for most people to realize, your business legacy includes not only your business but the rest of your life, too. Do you think Walt Disney would have the same professional legacy if he had been an alcoholic womanizer? Remember, in today's society your life is considered fair game by the media. It's a lot tougher to hide any part of your life that doesn't jibe with the legacy you're trying to create. On the other hand, you can use the parts of your life that on the surface are unconnected to business to help build your legacy. If you take a table at a big charity function, or sponsor a 5K race in your community, or buy uniforms for a Little League team, do you think that might help create a brand and a legacy for your business? The work I do with the Greater Delray Beach Youth Council probably won't bring me any business directly, but it certainly helps me establish my brand in the community. (That's not why I do it, but it is a side benefit.) And if any of those kids become entrepreneurs, that will be a part of my legacy, too.

The fourth element of an enduring legacy is that it must grow through time. You can't rest on your laurels; you've got to up the ante consistently. Every time I go to Disney World in Orlando, they've always improved something, or added a new ride, restaurant, or exhibit. The employees are always looking to see what else they can do to make the "Disney experience" better. To create your own legacy, you have to keep growing and getting better. This may or may not mean expanding what you do; if you're a real estate broker working in a small town, for example, there may be only so many opportunities to expand your business. But could you expand the range of services you offer? Perhaps you could add referrals to contractors or interior designers, or sources for second mortgages, or connections with other agents in other towns where people might be likely to move? Could you add tools that make you better at your job—Internet listings of your properties, mortgage calculation software? Would it be worthwhile to add another specialty to what you do? If you're running a beauty parlor, could you learn to give facials or massages? If you're a carpenter, could you learn to repair furniture? When you think about a legacy, you're thinking long-term. Allowing for growth will not only ensure a more enduring legacy, it will also help keep your interest in your business fresh and alive.

Finally, to create an enduring legacy, your business must make a difference in the lives of others. The truly successful companies have always gotten involved in the civic and charitable lives of the communities in which they operate. Expanding your business focus to include community service is one of the best ways I know to create a legacy. People may not remember who sold them their house, but they sure will remember that Patrick Smith's real estate firm endowed the high school gymnasium. They may not think much about where they decide to have their hair cut, but if they read an article about Joan Jones, the beauty salon owner, giving free haircuts to women on welfare who are going out to look for their first jobs, do you think they might just choose Joan's salon over someone else's? If you're selling homes in a particular community, how important do you think your civic and community identity might be to the legacy you wish to create? Not many of us in business have the luxury of making a difference in our jobs. That's why it's important for us to use our skills, abilities, money, time, and energy to make a difference whenever and wherever we can.

I believe being successful in business means you have an obligation to leave an enduring legacy. People are usually remembered for one thing: whatever they have done extremely well, or extremely poorly, in their lives. I believe it's possible to be remembered for your successes in business and in life, for what you did in your industry and what you did as a person. I would love it if at the end of my life, friends and critics alike would say, "Frank used his successes not only to provide the finest oceanfront homes in the world, but to make a difference for homeless people and young entrepreneurs everywhere. He touched a lot of lives." If your eulogy includes professional success and using that success to help others, then you will have left an enduring legacy—and you truly will have made it big.

Part Six

Enjoy the Ride

On June 16, 2000, the traffic was backed up for miles on A1A, the main road by the ocean in Palm Beach County. The Benzes, Bentleys, and Beemers of the invited guests were waiting to turn their cars over to the valets and stroll through the spotlit gates of my latest property, a $30 million estate built on spec. This was the grand unveiling ball, and I had pulled out all the stops. It was going to be the biggest, most spectacular event I had ever staged. I had invited a combination of Palm Beach County's society crowd, civic and business leaders, the media, plus the workers and their families. (I wanted to recognize all the people who had toiled such long hours to turn the house and grounds into a master-work, the complete realization of my vision.) Three hundred people had RSVP'd; five hundred people showed up.

Around the pool, bartenders were serving drinks, featuring the Manalapan martini, created especially for the evening—it had real 18-karat gold flecks in it. Waiters circulated with trays of amazing hors d'oeuvres to titillate the palates of the guests. At 9:10 P.M. the guests heard a drumroll, and that was my cue. As white smoke billowed from underneath the "rock" grotto wall structure next to the pool, I climbed the marble stairs to the top of the structure, which incorporated a water-fall and water slide. The spotlights snapped on, and there I was, standing about 15 feet above the crowd, with Nilsa next to me and Laura Kather-ine in her arms. I had on the coat from my wedding tuxedo (beaded black tails) and leather pants, demonstrating the "shabby chic" attire that was the theme of the ball. For me, that was like the opening night of

231

a Broadway play, something I had been planning and working toward for months. The words excited, nervous, and ecstatic don't begin to describe what I was feeling as I looked out at the crowd.

I took the opportunity to thank all the people who had contributed to the renovations, from the town council to the guys who laid the tile and planted the shubbery. I joked about having ordered the full moon, which guests could see rising over the ocean, especially for that night. I thanked God for being given both the opportunity and the ability to accomplish what I have done so far. And I invited everyone to enjoy the show, and then tour the house—"after you've sampled some of the Manalapan martinis!" I said. After my short speech, fireworks that were timed to live music performed by the Ink Spots exploded over the moonlit ocean. Then Nilsa and my mom, Katie, snipped the red ribbon that ran across the front door of the house. I invited people to come in (removing their shoes; the "shabby chic" theme meant going barefoot through the house, which kept the floors and carpeting immaculate) and see the luxurious atmosphere Nilsa and I had created. I've never had more fun in my life.

That opening night was an example of one of the driving principles of my life: to enjoy the ride every step along the way. I make a point of having a blast in both my business and my personal life. Our time on this earth is so short, we'd better make the most of it. I believe one of the true secrets of success is to figure out how to have a blast no matter what—whether you are at the end of your career or just beginning; whether you're applying the lunch pail approach and doing the job, day after day, or sitting in your rocking chair, happily retired; whether you're going through tough times or great times. The best way to keep the life in your life is to enjoy the process while you make it happen.

I know too many people who don't make having a good time a priority. They get locked into the role of the "responsible adult" and lose track of the child inside who's dying to come out and play every now and then. They get so focused on producing results, getting the promotion, raising the kids, finishing the project, they forget to enjoy the life they're experiencing while they go for the goal. Then all of a sudden they turn around and boom! they've turned 60 or 70 or 80. Sure, they've produced results, but at what cost—years of joyless drive? A life spent with no time for happiness and just plain fun? Is that the kind of life you want, or the example you want to set for your children?

I've got news for you: That little kid inside you can help you get further faster than any objective, plan, task, or effort. There's real power in play. Play releases our natural spontaneity, our curiosity, our drive to explore. It makes us fearless. It gives us resilience—we can take the inevitable knocks and bounce back, like a child who skins a knee and, after a few tears, gets a Band-Aid and keeps right on playing. It helps us keep things in perspective, too. When you view your efforts as a game and fun as part of the process, you learn not to take yourself so seriously (an extremely valuable lesson for any adult).

I hope the Philosophies in this section will help you unleash the child within and start having fun in your career and your life. You'll learn about enjoying the 97 percent of ordinary life as much as the 3 percent of extraordinary "golden moments." You'll appreciate the necessity of recharging your battery on a regular basis. I hope you'll discover how important it is to resist the temptation to act like an adult and instead let the little boy or girl inside you come out and play while you renew and reinvent yourself. You'll understand why I think falling in love and showing your affection is key to any kind of success. You'll learn to become the star of your own life as you step onto the concert stage each and every day, giving it your all with flair. You'll remember the power of laughter and why the first person you should laugh at is yourself. And finally, you'll learn how to live a life with minimal regrets, so you can sit, content, in your rocking chair at 90.

Throughout this book I've tried to give you ideas and advice about living by a vision, creating your own unique niche and brand, doing the job day after day, taking risks, and making a difference. This section is about adding joy to the mix. I believe that's the most important element of all when it comes to longevity. You can follow every Philosophy in this book, but without joy your life will be dry as dust and just as ephemeral. Put some life into your life—it's the last, best secret to making it big!

If We Are Fortunate, 97 Percent of Our Ordinary Life Is Spent Pursuing the Extraordinary 3 Percent. Enjoy the 97 Percent, and Recognize and Adore the 3 Percent as Extraordinary Golden Moments

Have you ever noticed how we can get caught up and often stuck in our daily routines? Our nine-to-five becomes monotonous and almost dreadful, as in the movie *Groundhog Day*, where Bill Murray wakes up each day to the exact same sequence of events. A daily regimen is normal for you and me, but how can we vary it and make it more enjoyable and fulfilling?

Most of us are motivated by a desire to attain goals that are important to us. The challenge is that so much of your life—97 percent—is spent pursuing the other 3 percent, what I call extraordinary golden moments. Those are the moments that you will remember for a lifetime: the day you get married, the day your first child is born or gets married, the day you close the deal you have been working on for months, or the day you land the job you have been searching for. If you focus only on those golden moments, however, you run the risk of becoming very depressed.

Have you ever known someone who rushed through life living only for the high points? First, such people can't wait to start school. Then they want to graduate from grade school and get into middle school, then high school. Then they focus on getting into college; then getting out of college and getting their first job. They focus on finding the right girl or guy to marry, then spend a year planning the wedding. Then it's the first child, the second child, the first promotion, the vice presidency, retirement. . . . Their entire lives rush by and they've actually lived only a few, fleeting moments! What a shame—and what a waste.

Why limit your enjoyment to the golden moments? Why not enjoy the 97 percent just as much? While I continue to pursue what is important to me, I constantly remind myself to take pleasure in everyday life. It's a good thing, too, because for me the time span between the extraordinary golden moments can sometimes be quite long. Certain years I may sell only one house that took me two years to create. And my triumph is short-lived, because I believe the joy is in the ride, the chase, the pursuit; it is found in the implementation of my idea or concept. It's important for me to focus as much on the 97 percent as I do on the 3 percent. That way, I remain driven and motivated.

If you don't learn to enjoy the 97 percent as much as the 3 percent, you run the risk of becoming a "success junkie." It's kind of like being a member of a successful rock band. I'm sure you've read about musicians who live for the moments they spend onstage. They love the high, the adrenaline rush, the adoration from the crowd. But when they get offstage and back into "real" life, they can't take it. They turn to drugs or alcohol or anything else that will give them that same high feeling. There are businesspeople like that, too; they always have to have at least six deals going at once. They push beyond any levels of financial or business prudence. As a moderately rehabilitated adrenaline junkie myself, I understand this temptation all too well. That's why I work hard to enjoy every single moment I go to the job site, take another client through a property, or have another Monday morning meeting with my team. You've got to learn to enjoy it all—the highs and the plateaus—for without the one you can't have the other.

Conversely, I'm afraid there are a lot of people who settle for the "97 percent life." They don't work to create golden moments; they live 100 percent of the time at an average level. That's being dead even though you're living, in my opinion. You've got to be able to live the 97 percent, everyday kind of life with appreciation and enjoyment, while directing your consistent efforts toward the creation of golden moments that can take your life to a whole new level.

The real secret to enjoying both the 97 percent and 3 percent is diversity. When your life includes professional achievement, great relationships, spiritual connection, personal growth, and making a difference in the lives of others, whether your day is average or extraordinary you're going to be living at a much higher level of satisfaction and enjoyment. Today you may have a golden moment with your kids; tomorrow it may be when you help a homeless person. The next day it might be in your business, and the day after in your personal introspection. When you have the potential for growth and achievement in many different areas, the odds of your living a golden life increase exponentially. The 97 percent and the 3 percent will move a lot closer to each other; the 3 percent will be filled with the steady enjoyment of the 97 percent; and even the dullest of the 97 percent will be filled with life.

We all spend most of our time on the climb before we reach the summit. Deciding to enjoy the scenery along the way will make attaining the peak more enjoyable. And when you reach the summit, celebrate—and I mean it! Adore the 3 percent; congratulate yourself on your achievement. I reward myself with little things that mean a lot to me: a trip to our vacation home in Colorado, a sushi dinner with my wife, even a Slurpee from 7-Eleven. Those golden moments don't have to be the sale of a $30 million spec home; the cause for celebration can be my daughter's first day at school, my wife's new interior design job, or the day my book deal was signed. But it's just as important to enjoy *getting* to those moments of success. True living is in the 97 percent. So enjoy every moment of life—golden, everyday, and in-between.

Actions

1. What have been some of your golden moments? Did you celebrate them for all they're worth?
2. How's your 97 percent, the everyday part of your life? How can you enrich your experience? Remember, diversity is one of the greatest secrets for enriching the 97 percent. Are you working toward fulfillment in your business or your relationships? Are you making a difference?

Deal Points

In business, it's smart to create golden moments for yourself and your team. How often do you reward the people who work with you and for you? Doing something that they will never forget in order to acknowledge their efforts helps build enormous loyalty. And creating "golden moments" throughout the year is a much better approach than an annual holiday party and once-a-year bonus. Most businesses have quarterly goals and regular reviews of progress, right? Why not create "golden moments" in conjunction with some of those? Perhaps a company picnic in the summer, an outing to a local theme park in the spring, an apple-picking day in the fall. Or do what a friend of mine did with his company: At the end of a particularly hard week, he called his 50 or so employees in, gave them each $100, and told them they had to spend it on themselves before the night was over. They could use it for anything as long as they treated themselves well with the money. That "golden moment" is something the company still talks about. Taking the incentive to create golden moments in your business will make your team a lot happier about spending the other 97 percent getting the job done.

Take Time to Recharge Your Battery. You Won't Get the Golden Egg without First Taking Care of the Goose

I meet a lot of very wealthy, successful people, many of whom have been working nonstop for 10, 20, 40 years to get where they are. The hardest thing for them to do is to relax. But what happens? They either trash themselves physically because they don't take care of their bodies and the constant stress does them in, or they burn out emotionally.

To make it big and enjoy your success for a good, long time, you have to take care of yourself, and that means taking time to recharge your battery. In the intense business climate of the past several years, it seems everyone is competing to work harder and longer than the next guy. The "B" word—balance—seems to have gotten lost. Yet balance is the only way anyone is going to make it big over the long haul. Even if you absolutely love what you do, you can't do it 24/7 and not lose your edge. Whether you're flying solo or you're a cog in the great corporate machine, you've got to take time to refresh and renew.

Frankly, this Philosophy is on my list because it's one of the most difficult lessons for me to remember. There is so much I want to accomplish in my life, professionally, spiritually, and emotionally; there isn't enough time in the day, week, or year for me to do one-tenth of it. And when you become successful, the demands on your time and energy increase. It takes a lot of strength of will to put aside time in a jam-packed schedule to do absolutely nothing, if that's what will help you recharge. Yet if you don't take care of yourself, you're gonna hit the wall, and hit hard.

Nowadays, with home computers and the Internet and telecommuting and PalmPilots and cell phones that can reach us anywhere and everywhere, it's harder than ever to get away from work, especially when you love what you do. But you've got to take a break from work to allow yourself to come back refreshed and renewed. When I leave my office for the day, that's it. I don't answer the phone at home; I don't even have an extension in my bedroom. If I need to work, I'll go back to my office, but I try to keep my home as a place where I can relax and renew.

What you do to renew is a very individual thing. Some people renew by going to the tennis court and beating the cover off the ball. Others take a nap in the middle of the day. I have one friend who unwinds by reading the newspaper comics every night. Many people have hobbies—everything from building model airplanes to flying real ones, from cooking to collecting antique toys. Whatever you choose for your leisure activities, I recommend you include things that renew your mind, your body, and your spirit, and also allow you to relax.

I work very long and very hard hours throughout the week, and spend Saturday introspecting and planning the next seven days. But unless there's a showing scheduled at one of our properties, Sunday is my day to renew. I get up at six o'clock instead of five, and I go to seven o'clock mass. My wife and I have a tradition of taking our three-year-old daughter to the Marriott for Sunday brunch. (She calls it the "treadmill place" because she has walked on the treadmill there since she could walk.) I take a nap Sunday afternoon. I might spend part of the day watching sports on TV. Nilsa calls this "brain-dead activity," and she's right: My brain completely turns off. I also spend time on Sunday playing with my daughter. (Children can help you renew faster than almost anything, as long as you're playing with them and not "watching" them. See Philosophy #43.) I even steal a few moments with my wife every now and then.

Other than attending the Indy 500 each year and an occasional weekend getaway, for the first five years of my real estate career I hardly ever took a vacation. I was too darn busy, and was putting every dime back into my properties. But about four years ago I realized a lifelong dream and bought a vacation home in Colorado, not too far from the Benedictine monastery where I went to school for a year. It's a pretty primitive place, but the location is fantastic, and it allows me to get away completely with my family and a few close friends. It's great—I'll ride my dirt bike or all-terrain vehicle, run through the hills, go camping or river rafting. I'll take my daughter to visit the monks and the farm that's part of the monastery grounds, or eat a $1.99 breakfast at the local coffee shop. I can feel myself relaxing when I'm there, especially since I make sure to tie up every loose end before leaving Florida, so I don't have to think about work while I'm gone.

Another great way to renew is to follow Philosophy #31 and celebrate your humble victories. Since I buy or sell a property only once every couple of years, I do my best to look for excuses to celebrate along the way. A great way to renew your relationship, for example, is to take your significant other out to dinner when he or she closes a deal or finishes a project. How about celebrating with your child when he or she gets an A in math or makes the soccer team? Life provides us with a myriad of opportunities to renew our emotional resources by celebrating the little things in life. And if you can celebrate with those you love, so much the better.

Strange as it may seem, living a disciplined life (see Philosophy #23) is an essential part of taking care of the goose. You've got to take care of the vehicle. Yes, it's important to take a break every now and then, but without discipline your body isn't going to be up to the demands you place upon it. When you get eight hours of sleep a night, exercise every day, eat well, and don't trash your body with undue consumption of alcohol, then you can maintain your energy and focus at a high level consistently. And when it's time to renew, you can relax knowing you can bounce back quickly.

Stephen Covey calls this area of life "sharpening the saw." It's an apt metaphor. Taking time to relax and renew allows me to keep my edge in business and in life. Make sure you include this philosophy in planning your week. Strange as it may seem, taking time off may very well be the best way to make it big even faster.

Actions

1. What kinds of activities help you renew? Make a list of everything you do to take care of the goose, and make sure it has items on it that will refresh you physically, emotionally, and intellectually, as well as "fun for no reason" stuff.

2. If you don't do it already, develop the discipline to take care of yourself physically. This should include regular exercise, diet, and moderation or elimination of any unhealthful habits.
3. When's the last time you had a vacation or celebrated a humble victory? Take advantage of these important ways to refresh and renew.
4. When you leave the office, leave the office. Set rules for yourself in terms of when and how you can be reached. If your rule is to spend Sunday mornings with your family, stick to it. Then forget about work for a few hours. It'll still be there when you get back, but you'll be better equipped to do it.

Deal Points

The absolute best thing you can do when it comes to taking care of the goose is to gather a great support team. Whether I'm spending an afternoon in the park with my daughter or going off to Colorado for a weekend, I'm confident my team knows where things stand in terms of our projects and what my wishes would be in almost every eventuality. I also know that if they run into anything they're not certain about, they'll let me know. When I drive away from a job site I can take a deep breath and leave work behind, because I know many other hands, hearts, and minds are looking out for the business.

What kind of team can you create for yourself? Even if it's as rudimentary as hiring a college kid to answer your phone, or getting an associate to cover your calls when you take an afternoon off, there are many different support systems that will allow you to leave your business in good hands while you sharpen your saw. Figure out what you need, get it, and then get going. Take care of the goose before your goose is cooked!

Never Grow Up, and Consistently Renew

One of the greatest compliments I was ever paid came from my cousin, Greggie, who was 10 years old at the time. When Nilsa became pregnant with our daughter, we had a big party and invited a lot of our friends over to make the announcement. Afterward, we found Greggie in the corner of the room, bawling his eyes out. We kept asking him, "What's wrong?" but he wouldn't say. The next day his mom called and said, "Greggie's afraid you're going to be a different person now that you're going to have a baby. He's afraid he's going to lose you as a friend." I went right over to his house and reassured him I wasn't going to grow up and stop being his friend just because I was going to be a dad. And I haven't.

As kids, we're always saying, "When I grow up. . . ." We think that's when we'll be able to do what we like, when we like, without anybody telling us what to do. Yeah, right. As anyone reading this book knows, while most adults have the capacity to do almost anything, we are a lot less free than we were when we were kids. We lose our spontaneity. We lose our sense of fun. We get "responsible." We lose some of the very elements of our personalities that allow us to make it big.

I believe we all have an instinctive drive to explore, to find out more about our world and stretch our natural abilities in the process. We see mountains and want to scale them. We look at the ocean and wonder what's on the other side. When we're kids, that instinct is right on the surface. I am astounded at my daughter's continual desire to explore everything and test her limits. "Let me do it!" she tells me. "I'm a big girl." She jumps at the chance to try something new. If she fails, she tries again. If she falls she may cry for a moment, then she's back in the game. Unfortunately, most of us lose track of this natural instinct to explore and test our limits. We settle for a very mundane, unexciting life of mediocrity. I want to approach life with the same enthusiasm, desire to explore, and wish to grow that my daughter has; and if growing up means losing that, then you can leave me out.

I'm not saying you should act like a kid all the time. After all, I did a lot of reeeeeeeeally stupid things when I was a teenager. If I was still doing those things I'd probably be dead, and I certainly wouldn't be successful. But I've seen far too many of my contemporaries who are stuck in the straitjacket of responsibility, of being grown-up. I live a very disciplined life, but I can still enjoy a Slurpee and play games with my daughter. If you can't be disciplined Monday through Friday and then ride dirt bikes with your cousins on the weekend, then you've lost a part of yourself that's very precious and valuable.

Even if I can't let it out to play all the time, I work hard to stay in touch with that nonadult part of my personality regularly, and for me it's not that difficult. I don't take many friends with me when I go to Colorado, mostly because they can't keep up with me! Given the choice, I'll be out every day river rafting, dirt biking, four-wheeling, mountain climbing, and so on. Now, I know that if my daughter were a little older she'd be right there with me, because she's game for anything. And I plan to keep doing that kind of stuff until I'm so old I can't walk anymore or see the rapids. I figure you can always sleep when you're dead, so why do it now?

Not growing up has another advantage, too: It allows me to be on the same level as the kids I mentor in the Greater Delray Beach Youth Council. If you want to be able to talk to your kids, I strongly suggest you cultivate that part of your personality that never grows up and stays young, fresh, and a little wild. When you were a kid, did you *ever* listen to an adult telling you that you were on the wrong path? I sure didn't. Who did you listen to when you were young? Your peers. I may not be the same age as the kids I counsel, but they sense there's part of me that is basically just like them. Maybe it could make a difference for you, too, when you're talking to your own kids.

The second part of this philosophy is the means by which you can keep yourself from getting locked in that "adult" straitjacket. You have to renew or reinvent yourself consistently. As I have said before, I have enormous admiration for Madonna, the pop star. She reinvents herself completely every year or so, changing her life, her look, her music, everything. Metallica's another example of a band that has changed its music repeatedly to attract new audiences. Businesses, too, can reinvent themselves: Under Jack Welch, General Electric changed from being an appliance- and technology-based company to being an economic powerhouse. It moved into media, into financing, into all sorts of other business areas.

You've got to be willing to renew yourself and your approach to life frequently. I have this sneaking suspicion that one of these days when I've hit the limit as far as ultra-high-end property is concerned, I'll change completely. I may decide to become a deacon (close to a priest, but married). I may purchase an entire oceanfront town and rebuild it. I may focus solely on homeless causes; I may try to qualify for the Indy 500 or get involved in the Eco-Challenge endurance race. I'm not afraid to let everything go and start fresh. And that gives me an energy, a freshness, a spontaneity that few of my contemporaries can match.

When I die, I'll bet whoever's giving the eulogy will talk about the way I preferred to spend my time with young people, and how it seemed I was always one of them. And I hope I kick the bucket at 90 while riding a dirt bike with my great-grandkids. May you, too, avoid the straitjacket of "acting like an adult" and keep in touch with your sense of spontaneity, wonder, and renewal.

Actions

1. What can you do to keep in touch with your spontaneity? Make time to do something an adult would never do, then do it frequently.
2. Look at your life and your business. Have you become what you loathed as a young person? Look for fresh approaches to common occurrences; discover different ways to dress, act, learn, or do business. Find strategies that excite you and take you out of your comfort zone.

Deal Points

While never growing up will give you a lot more joy and fun in your business, the willingness to renew and reinvent yourself is essential, given today's economic climate. Even in my profession, real estate, things are changing so rapidly that you have to be willing to approach everything in a new and different way at the drop of a hat. For example, five years ago how many real estate professionals had web sites? How many thought that virtual-reality house tours on the Internet would draw clients from around the world?

Part of my obsession with always getting better has been to take advantage of every opportunity to renew and reinvent my business. With each project I undertake I am looking for new ways to understand my marketplace, new features that will titillate the client, and a new level of "wow" factor. Now that the economy appears to be slowing, I am absolutely looking to renew my approach to the houses I design and build. With my latest project, a 10,000-square-foot house on a large ocean-front lot, I am insisting the architect keep the house at exactly 10,000 square feet while making it as luxurious and inviting as possible. I'm shifting the focus of design more toward creating unforgettable grounds in addition to an unbelievably beautiful house. And the project I undertake after this one may end up going in a completely different direction; it all depends on the marketplace and my vision of the next new trend. Leading the marketplace rather than following it is a powerful impetus to keep refreshing and renewing your approach to business. It certainly has helped keep me ahead of the pack.

Resist the Temptation to Act like an Adult. Never Lose the Little Girl or Boy Inside

A lot of people change drastically as they grow older. They think they have to be the adult, wear the suit and tie, act like a person they're really not. They lose touch with who they were at the beginning of life, that little boy or girl who explored the world and faced the future with boundless energy and excitement. And that is a terrible loss.

Let's face it: Most of us have a lot riding on who we are and what we do. We have responsibilities; people and companies are depending on us. We can get caught up in the seriousness of what we want and need to accomplish, and stuck in the fear of "What if it doesn't work out?" But sometimes the best thing we can do to fulfill our responsibilities is to lighten the heck up and remember who we really are. We need to keep in touch with the little boy or girl we once were, because that child still has a lot to offer.

Even though my mother sometimes despairs of the way I act, to me it's important to resist the temptation to act like an adult because every time I've tried it I've regretted it. I remember not too long after my dad died in 1992 I decided I would go into banking like him. (I guess in some strange way, I thought I was honoring his memory.) I cut my hair, bought a couple of banker's suits, and started negotiations to buy a failed savings and loan on the west coast of Florida. Thank God I changed my mind. The idea of my having to act conservative, stifling every bit of drive and fun and excitement I get from what I do now, feels like someone is putting me in a straitjacket, pinning my arms behind me, and locking me in a padded cell.

On the other hand, when I closed the deal to buy the property I eventually sold for $30 million, I was ecstatic. It was one of the biggest opportunities I'd ever had. The vision for the renovated estate was already percolating in my mind. So what did I do? I drove over to the house and went down the slide into their pool with all my clothes on. It was the best celebration I ever could have come up with, because I allowed that little kid to come out and play. When I bring that kid's spontaneity, willingness to explore, and boundless joy to my work and my life, I not only succeed at a much higher level, I have a ball while doing it.

How many people have you seen whose idea of a celebration is sending a letter to their shareholders? Or having a big announcement party where everyone dresses up in their most uncomfortable clothing and pretends to like each other? I'd rather chew nails. Sure, I can celebrate by taking my wife out to a great dinner in a fine restaurant, but I'd much rather do something where I can let loose and really have fun. After all, who knows more about celebrating and having a good time than a kid?

One of the greatest things about thinking and acting young is the almost medicinal effect it has on your creativity. Many creative people are often quite childlike in their approach to life. When you can retain that youthful exuberance, that willingness to approach everything as if it were the first time, your creativity can't help but expand. Thinking and acting young allows you to stay in touch with a truly vital part of yourself.

Letting the kid inside you come out is also a great way to deal with the stresses and strains of everyday life. Say you're an accountant during tax season. You've been in an office with no windows, hunched over your computer screen for the last week. Sure, you could go to the nearest bar and knock back a few to unwind—but what if you took a couple of friends to Grand Prix Race-a-Rama and challenged them to a go-cart match? You could spend the night vegging out in front of the TV—but how about asking your kids to teach you how to play the latest video game? You might love your weekly golf game—but could you take your family out for a night of miniature golf, too? I think these "nonadult" types of recreation access a completely different part of our personalities. They let us laugh more, have more fun, and blow off steam.

When you resist the temptation to act like an adult, there's an opportunity for a kid's sense of humor and irreverence to come out. Remember the scene in the movie, *Liar, Liar*, with Jim Carrey, where his coworker brings him into the boardroom and asks him what he thinks of the CEO? Now, Carrey's character has been hexed so he can't tell a lie, so he tells the CEO, "You're a pompous ass." There's a moment of silence as all the adults in the room sit horrified. Then the CEO starts laughing like crazy; and everyone else does, too. I believe there's part of each of us that secretly loves irreverence when it shows up. If I'm speaking at a gathering, inherently I tend to be a little bit irreverent, letting that rebellious little boy inside of me out. Too many times we're tempted to "make nice" and say what everyone expects us to say instead of telling the truth. Well, I vote for shock value every time. I can't tell you how many times people have come up after board meetings, or city council meetings, or negotiations and told me, "Boy, I wish I could have said what you did!" With irreverence and humor, you can get away with telling truths you could never express otherwise. And sometimes those truths need badly to be said.

Take a look at situations where you've been tempted to act like an adult when you didn't need to. I'm proud of the fact that my younger cousins like hanging around with me and want me to sit with them at the kids' table at family gatherings. "Mickey's fun," they say. "He doesn't act like an adult. He's like us." The people I've found who are the happiest are the ones who resist that temptation and bring a bit of irreverence to places where others are acting like adults. Maybe you, too, should let that little girl or boy inside loose, and see what he or she might do.

Actions

1. Go play with some kids. They're the best antidote I know for the "adult" straitjacket.
2. How do you let off steam? Come up with some nonadult recreations and celebrations that you can indulge in.
3. Cultivate your sense of irreverence. Even if you don't voice your comments like Jim Carrey did, make them in your head. Keep in mind the advice you find in many speakers' handbooks: Imagine other people sitting there in their underwear, and see if your attitude doesn't take a turn for the lighter.

Deal Points

In business, there are a lot of times when you have to be responsible. You have to apply the lunch pail approach and get the job done. This Philosophy deals more with *how* you approach your job. I look for ways to have fun in my business. Why do you think I do outrageous things like dressing in a loincloth for a publicity photo? Or hire bands like the Ink Spots for a grand opening? When you have fun, your customers are more likely to have fun, too, and they're a lot more likely to give you their business.

Certainly, when I first meet a client, I'm a little more well-behaved and sedate. I don't joke right away. I don't want to express too much of who I am because I'm focused on learning as much as possible about the other person. But once the relationship is established, I start to let that irreverent side of me out little by little. And most clients appreciate it. The older gentleman who bought one of our properties a few years ago calls me his "super hero." Another friend, a CEO of a multinational corporation, has told me he admires my wearing wildly colored jackets to the big stuffy parties where we usually see each other. There's something very attractive about a person who's willing to show the side of him- or herself that is joyful, eager, buoyant—the little kid inside. I let that side out a lot more than most people.

At the same time, I'm careful when and how that kid comes out. It's like the salt and pepper you put on mashed potatoes. If you had just the salt and pepper, it wouldn't make a meal; but without the seasoning, the meal would be unbelievably boring. So I season my business with a little irreverence here, a little playfulness there, all the while serving the client a big helping of quality results.

One of the things from this Philosophy that you can apply directly to business is the joy and eagerness to learn that most kids bring to their endeavors. Let's use the example of a five-year-old learning to ride a bicycle. If you were to approach your business like that kid approaches the bike, what kind of energy would you have? How open would you be to trying new things? How easy would it be for you to recover from the inevitable tumbles every kid—and every business—takes? How would you celebrate when you are able to wobble a few feet down the driveway, metaphorically speaking? If you want to keep your approach to business fresh, alive, and vital, let the kid inside you out. Resist the temptation to be sedate, cautious, or adult; try new things with eagerness, knowing you can always get back up on the bike and try again.

Fall in Love; Don't Hesitate to Show Your Affection; Don't Hesitate on Anything

I thank God for my wife, Nilsa, all the time. I've been with her for 14 years and I can still remember the feeling of falling in love with her. I would never have succeeded as much as I have, nor be living the life I'm so grateful for, if it hadn't been for her inspiration, love, and support.

When I met Nilsa, however, I had absolutely no intention to get married for a long, long time. I was 24 years old, on my own since I was 18, and I was pretty successful for my age group. There had been a lot of girlfriends along the way, and you'd better believe I enjoyed my single life to the hilt! But when I met Nilsa, that was it. I knew right away she was a special lady, and in very short order I knew I wanted her to be my wife. Nilsa, however, took a little more persuading. She was a very successful interior designer, far more established in her career than I was in mine. It took her quite a while to believe I was serious.

Most guys aren't good at showing their emotions. We're not brought up to do it. We're far more likely to slap a guy's butt than hug him, or take our anger, hurt, or frustration out by beating a tennis ball to smithereens instead of telling someone how we feel. But when a guy falls in love, it's one of the few times it's actually to his advantage to show his emotions. And I did. I wooed Nilsa. I took her out; I bought her flowers; I treated her as well as I could, given my finances and circumstances. (Remember, at the time I was buying and selling foreclosures and working 70- and 80-hour weeks—not exactly the best situation for spending a lot of time with a girlfriend.)

For anyone, but especially for a guy, showing affection means taking an awful risk. But I was determined to make my proposal to Nilsa one of the most memorable moments of both our lives. I set it up way in advance: I got an enormous banner made saying, "Nilsa, will you marry me?" and strung it across a 100-foot-tall water tower on the outskirts of Palm Beach. Earlier in the evening I had actually donned camouflage clothing and scaled the tower without benefit of a ladder to secure the banner myself. The night I planned to pop the question, first I took Nilsa out for a romantic dinner, brought her flowers, the whole works. Then I blindfolded her and drove to where the banner was hung. She had no idea what was coming.

I pulled up next to where the tower was, and with a lot of talking, persuaded Nilsa to get out of the car. As I walked with her toward the tower, she took off her blindfold because she was getting tired of the anticipation. Just then a friend of mine threw the switch on two huge spotlights that were pointed straight at the banner. Nilsa stopped dead in her tracks and gasped. I turned to her, pulled out the engagement ring I had been carrying for several days, and said, "Nilsa, I love you. Will you marry me?" Before she could respond, there was a loud cheer from the other side of the water tower. Some of the neighbors had come out when the spotlights went on. At that point, Nilsa looked at me and said yes. I was ecstatically happy and relieved—if she'd said no I had vowed to climb back up to the top of the tower and stay there until she said yes.

Falling in love is one of the greatest experiences we can have. And I'm not just talking romantically. We can love our friends, our kids, our hobbies, charities, and communities. We can love going out for runs in the morning. And to make it big professionally, I believe we absolutely must fall in love with what we do. We have to have that eager, swept-off-our-feet kind of passion about our careers.

If you've ever been happily in love, didn't you find that the rest of your life just seemed to go really, really well? When I was courting Nilsa, I had so much going on—just getting started in the real estate business, still running my tennis business but making a transition out of that. I was burning the candle at both ends and the middle, living on adrenaline, and yet I felt great! It was one of the most productive times in my life, and I attribute that directly to the energy and joy that came from falling in love. Allowing that emotional part of yourself to come into its own can kick your life into another gear entirely.

There's a reason it's called "falling" in love instead of "creeping" in love, however: You have to be willing to go for it with your whole heart. Yes, you can get hurt. The other person might not love you, or not love you as much. Certainly your job or career or profession may not love you back (as many would-be actors, musicians, writers, and athletes discover). There's a risk inherent in loving anything or anyone. But just imagine the risk you take if you *never* fall in love. Imagine going your entire life without saying "I love you" to another person, or "I love this!" about some activity. That isn't life—it's a living death. I vote for having passion and love every time.

I admit this is a Philosophy I have to work on. I don't show my affection enough, especially where friends and family are concerned. Like many people, I've got the "What if they don't love me like I love them?" tape running. But then I say to myself, "So what? Who cares if affection doesn't come back? I'll never know unless I give it a shot." When it comes to showing affection and falling in love, hesitation comes mostly from fearing for your ego. Just go for it. Whenever you express your affection the odds are on your side anyway, because there's never enough love in this world. Anything you can add to the mix will probably be welcomed with open arms.

Nilsa is still the love of my life, but I must confess now there's another woman: my daughter, Laura Katherine. I just look at her sometimes and I get teary-eyed. I want to let her know how much Daddy loves her. When you don't hesitate to show your affection, you can live the richest life in the world regardless of whether you have a dime in the bank or a roof over your head.

Actions

1. Who do you love? What do you love to do? What does love feel like for you? You might want to make a list and then spend a few moments thinking about why you love this person or that activity. Connect with that inner excitement of falling in love all over again.

2. Create ways you can show your affection for the people in your life. Find something that will make them feel special, and do it. For some, you can just tell them; others love flowers; others need to be held. And remember, it's not about them reciprocating; it's about your sharing the love in your heart.

Deal Points

I fell in love with being an entrepreneur, and buying and selling property, even before I fell in love with Nilsa. I don't think I will ever stop loving the exhilaration of doing deals—creating a vision for a property and then making that vision real. I love the excitement of figuring out how I can make the next project better than the last. I love creating a marketplace and building the Frank McKinney brand. And I don't hesitate to show my affection about my career; that's one of the reasons I'm asked to speak to a lot of real estate and entrepreneur classes, clubs, and associations.

But at the end of the day, I also know business is business, and if you let your heart get too wrapped up in it, you're going to be in trouble. I can't tell you how many people come up to me at the grand opening for one of our multimillion-dollar properties and say, "Frank, how can you sell this? You've poured two years of your heart and soul into it, and look what you've created. Don't you want to live here yourself?" No, I don't. I love the creation and the challenge, but when the project is done, I can let the place go immediately. If someone were to walk up right before the grand opening and make me a good offer, I'd take it in a heartbeat—and the party would become a celebration. Actually, what I absolutely love most, what keeps me going from deal to deal, is the fact that my vision has been validated when someone buys the house.

In business, the smart way to fall in love is with the process of the business itself. If you're a realtor, sure, you can love real estate, but you should love selling or renting houses more than your particular office. If you're building a team as part of your business, you should love the process of team building even more than you do the team members. Your team members can and will leave for reasons of their own; if you're fixated on the people instead of the team, you'll find yourself sunk in feelings of disloyalty, betrayal, and anger. But if your love is for the overall team and the process of team building, then the members can come and go, and your love for what you do will stay intact.

I'm not saying you can't care for the people in your team. Some of my strongest relationships are with people like Bob, my president of construction, or Phyllis, who's been my company bookkeeper and personal assistant for many years. But I believe one of the ways you should express affection for your team is by giving them the chance to learn and grow, even though they may grow themselves into another job with another company as a result. It's a fine line to keep personal affection separate from your regard for someone's contribution to your business. I do my best to keep the first for a long, long time, and enjoy the second while it lasts.

But I do think the attitude of being in love with your business shows through, both in your approach and in your results. In the same way being in love with your spouse makes the day-to-day of a marriage possible, being in love with your profession makes the lunch pail approach we discussed in Part Three possible. When you love what you do, it's a lot easier to get in there day after day and do the unglamorous stuff. And I also believe you'll put a lot more of yourself into the job. I love creating one-of-a-kind mansions; my taste and my fingerprints are on every square inch of the properties I design. I love trying new design elements and seeing if they create the kind of "wow" factor my clients expect. I put a lot of heart into each property, but I always remember it's the vision and the process I love, not the result. So I can sell with a happy heart and start looking for the next project to fall in love with!

Approach Each Day with Flair

When I was growing up, I used to love the New York Seltzer Company guy. The owner was young, and he used to promote his seltzer by doing all kinds of crazy stunts. He'd jump out of buildings; he had a bunch of leopards; he'd race cars and go in shark cages and do anything else he could think of to get people to remember New York

Seltzer. I thought his approach was impressive. (He had long hair, too.)

To me, the New York Seltzer guy demonstrated flair. Flair takes what is ordinary—like building houses, or raising kids, or selling clothing—and gives it a spin that makes it interesting. Flair is the reason people watch soap operas—as if real doctors and lawyers and businesspeople looked and acted like that every day! But why have soaps been on the air for as long as TV has been broadcasting? Flair—ordinary life lived at heightened levels. When you approach most businesses or lives, what's special about them? My profession is building houses: What's romantic, flamboyant, or Hollywood about that? But when you approach your work and life with a little outrageousness, a little extra energy, a little extra enjoyment, then all of a sudden you (and it) become interesting, special, unusual. That's flair. And I think everyone should make flair part of daily life.

I believe flair starts with a person, not a particular profession or task. And everybody's got it; it's not just the Siegfrieds and Roys, the supermodels, the beautiful, wealthy, successful people. In fact, I'll argue that one of the reasons that certain individuals become successful is through flair. Look at Bruce Willis. He's kind of average-looking—medium build, going a little bald, not particularly athletic—yet his energy and the aura he puts out on-screen make you want to watch him. That's flair.

A lot of people don't like Donald Trump, but you have to agree the man does things with flair. He's not afraid of being outrageous and making himself seen and heard. He was one of my role models in that he was the only "celebrity developer" I'd ever seen. I liked the fact that Trump was creating huge and beautiful buildings while making sure everyone knew who was doing it. If you had an apartment in Trump Towers in New York, it meant you had arrived.

It's up to you to find your own particular special quality, your flair, and then apply it. Someone once asked fight promoter Don King about his hair. Don shrugged and said, "It's natural." Well, it's not; I've been to dinner with him and you can tell, he does *something* to his hair to make it stand up like that. But his hair is a distinguishing physical characteristic and, as he told me, it helps set him apart. That's what flair does for you: sets you apart from the crowd. Your flair will be something in your personality or appearance that you can emphasize and exploit (yes, exploit—meaning use productively). Flair could be your verbal presentation or your ability to take charge of a situation. Your appearance or the way you approach business could be part of your flair. Everybody has something that can be kicked up a notch or two and turned into their own, unique, personal flair. You just have to find yours and then put it out there for everyone to see.

As I think should be pretty clear by now, I have a rather unique personal style. It extends not only to my appearance and the way I promote my houses, but it also includes what I drive: a 1974 Cadillac station wagon. The guys who work for me love it. I can hear them when I drive out to the site: "You see that? The boss doesn't drive around in a fancy Mercedes. He's got himself an old Cadillac station wagon!" No matter what I've done in my life, it's always been done with an unusual twist that will make me stand out. But I put that flair to work for me, to help create publicity for my properties or my causes. If the way I dress and the theatrical way I approach things will get more people involved with the homeless or with helping young people get a positive start, then I'll be as theatrical as I can be.

The problem is that most of us get the flair knocked out of us when we're kids. You see, flair makes you stand out from the crowd, and that takes a lot of certainty and a lot of strength. Flair is the opposite of conformity—and that's why it's so important if you want to make it big. By definition, to make it big you're going to have to stand out, you're going to have to be noticed, you're going to have to make your mark on the world. And that's not always easy. There have been times when the sense of personal style I bring to my work has created alienation and envy: the "who the hell does he think he is?" attitude. If my style makes my work more visible, helping me to sell my properties and support the causes I care about, and also gives me (and others) a lot more fun along the way, what's wrong with that? And if others find something wrong with my style, that's okay—they're entitled to their opinions.

If you find, accept, and develop your own sense of flair, you can actually enjoy taking the lead in your profession. You can step onto the concert stage of life (see Philosophy #46) and have a blast. So find your own unique personal style, and don't be afraid to express it. Then you can walk up to someone like Don King and say with admiration (as I did), "Nice hair!"

Actions

1. What's your flair? Find something in your personality that you can bring out to help you stand out from the crowd. In the 1970s, Congresswoman Bella Abzug used hats. Don King

has his hair. The New York Seltzer guy used outrageous stunts. What is it about you that you can augment, emphasize, enjoy more?

2. How can you apply your flair to make you and/or your endeavors more noticed in your marketplace? (By the way, reporters like people with flair, because they're a good source of copy. You can use this to your advantage when it comes to publicizing your business, civic, or charitable efforts.)

Deal Points

In your professional life, flair can make you more visible than your competition. In my industry, there are other estates and other estate builders out there. And remember, while only 50,000 people out of approximately seven billion can afford the properties I create, they also can buy almost anything they want in any location in the world. So I try to make myself and my properties memorable. I have a distinctive physical appearance—I certainly don't look like your average developer in a suit. Whenever a property is shown, everything possible is done to make the experience something that will stick in the client's mind (see Philosophy #37). Our grand openings are a combination of the world's best party and a Vegas show.

All these efforts are in service to two objectives. The first is to sell properties. My houses are lifeless; they can't speak on their own. The only voice they have is the way in which they are presented to the clients and the marketplace as a whole. That brings me to the second objective: to build the brand that is Frank McKinney (see Part Two). I am the voice and image that sells properties. If they remember the "rock 'n' roll developer" or chuckle at my long hair or brightly colored jackets, great—as long as they remember me. Because I'll always lead them right back to my product: the houses I create.

I don't know if approaching each day with flair is necessary to be successful in every profession. If you're an accountant or tax attorney, you might think that flair isn't something that will help you do your job. But I do think flair helps you have fun whatever your profession. And it helps you stand out from all the other accountants, tax attorneys, soldiers, sailors, postal workers, cleaning people, and so on. In some professions, flair may be doing the job better, quicker, faster than anyone else. No matter what, I believe it will be to your benefit to find your own bit of individuality and bring it out.

Each Day You Are on the Concert Stage of Life, So You'd Better Make It Rock!

One day about five years ago I was watching A&E—one of my favorite channels because it is very educational and often features biographies of well-known people. This particular show was on KISS. (Yes, the band whose members wear character makeup and costumes, and whose guitar player spews fake blood.) KISS was formed in New York in the early 1970s, and two of its original members, Gene Simmons and Paul Stanley, are now in their early fifties.

The program talked a lot about the band's trials and tribulations, and what it takes to stay on top of an industry as fickle as rock music for 30 years, as KISS has managed to do. When they first started performing, the Bee Gees and Donna Summer were hot. They've lasted through techno and punk and hip-hop and rap and everything in between. Critics have proclaimed again and again that KISS was washed up. What made the difference? What made the band last? I believe it's a common creed each band member talked about backstage: They're committed to giving their absolute best at each concert. They vow to give concertgoers their money's worth and leave everything on the stage.

The TV program continued with concert footage—and what a show KISS gave the audience! As I watched, I remembered a KISS concert I had attended when I was a teenager, and how entertaining I thought it was then. A short time after I watched the TV program, I saw that KISS was touring yet again and making a stop in West Palm Beach. My wife Nilsa and I went to the concert, and to my amazement the show was every bit as great as both my memory and the TV program had indicated. These guys, who are in their fifties and who've been doing the same thing for the past 30 years, put more energy out and gave a better show than almost anyone I've ever seen. They left 15,000 concertgoers in a frenzy.

I've seen the animal tamers Siegfried and Roy perform only once, but they're another example of performers who give it their all every day. Their act is one of the longest-running in Las Vegas; they've per-formed thousands and thousands of times. The night I was there, I met a couple celebrating their fifteenth wedding anniversary. They had hon-eymooned in Vegas and seen Siegfried and Roy then, too. They told me they thought the act had only gotten better! Siegfried and Roy are amazing: Their energy level and showmanship are incredible. They are giving their all on the concert stage night after night after night.

You, too, are on a "concert stage" daily. It may not be in front of thousands of screaming fans, but aren't you performing for your company, clients, family, and, more important, yourself? You have the opportunity to get up, style your hair, put on your makeup and costume (i.e., your business suit, apron, or work boots), grab your instrument (your briefcase, hammer, cooking spoon, or textbook) and hit the concert stage of your life.

Once you are there, you can choose to just go through the motions or you can make it *rock*—which to me means giving it your all, doing the best you can, making it fun, exciting, and special, making it happen in a big way. I try to get some kind of excitement out of every day. It puts life in my life, and I believe it's a really good approach to almost any 16-hour period. If I've got a meeting in the afternoon with a client, that's an op-portunity to be on the concert stage of life and I'm going to make that meeting rock. If I go out to the job site to check in with my guys, I'm going to do my best to make our time together great.

This approach can enhance every part of your life. How much would your spouse or significant other enjoy it if you added some excitement to your relationship? How about your kids? Even in charity work, I find a rock 'n' roll attitude can make a major difference. When I was chairing the fund-raising drive at my church, for example, I'd give updates on our progress to the congregation, and I'd do all kinds of crazy things. Once I dressed up as a priest—all in black, clerical collar, the whole bit. (With my long hair, it was quite a picture.) Some of the older parishioners who couldn't see very well thought I was a real priest and called me "Father." Another Sunday, I walked up to the pulpit with a big white bandage on my nose. Everybody was whispering things like, "What happened to Frank?" "Shhh, don't say anything, it's not polite." I looked at the congregation solemnly and said, "With this fund-raising drive I've had so many doors slammed in my face, I finally ran into one and broke my nose." Silly? Yes. Outrageous? Yes. Memorable? Absolutely. Did I have fun? You bet. More important, did the congregation have fun? You'd better believe it. Most important, we raised $500,000 more than our $3 million goal.

You might not feel very comfortable making it rock on the concert stage of your life. I know what that's like, too. Quite honestly, I am still uncomfortable speaking in front of groups. When I was in high school and had to give speeches for one of my classes, I used to knock back a few beers just so I could get up in front of people. What helped me was to create a personality for myself: "Frank McKinney, the rock 'n' roll developer." That Frank loves being in front of people. It's kind of like being an actor, like the guy who used to do the "Crazy Eddie" TV commercials, or being able to put on makeup and costumes like the KISS band members do. It gives you the freedom to be outrageous. Maybe your performing personality is "Robert the Radical Realtor" or "Connie the Superconsultant." It's just taking part of your own personality and giving it a little pizzazz, a little freedom, and a little latitude to get out there and give the customers a good show.

Now, you don't have to act like you're on the concert stage of life 24/7. The KISS band members pull out all the stops when they need to perform, and the rest of the time they're just normal people. If you've ever seen interviews with Michael Jackson, he's pretty quiet and meek. But onstage—watch out! For most of us, however, we spend all our time in that "normal" mode. We think it's fake to "put on an act," or "get above ourselves," or even to have a good time at what we do. But I believe you should make it rock when you can, because you can always go back to "normal." This philosophy is about creating excitement in your own life and pulling out all the stops when required. When I have the opportunity to perform, I perform. That opportunity can be in my profession, with a client, talking to a reporter, turning a staff meeting into an event rather than a Monday-morning chore; or it can be with my family, turning a play date with my daughter or an adult date with my wife into something memorable. But when the concert is over, it's over. I'm back to being Frank the guy, just like KISS is back to being two guys named Gene Simmons and Paul Stanley.

You are the star of your life; it's your responsibility to take the stage and do what you can with it. It means you'll have to put more of yourself, your energy, your drive into your day. But isn't that a more exciting way to live? I guarantee you, it's definitely the way to extreme success.

Actions

1. Where's your concert stage? What are the moments in your business, your relationships, your family, your hobbies, that you can make special, unique, and exciting?

2. How will you make those moments rock? Perhaps you need to create a "personality" to give you the freedom to really let go. What aspects of who you are do you want to exaggerate or focus on developing?
3. Remember, knowing when to step off the concert stage is almost as important as knowing when to step on. You don't have to perform 24/7. Kick back when you can, and you'll be fresher and more ready to give it your all when your audience is there.

Deal Points

One of the key aspects to KISS's long-term success is the band's desire to give people their money's worth at every concert. I do the same thing with our properties. If someone goes through a showing, they're going to get a show. All five of their senses are going to be involved, as I talked about in Philosophy #37. Even with people who might not be qualified buyers, I don't take anything for granted; I make sure we crank it up just as if they could buy a $30 million property out of petty cash.

Do you remember the grand opening event for the $30 million property, which I described at the beginning of this section? Even back when I was buying and renovating $30,000 foreclosures, I used to make those open houses as much of an event as I could. I'd have fuchsia-colored Mylar hanging on the outside of the house. I'd tie helium balloons to the chimney, like you see in car lots. My signs would be the biggest and most visible. Of course the place would be immaculately clean, the lawn would be freshly cut, and the driveway and walkways pressure-cleaned. I'd even open up the air-conditioning units and stick an air freshener on the back of the filter, so the fragrance would waft throughout the house. All day long, Nilsa and I would be there to welcome people with cookies or soft drinks (served outside so the house stayed clean). We made sure everyone who walked through one of our properties would remember the experience.

In business, there are so many moments of truth, when you've got only one shot to make the presentation, close the deal, get the client, sway the city council, and so on. I approach those moments like Jimmy Connors stepping onto the court at Wimbledon, or KISS getting ready to walk onstage. All my senses are heightened. I bring everything I have into play. I put on my "game face" or performer's makeup: that attitude which says, "I'm here to get it done." I'm committed to making it happen right here, right now. And people sense that. It creates an excitement about what could otherwise be a ho-hum business meeting or negotiation or permit presentation. When I walk in like I'm on the concert stage of life and ready to rock, clients, employees, and buyers love it.

Conversely, when those same people meet me outside of that context and they see a more laid-back Frank McKinney, it creates a little mystery—and that's good. I don't want them to think that all I am is this outrageous guy who spends his day lounging around a $30 million mansion in nothing but a loincloth and a smile. Clients will keep coming back to you again and again if you give them a great time and then keep 'em guessing.

Even on the days they don't feel like performing, do you think bands like KISS and performers like Siegfried and Roy let it slide? They can't—and neither can you. So put on your concert personality and give it everything you've got, and you might end up with the ultimate "standing ovation": success beyond your wildest dreams.

Laugh Often—and Make Sure You're Able to Laugh at Yourself

I'm a big believer in laughter. How many books have been written about laughter and what it does for the soul? I think it was Jimmy Valvano, the amazing Villanova basketball coach who died of cancer, who once said, "To live a full life, you should laugh once a day, cry once a day, and hug somebody once a day." I agree with him, and I try to follow his advice.

Laughing is an absolutely essential component of making it big. There are dozens of people out there who work very hard to achieve their successes; but if you take things too seriously, you run the risk of having your work consume you. If you're in life for the long run, laughter makes the run a lot more pleasant. I think we can work longer and harder and get better results when we leaven our efforts with laughter and enjoyment.

But the real key to this Philosophy is being able to laugh at yourself. If you can't, that's a sure sign your ego is out of control. And what happens when your ego rages? You start making stupid decisions based only on ego. You become Mr. (or Ms.) "I'm So Important"; you start acting like you're God's gift to the world. (It's okay to believe in your heart that you are God's gift, but don't act like it!) You've lost touch with any humility you once had, and probably a lot of your humanity, too.

Laughing at yourself means you're able to separate who you are from the role or image you've created. Think of it as the difference between being dressed and seeing yourself standing in front of the mirror in your polka-dotted underwear. Being able to see how ridiculous you are is the best antidote to ego I know of. When I speak in public, I make jokes about my attire, my hair, my attitude, my background. It keeps me loose, and also helps the audience get past anything they might be thinking about me in the same vein.

I like laughing at myself—I'm a pretty ridiculous guy. I mean really: a grown man who wears his hair longer than most women; a fellow who can't go to a party without putting on a gold or red or yellow jacket and then ordering his favorite drink, a Shirley Temple; a dude without a college education who still has the nerve to build multimillion-dollar estates on spec. Who wouldn't have a good laugh at him? Sometimes I think I'm like those caricatures you see artists drawing at the fair, the ones where all your worst features are exaggerated for everyone to see. I laugh at myself a lot, because there's stuff to laugh at. And it's part of what keeps my head from getting too big and cuts me down to size when I start making grandiose plans.

Laughter also helps me get past some of my faults, foibles, and hot buttons. I'm known around my office as having a short fuse on certain issues. If someone brings me a problem without proposing a solution, for example, I can get pretty steamed. But lately, instead of tearing into someone, I just laugh at my own overreaction. *How stupid it is for me to get mad about something so trivial!* I'll think, chuckling. I'll go to the assistant or the foreman or whoever and say, "Your dog must have indigestion. There's a page missing from this memo you gave me—the page where you wrote the solution. I'm sure your dog ate it, right?" Now, my humor may seem feeble to you (and probably to them as well), but it's a lot better than my yelling and screaming and making a big deal over a simple omission.

I also use laughter to help diffuse and cushion disappointments. When I'm at a city council meeting where I'm trying to get permits to build homeless housing and I'm getting stonewalled, I'll argue my case strongly and positively, but afterward I'll just shake my head and laugh at how stubborn people can be sometimes. Taking that moment to laugh at the situation takes me out of frustration and lets me look at things in a different way.

I believe every interaction can benefit from a little humor and laughter. Laughter is a great leveler; it creates an instant relationship. If you take yourself, your business, and your life too seriously, you stand a much greater chance of being consumed by what you do. Sure, work your butt off to get things accomplished, but have a lot of laughs along the way. And for heaven's sake, laugh at yourself. You'll be a lot easier to be around, and you'll like yourself better, too.

Actions

1. Stand in front of a mirror in your underwear and have a good laugh. Pretty impressive, aren't you?
2. What faults and foibles could you learn to diffuse through laughter? Come up with at least five situations where laughter would make things easier and help them go more smoothly. Concentrate on the situations where you can absolutely laugh at yourself.
3. Think of a situation where it would have been valuable to laugh about it afterward. If you didn't then, what's stopping you now? Find something you can laugh about in that event. (There's always something. Have you ever seen anyone crack up during a funeral? Laughter is nature's way of telling us to relax and let go.)

Deal Points

Laughter is one of your best business tools—not just in keeping a good relationship with customers, not just in creating a greater sense of team with your people (although, as I said earlier, it can do both). In today's business climate, you can use laughter and humor very effectively in marketing your product or service.

Think about all the commercials you've seen. Which ones do you remember? Mostly the funny ones. If you go back as far as the old Burma Shave signs that used to line the roads, why were they so memorable? They were limericks: jokes with a punch line of "Burma Shave."

Every business can use a sense of lightness when creating its advertising. For example, in the Los Angeles area Forest Lawn Cemeteries runs radio ads promoting its services. Not exactly the kind of business you'd think levity would work for, right? But one of their best ads talks about Betty Sue, who was a rabid bingo player. When it came time for her service, what did the family do? They had a prayer printed on the back of a bingo card. Another ad talks about Harry the Harley rider, and how all his buddies rode around the church on their "hogs" in his honor. No matter what your business, incorporating a sense of humor into your brand will draw customers your way.

And don't be afraid to let your business laugh at itself, either. People like self-deprecation; they're suspicious of a business or businessperson that takes itself, himself, or herself too seriously. But if people see you aren't full of yourself, that you're able to recognize your own foibles and laugh at them, they're more likely to see you as someone they can relate to no matter how successful you are. Remember, to make it big you need to attract customers and keep 'em happy. Laughter can help you do both, and give you and your customers a good time in the process.

Live Your Life with No Regrets. When You Are Older, What Will You Say from Your Rocking Chair?

Not too long ago, I was buying a house on the ocean from a couple who had lived in it for 35 years. The gentleman had built the house himself when he was 35. Now he was 70 and in a wheelchair. He had suffered some kind of a stroke, and his wife was devoting herself to taking care of him. The house had that stale, musty, ammonia-like smell that reminds me of sickrooms. The man barely knew who I was. He was sitting in a dark, sealed-up room with a thick blanket draped over his legs in the middle of summer. I had to work very hard to make sure he understood what was happening, how his wife had decided to sell me the house because she couldn't take care of it and him anymore.

While I was sitting there, it hit me: This guy had built this house when he was my age, 35. He had been successful enough to be able to afford a house on the oceanfront. I'll bet he was sharp; I'll bet he thought he had the world on a string and he'd be that way forever (exactly the way I was feeling about myself at the time). And look at how he ended up. I thought, *I wonder what regrets he has. I wonder if there was anything in his life he wished he'd done and didn't.* I said good-bye to the couple and instead of going back to work, I went for a walk on the beach. I resolved then and there to make sure I lived in such a way that I would have no regrets. The only regret I would allow was in taking a risk and having it not work out. But I vowed I would not end up in my rocking chair singing the "shoulda–woulda–coulda" blues. I was going to go for it with every ounce of my being.

The "no regrets" Philosophy has become the standard by which I judge every opportunity. Whether it's personal or professional, deciding to buy the fastest motorcycle made in the world or to invest several million dollars in another new project when we're already fully committed, I don't ask, "Will I regret this?" Instead, the question is always, "Am I going to regret *not* pursuing this opportunity?" And most of the time, I decide to go for it. Even if the opportunity doesn't pan out, I never regret making the decision to try.

In my family, there were two stories that made me determined to seize every opportunity that came my way, no matter how crazy it might sound at the time. The first was when my grandfather turned down Walt Disney's invitation to invest in Disney World. (I told you that story in Part One.) The other was about my dad and the chance he had to buy almost the entire Kona coast of the island of Hawaii in the early 1960s (see Philosophy #28). Having heard those stories early on, I was determined not to make the same kind of mistake. The only thing I wanted to regret was going for it and having it not work. And that's happened. I've gone after some things and regretted doing so; in other cases, I've spent a lot of time researching a particular deal and then had to walk away because it didn't meet my criteria of profit. Do I regret the time spent? Yes—but in every case, I would regret not spending it a whole lot more.

I'm not advocating a "just do it because it's there" philosophy. You've got to fit your actions into the context of what you want your entire life to be about, the vision you want to create, how you want to view life when you're sitting in that rocking chair. Vision gives you a clear idea of who you want to be and what you want to accomplish in your lifetime. (Here we are, coming full circle to the vision from Part One.) What is it you want somebody to say at your eulogy? Is that the way you're living right now? If not, you'd better make some alterations.

When I think of my vision, I imagine myself at 90 or so. I'm sitting in a rocking chair on a porch somewhere, maybe in Colorado, surrounded by my great-grandkids. They're asking me, "Grandpa, what was your life like? Did you accomplish everything you wanted? Are you happy?" I want to be able to tell them, "Kids, your grandpa doesn't regret very much. I had a vision and tried to make it come true. I lived by philosophies I thought were important. I tried to be a good man and make a difference. And I had a lot of fun, too! Yes, your grandpa's happy."

Of course "no regrets" is usually a goal instead of a reality. Quite honestly, I do regret losing four years as a teenager to drugs, alcohol, and rebellion. I regret my dad died before he could see the success I've created over the past decade. I have regrets about relationships that have been strained and need to be healed. There even have been a few professional regrets, like the time I was offered $1.9 million for the first oceanfront property I renovated. I thought the amount was too low and turned it down, only to take the same amount of money on the sale 19 months later. (I don't regret the lesson I learned, which is to know your market and your profit margin, and don't let pride get in the way of closing a deal.) But today, looking back at this point in my life, I can honestly say that I've avoided most of the "shoulda–woulda–couldas," even when things didn't work out the way I planned. Regrets are like cancer; and the more you have, the more I think you're going to suffer as you get older.

But here's the good news: If you don't want to have regrets when you're in your rocking chair, you can change, starting right now. What haven't you done yet that you will regret missing out on? Don't regret it, do it. What are you doing right now that you will probably regret later—like bad habits, or bad relationships, or being stuck in a bad job or profession? Change it today; don't wait. Every moment between now and that rocking chair is a chance for you to rewrite your own eulogy. At my funeral, I hope they'll say, "No matter what you may think about Frank McKinney, he certainly went after everything with enthusiasm and gusto."

Someone once said it's never too late to have a happy childhood—well, I believe it's never too late to create a regret-free future. And isn't that the best kind of legacy to leave the world?

Actions

1. When you're faced with an opportunity, instead of asking, "Will I regret doing this?" ask, "Will I regret missing out on this chance? Will this help me fulfill the vision for my life?" Then choose accordingly.
2. Take a look at your life so far from the perspective of sitting in your rocking chair at 90. Is there anything you regret? Is it something you can change? If so, change it—starting right now.
3. Regrets are useful only if they are lessons rather than road-blocks. Don't get caught in the "shoulda–woulda–couldas." If you do have regrets from the past, learn from them and let them go.

Deal Points

It's vitally important that in business you never waste your time on re-grets. If the deal doesn't work out, cut your losses and move on. If the job doesn't pan out the way you want it to, leave and find a new one. I learned this lesson when I was buying and selling foreclosures. There were so many deals I missed out on because someone else outbid me or I wasn't in the right place at the right time. If I had wasted my time re-gretting the ones that got away, I never would have been open to seize the ones that were just around the corner.

As I said earlier, however, I tend to take rather than skip the oppor-tunities I'm presented with. I'd rather regret taking on too much than miss something I could have turned to my advantage. For example, when I sold the $30 million property, the buyer offered me two choices: a slightly lesser amount completely in cash, or the full amount partly in cash and partly in trade. He owned a 17,000-square-foot house on nearly two oceanfront acres in Gulf Stream, Florida, that was worth at least $9 million in its as-is condition. I knew I could renovate the property and get at least $13 million for it. I thought, *The only thing I'll regret is if I don't take this house!* I certainly didn't regret my decision, as the house sold for $13 million a mere 25 days after renovations were completed.

Remember, however, that I also evaluate each opportunity against my overall vision for my business and my life. Every single property I buy is part of my vision for creating the Frank McKinney brand as the top in ultra-high-end real estate. Each property has a vision for it, too, and is built or renovated accordingly. Your business and career should always have that long-term vision to guide it. What kind of reputation and legacy are you building? Are you going to look back on a lifetime spent at work (since most of us spend the majority of our life working at something) and feel good about yourself and what you've done? Or are you going to be caught with the "shoulda–woulda–coulda" curse when you retire?

There are a lot of TV commercials that show happy people enjoying their retirement because they've prepared themselves financially. I believe it's just as important to prepare our lives with a regret-free retirement plan. Seize the opportunities that come your way. Don't stay in something you'll regret wasting your time over. Sitting on the porch in that rocking chair, you're going to have a lot of time to contemplate how you spent your life. Make it something that will bring a smile to your face and joy to your heart, something you'll be proud to leave as part of your legacy.

Part Seven

The Last Secret:
There's Always One More

My grandfather (the other entrepreneurial McKinney) kept a sign above his desk. It was one of baseball player Satchel Paige's rules for staying young: "Don't look back. Something might be gaining on you." Underneath it Granddad had scribbled, "Or you can just keep running faster and farther than the sons-of-bitches." That's kind of the basis of the Philosophy, "There's always one more."

As I said at the very beginning of this book, all of these Philosophies are meant to focus us on our better natures. They are not meant to come easily; they are supposed to challenge us. For example, the ultimate score in golf is an 18, or a hole in one on every hole. An impossibility, right? But every round even the worst hackers are striving for that hole in one. The same is true with these Philosophies. If we strive to master them, even if we don't reach perfection our lives and the lives of those around us will dramatically improve.

This list is a living, evolving thing; a broadcast rather than a billboard. It took me this long to come up with 49 Philosophies, and my life might present me with 49 more by the time I'm through. I meet new people, and they share something important with me. I learn something about myself, and add it to the list. I'm always learning, looking at things from new perspectives. The only way we keep ahead of the pack is to be willing to keep running, working, and making ourselves better. But it's also the best way I know of to stay young and vital for a long, long time.

As you achieve certain levels of success, sometimes the hardest thing is to keep pushing. It's easy when you're young and you can clearly see where you have to climb. As a young entrepreneur at 18 or 20 or 23, I knew where I was going and I wanted to get there fast. I still have the same drive and initiative, but how can anyone maintain it? The answer is to keep finding new challenges—within yourself, within your profession, or even within new fields of endeavor. You must realize there is no pinnacle to reach, no top to the mountain. The climb continues; and that is where the drive is found. When you live by the Philosophy "There's always one more," you see the opportunities that come your way rather than passing them by. You look to stretch yourself rather than settling for what you already have accomplished. You keep growing inside even if you're sitting in a rocking chair on that porch at 90.

You've not only got to be willing to stretch, however; you've also got to be willing to change completely. We are such creatures of habit, and success builds habits we are very loath to examine. Yet sometimes the only way to break through to that next secret, that new level, is to change the very things that have worked for us in the past. The premise behind "There's always one more" isn't like your mother offering you one more cookie; it's more like a personal trainer challenging you to try a whole new machine that will build a different set of muscles. But if you're up to the challenge, if you're willing to leave what you know behind and plunge into the unknown, you stand the chance of astounding yourself. You may reach heights of success you could never have dreamed of otherwise.

Goals are the rewards we give ourselves in the process of becoming more than we were. Happiness occurs when we live up to our own expectations or meet our self-imposed goals, but *greatness* occurs when we exceed them. We're put on this earth to keep learning and growing, to take bigger risks, build bigger things, and create more success. When you really make it big, however, you realize, as someone once put it, there is no "there" to success. The real secret of making it big is to enjoy your efforts so much that you never want to stop. Every second of your life is devoted to discovering how much more you can be, how much more you can do, how much more you can give to others. It's the ultimate exploration, because you're discovering the best of who you are.

I wish you the joy of the exploration and discovery. May all your efforts create a life lived on the biggest possible terms. And I look forward to meeting you as we do our best and make it big!

Index

273

Trying new things, 41
Turner, Ted, 198

Ultra-high-end real estate
  fostering relationships with buyers,
    62–63, 132
  as niche in marketplace, 67–68
  psychology of likely buyer, 81
Unremitting effort and success, 110

Vacations, 83
Valassis, George, 208–209
Valvano, Jimmy, 260
Van Halen, 8
Vices, avoiding, 137–141
Vision
  description of, 22–30
  imagining self in future and,
    264–265

objectives, setting, 147
passion and, 13–16, 83, 84
reviewing, 31–32
Visionary, 15

Warranties, 219
Wealth, giving of, 198
Web site, 95
Weekly organizational chart, 25–27,
  31–32, 148–150
Welch, Jack, 242–243
Willis, Bruce, 96, 253
Win-win thinking, 133–137

"Yes," committing self to say,
  174–178
Young Entrepreneurial Society of
  Palm Beach County, 10, 56, 66,
  87–88, 94, 100–101, 221